A FEW
WORDS FROM
AN ABSOLUTE
NOBODY

I would like to start off by saying: in this book, I rarely mention my name and that is because it is just a name. It certainly has nothing to do with who I truly am, it means absolutely nothing, and also because none of you know me.

I am an absolute nobody!

YOPO: THE END

I had my first serving of Yopo delivered by a pipe that shaman Juan Pablo used to blow the ancestral medicine up my nose. It wasn't long until I felt very heavy in my body, tingles all over and within me, and I was scared. As had previously been the case when feeling fear, I tried to push it away, to ignore it ... but I couldn't; and as the medicine took hold of me even more, I laid there asking myself what I was so scared of. As I sat there with this question, it became clear – I was afraid of the unknown.

I was no longer in control of my body, was completely at the mercy of the Yopo, and questioned what was going to happen here today? For me, this was very hard, because I've always had this bravado perception of myself as a strong man who fears nothing, and who provides protection and comfort to those who do. Well, in this moment, the very core of me, the sum total of all that I am, was struck by the revelation that hey, it's okay to be scared, and it's okay to admit it to myself.

Why is the harmonica so amazing? The harmonica is one of the languages of life, it speaks to the heart and to the soul.

Why is life so special?!

It's okay not to understand! I understand that it's okay not to understand.

Breath is life.

Why do I always doubt myself?

It doesn't matter if my book is successful, it will be what it needs to be.

It doesn't matter because nothing matters.

Everything will always be exactly as it's meant to be.

The medicine made me feel like I wanted to be sick, but when I grabbed the bucket provided for this purpose, the feeling was gone. Instead, looking at a fragment of dirt inside the bucket, my higher self explained to me: "That has to be that, so that this can be this ('this' being everything we perceive; 'this' being life). Everything has its place in the universe, everything has to be exactly as it is for everything else to exist. I have to be me so that this can be this ('this' being existence; 'this' being everything outside of me). Everything exists exactly how it exists in every moment that it exists, so that everything can be. If I don't do what I'm doing right now, then the world can't be. Everything breathes together in the moment of now, the present moment. If I wasn't here doing what I'm doing in the moment that I'm supposed to be doing it, nothing else could be.

"When we don't accept the present moment, things still exist, but in a state of disharmony. Everything will always exist, but it's up to us whether they exist in positive or negative harmony, although this is from the human perspective, because when we zoom out and see things from the universe's perspective, all there is, is harmony; everything is growth … growth from what we humans call negative, and growth from what we call positive."

As the medicine took over my body, I watched my right hand dart out towards the sky, reaching, pointing and grabbing. I was made to see that I am constantly reaching for something out there, when actually everything exists right here within me. My finger began to change the direction in which it was pointing, from the sky back towards me, repeatedly prodding me harshly in the chest with the message: "Look within, for that is the answer to everything. Do aliens exits? Of course they do, they exist within me. Because for me to be able to see something out there, I first have to imagine it within, and what is imagination? Just another way of perceiving something. Nothing exists without it existing within beforehand.

Things can only exist in the way that they do because I will them to be that way. This cannot and will not ever be understood by the human mind. Everything I want is right there at the tip of my finger, but it's not within my human grasp. Everything I want to understand about life is right here, but I will never understand it as long as I'm alive."

A small Yorkshire terrier dog that was there, wandering in and out of the ceremonial space, came over to me, and as I stared into its eyes, it was explained to me that this dog, with what I would label as a most simplistic level of understanding, knew exactly what life was and accepted it, which is why it was so happy being what I would describe as 'just' a dog.

My hand involuntarily shot out in front of my face and, as it moved and I followed it with my gaze, it stopped directly at the point where I could see the face of the lady in ceremony beside me. As it dropped away, and my view of her face was clear to see, the message was: 'You, me … we are beautiful just as we are'.

Then I was reminded of all of the women in my life with whom I had had a real chance to be with, but had found reasons as to why they hadn't met the superficial requirements that I had imposed on them. My higher consciousness explained to me that this is why romantic love will always be that little bit outside of my grasp, because as a human I'm flawed, and that's okay … this is the journey.

I was shown that it's okay for my life to turn out exactly the way that it's going to, because this is the journey! Hallelujah, what a relief. It's okay for my life to turn out to be absolutely shit, if that's the way it turns out, because 'shit' is just another label and that's why I came here – for the journey, not the end!

I love everybody so much; love is the key, love my thoughts, love myself.

I love sadness so much. Why do I find such profound beauty within the despair of sadness?

I vomited into the bucket, and when I was done, I asked it: "What are you?" The reply I got was: "The understanding of life." It made me vomit out every last bit of it. 'It' being the understanding of life, in the totality of the degree to which it had immersed me during the peak of the experience.

"Wherever you are, whatever you're doing, however you're feeling and whatever you're going through, right here right now, is all part of the experience that you came here for."

BAKES & DUMPLINGS: THE BEGINNING

"Stop your fucking crying or I'll give you something to cry about!"

The earliest memories I have are of me, my brother and my pregnant mum living in a two-bedroom flat in Walthamstow, London. I guess this must have been when I was five, as my mum was pregnant with my sister and there are six years between us.

I believed that we grew up happy, although my father was never really there. He would turn up randomly from time to time, and sometimes even spend the night; but, looking back on this now, I realise that at the time, I thought it was normal and that this was just how relationships were between fathers and their families.

My mum is from Barbados, having emigrated to the UK in the seventies with some of her siblings, following their mum, my grandmother, who had come over a few years before, managing to secure a job as a care giver. My mum tried to instil in us the same values that were instilled in her as a child in Barbados, so she took us to church every Sunday, dressed in our best clothes, which we weren't allowed to wear anywhere else. My mum struggled with money as a single parent, raising three children with no real help from my father, who occasionally gave her sixty pounds – or maybe even a hundred or so, if she was lucky – whenever he decided to show up.

There was a loan shark, Terry, who turned up every Saturday without fail to collect money that most of the time my mum didn't have, and I would hear her pleading with him to let her pay him at a later date. I remember weekends, when the milkman would come by and mum would tell us to be quiet, and not to move, as he peered through the letterbox calling her name, wanting to collect the money that was due for the milk that had been delivered. There were times when he would no longer deliver and mum would have just enough money to buy a tin of carnation milk, which had to last the rest of the week and serve us all. There was a ratio of carnation milk to hot water that made up the contents of our bowl of Weetabix in the mornings, and she had it down to a fine art.

I'm not sure how many people have had to endure this, if any at all, but carnation milk has a very rich taste – definitely not one that you would want to become accustomed to – and when hot water is added to it, it mutates into this weird, transparent, watery looking thing. We would complain and tell mum that we didn't want to eat it, and she would say: "You'll blasted well eat it or you'll starve!" in her Bajan accent that, to me, has faded somewhat over the years, though maybe not, to the amusement of my friends, who found its timbre very different to what they were used to.

Mum was, and still is, a very good cook, as was my father, who would sometimes cook whenever he chose to grace us with his presence. Mum often cooked chicken, rice and peas on a Sunday, along with roast potatoes, which I loved. She would always apologise for the food having no taste, but it always tasted good to me and, to this day, mum remains one of the best cooks I know, especially when it comes to Caribbean food.

Sometimes, when money was even scarcer than normal, we had to make do with corned beef and rice. One of the cheapest dishes that anybody can make, it was something we became used to, bearing in mind she had three mouths to feed. There were times, however, when even the culinary delights of corned beef and rice were beyond mum's budget, and we became acquainted with what West Indian people call bakes, or dumplings. This is probably hands down the cheapest meal that one could prepare, consisting of only flour and water (sugar can also be added to spice up the taste a little), but even putting such a simple dish on the table was at times a stretch, especially when gas and electricity were unaffordable.

My Uncle Richard was one of the strongest male figures in our lives, who occasionally passed by to give mum some money to help out, and without him we would have spent many a night without electricity to keep the lights on, gas to keep us warm, and food to eat. My Auntie Pauline was also a very strong figure in our lives. A social worker, she and mum had a very close, sisterly bond, and when one of them had money or food, and the other didn't, they shared and helped each other. Sometimes, though, there was no help to be had, so we had to spend a day or night with no food, electricity or gas.

These were tough times, but mum was always there, showing us love; and there was a sense that, even though things were hard at times, everything would be alright because she was taking care of us as best she could. I don't remember my dad ever experiencing any of the hard times with us, though. I'm sure he had tough times too, but he was never there during ours, and we very rarely knew what sort of life he was leading, where he was, or who he was with.

As we got older, me and my brother, Richard, became very mischievous. I guess we did what young boys do growing up – we played with matches, we fought each other, we created chaos, mayhem and lots of noise, and sometimes some of these things deserved a good punishing. I remember times when we had done something naughty and got 'the beats' – and I'm not talking about a little slap to the bum.

To be fair, some of the things we did were very naughty, and the standard beating for such things called for the belt. Mum would tell us to go and get a belt and bring it back to her. We would be in her wardrobe, looking for the flimsiest belt because, believe me, for those of you who have never had a belt beating, they are absolutely no fun at all – they leave whip-like, raised marks and bruises on your skin, which can remain sensitive for days afterwards.

Me and Richard have also had the pleasure of being beaten with a wire hanger and, let me tell you, that is no joke – it too leaves risen lines of bruising all over your skin. My brother got the wet dishcloth once and – wow! – I'm glad it was him, not me. It would amaze me how something so simple could inflict such pain and devastation.

Once, me and my brother were jumping on our bed whilst my mum was cooking, and either the noise or commotion of it all got to her. She came storming into the bedroom and told us to stop, but being mischievous young boys, we gave it a few minutes then were straight back at it. My mum flew back into the room like a wild force, shouted at me to come over, then beat me with her hands … and it was quite the generous beating, for there was plenty to go round.

When she had finished with me, she called my brother over. By now, he had backed himself into the corner by the bedhead and wall, and was pleading for his life: "Mummy no! Mummy no!" I still chuckle to this day whenever I think of it … pussy!

Mum got on the bed, grabbed him, pulled him over to her and gave him quite the plentiful beating – a little more than initially planned, I believe, for having the sheer audacity to refuse his punishment willingly. The beatings would sometimes be accompanied by vocals from my mum.

"You're just like your father!" she would rage. "When I look at you, all I see is your fucking father!"

There were a couple times when, instead of getting a beating, or maybe in its aftermath, the cool down period just after one, she would say: "Don't think you know me, you know! Just because I'm your mother, don't think I won't get a fucking gun and shoot you!"

I remember, as a child in junior school, going to my gran's house for the weekend and saying that I was going upstairs to use the toilet; but; instead, what I did was go around the different bedrooms looking through drawers and wardrobes. After checking the master room and the next room down, I went into the smallest bedroom, which was right next to the toilet, and came across what appeared to be a gold watch. It was so shiny, and I loved the way it looked, so I took it and put it in my pocket, then went downstairs and acted as if butter wouldn't melt in my mouth.

Over the next few days, I had been busy looking through my mum's room and found sixty pounds in a chest of drawers, so I took it. The following day, I carried them both with me as I made the journey to school. My mum would go to work early, so had to leave me with a lady who lived downstairs, called Debbie, who walked me, Richard and her daughter to school. On this particular morning, I asked to stop at a bakery shop to buy something, and when we got there, I removed the sixty pounds from my pocket and paid for an ice finger and a desiccated coconut cake, and I absolutely loved them.

"Where did you get all that money from?" Debbie asked with a frown.

"Oh, I found it," I lied.

I could tell from her expression that she didn't believe me, but probably felt that she had no jurisdiction on the matter, and so we continued onto school whilst I ate and happily enjoyed the two cakes I bought with the money I had stolen from my single mother, who fought daily to make ends meet. At the back of the classroom were a set of drawers, and each child had one to store books and stationery. It was here that I stashed the money and watch, assuming they'd be safe there.

Well, later on that day, somebody had a book or something go missing, so the teacher, Mr Smith, ordered us all to check our drawers, to see if we could find it. I was so worried about the money and watch being found that I made myself busy, pretending to help other children check theirs. The craziest thing is, my best friend at the time, a Turkish boy called Errol, went up to the teacher and told him that I hadn't checked my drawer. Mr Smith went over to my drawer and opened it to find a shiny gold Rotary watch, which I now know to be my grandad's retirement gift from 20 odd years' service to the Royal Mail, and the money I stole.

When he asked me where I had got them, I told him the best lie I could think of at the time … the same lie I told Debbie; the one that every young thief uses and one that, to this day, I don't think has ever been believed: "I found them." With that, I was taken to the school office, where the head teacher phoned my mum at work.

I already knew that that call alone was worth a serious beating. Around that time, I had already been in trouble for fighting, after another child and I had an argument. Whilst we were shouting at each other, he told me that he had fucked my mum. All the other kids were laughing, as if they believed him. I was so upset and enraged, I lunged at him and punched him in his face to defend my mum's honour. She, however, saw it very differently, and the incident ended in pretty much the same way as this story ends now.

Mum came to pick us up after school, and to speak to the teachers about the stolen property, which meant she had to leave work early – something that I knew would add another level of severity to the beating coming my way. But to my surprise, she calmly walked us from school to the nursery where we collected Gina, my younger sister. Mum's calmness continued as we walked home, and I remember thinking: 'Wow, I'm going to get battered when we get back', feeling scared of what was about to go down. Even more bizarrely, nothing happened when we got home, which was really unsettling for me. It was like waiting for a volcano to erupt, so I ate, then went straight to bed. My thinking was that she wouldn't beat me in my sleep, which she did not.

The next day, upon waking, the morning routine of getting up and getting ready for school began, while mum prepared for work. Readying myself to go downstairs to Debbie's, and then onto school, I went into our bedroom to get something, and to my horror my mum walked in behind me, combing her hair with a hot comb. A hot comb is a solid iron comb, used mostly by black women, I believe, and which is left on an open gas fire to heat up, to be combed through the hair, which straightens out.

The minute she came in, I did my rapid battle assessment of the situation – there was no smile on her face, she looked awfully vexed, and then she closed the door … and I knew it was go time. That morning, she gave me a good, thorough beating, whilst simultaneously spelling out to me: "Do … you … think

13

…. that … I … want ... to … be … receiving … phone calls … from … your … fucking … school … whilst … I … am … at … work … trying … to … make … money … so … that … I … can … buy … food … for … the … house … you … fucking … little … thief!" There was a bit of "Oh, stop your crying! Stop your fucking crying or I'll give you something to *really* cry about!"' and the beating continued, amid more vocalisation of how embarrassing it was that I stole from her mum, my grandmother.

I couldn't argue with any of her reasoning, and even if I could, I wouldn't have, as the only thing worse than being naughty was speaking back to her or any elder when they were telling you something. Once the beating was concluded, I stopped crying and finished getting ready for school, and our day continued as usual. To this day, I don't know why I stole from my gran or mum. I knew it was wrong when I did it, but the watch was so shiny and gold, and there was so much money, I guess I just wanted it for myself. The money was handed back to my mum and the watch was returned to my gran, and the shame I felt when I next saw her was worse than the beating I took from my mum.

During our childhood, mum would go through phases of having to work two jobs – a cashier for the local council during the day, before cleaning in the evenings with my Auntie Pauline. I never truly realised what some single mothers have to go through to raise their kids, until I was older and able to look back, see and appreciate all of the sacrifices mum made for her children.

I don't remember mum ever having another relationship, though when we were a lot older, she had begun renting an allotment, where she planted flowers and vegetables. I guess it was the only time she got a moment to herself, and maybe have a little time to enjoy her life, doing something she wanted. During this phase, she met a man who had an allotment, with whom she became friends. I remember her asking us how we would feel if she had a relationship with him, and I voiced a very immature opinion that makes me feel sad and ashamed every time I think of it.

"I don't want another man in the house," I whined. "That would make me feel weird, and I never want to come downstairs to find a man in the kitchen with just his boxers on."

I don't remember her saying anything in response, and nothing materialised between them. Now I realise my mum deserved a chance to be happy, and even if he wasn't the guy for the rest of her life, she deserved to be able to enjoy a romantic relationship, if that's what she wanted. In hindsight, I'm so disappointed in myself that I would want to deny my mum the small pleasure of being able to have a potential relationship after all of the sacrifices she made for us, day after day, for so many years.

Mum didn't have lots of friends, and in hindsight I can see that all of her time was taken up with raising us and working two jobs, constantly trying to make ends meet. Everywhere she went outside of the working day, when we weren't at school, mum would either have to take us with her or find childcare, which she definitely couldn't afford. She didn't have money for much of a social life either, but something like a walk in the park, or a coffee with some work colleagues every once in a while, without her kids, would have at least allowed her to enjoy her life outside of being a mother a little.

Mum has told me many stories about her life, but two of them stuck with me deeply and have stayed ingrained in me to this day. The first one dates back to when she worked at a bank in King's Cross, whilst she was pregnant with me. My dad would sometimes surface from God knows where and pick her up from work, but there was one day in particular, during the winter, that he said he was going to collect her, and didn't turn up. Because mum was so broke, she had to walk the entire distance, all the way from King's Cross back to Leytonstone, where she lived at the time, in the freezing cold. On the way back, she was really hungry and saw an apple for sale at a fruit stall for four pence, but only had three pence on her, and the guy who owned the stall wouldn't let her have it for a penny cheaper. It breaks my heart to know that my mum had to go through moments like these, all alone in the winter, and pregnant.

The second story involved a work colleague she considered a friend, called Julie. This was before I was born, and at some point mum introduced her to my dad. They reached out to one another and started to communicate on the phone, I guess one thing led to another, and they had a full-blown affair. I'm not sure how or when mum found out, but I can only imagine how hurtful and heart shattering this must have been. To rub salt into the wound, she later discovered that whilst she and Julie went to lunch, Julie would sometimes say that she needed to make a private phone call. It was not until later that mum found out that the recipient of Julie's calls was my dad.

Mum didn't fall pregnant easily with me, she and my father had been trying for a while, and after she finally conceived, on the day of my birth, he visited the hospital with the daughter he had with Julie. Mum later told me of the mixed emotions she felt, watching him run around after his child from this other woman, whilst she was bringing me into the world.

Those of you with an interest in medicine, spirituality or psychology will probably know about the concept of an inner child. I only learned about it during my first retreat at Rythmia in Costa Rica, and it pertains to the notion that an inner child dwells inside all of us – forming part of our subconsciousness, I guess – containing our formative emotions, memories and beliefs, as well as our hopes and dreams for the future. In ceremonies related to this ideology, you will often hear a shaman, or their helpers, tell people to be kind to their inner child and show it love. As I write this, aged 40, I still feel the inner child inside of me, and the dreams and aspirations I had in those early years. I've heard it said that no matter how old we get, most people still feel young inside, so when I think of my mum and her inner child, I imagine what she would have wanted as a little girl growing up in a world that seemed full of opportunities.

I believe she wanted to meet and fall in love with a man who would love her equally; that they'd be able to open up to each other, be vulnerable, show each other their insecurities and trust each other with them. I imagine she wanted to create new life, to have children with the man she loved, and see elements of them both resembled in their progeny; to have a nice home for those children to grow up in, and for them to be treasured by two loving parents capable of demonstrating the true nature of love and how potent an emotion it is. I suspect she wanted to make plans together, travel together, and be a family together.

What she got instead was perhaps the worst possible version of her inner child's dream. She met a man she fell in love with, who said he loved her back, but after they were wed, he had an affair with a friend of hers. She struggled to conceive, then finally got pregnant, only for my father to have a child with Julie, and then run around after their daughter while mum was giving birth to me – and to make matters so much worse, this took place whilst her mother, my grandmother, was there, demonstrating a complete lack of respect or decency. Dad would go on to have another two children with Julie, and one with another love interest – not that I've ever held anything against my brothers and sisters, all of whom I know and love.

Dad continued his random appearing acts, as mum called them, for many years. During this time, he offered no real financial support to a wife and three children who truly needed it. We witnessed many arguments between them, some of which were public. On one such occasion, mum shouted down from her bedroom window at dad, telling him to "fuck off," having thrown out the few belongings he had left at the house; and after that, he didn't return. We didn't see dad for many years, until my brother, Richard, randomly bumped into him on the street.

He re-entered our lives, but this time there was nothing between him and mum. They got a divorce and she removed his name from the property, which he hadn't ever contributed to anyway. He would come and go, just like before, but never stayed over. I don't think mum would allow it, and I suspect my father felt a little ashamed for having completely abandoned us. I often ask myself the following question: if Richard hadn't bumped into him on the street, would we ever have seen him again?

All of this is to say that although there were some hard truths pertaining to mum disciplining us quite harshly, she's human too, with an inner child who had dreamed of having a loving, fulfilling life. Instead, her dreams were violated, and yet she still showed her children as much love as possible each and every day. I remember stuttering at school, which was really hard for me, because the other kids always tried to finish my sentences for me, since I was taking too long. Sometimes I would go to say something, and it was as if my mouth and tongue just weren't ready to spit the words out. Words beginning with m, t and s were particularly hard for me, my eyelids would close, and my whole face and head shook, as if I was having a spasm or a fit.

Mum would call me by my complete first name, which she only ever did if annoyed or when trying to help me in moments like these.

"Stop, count to ten and try again slowly," she would say.

I never forgot how little demonstrations of love like this can mean so much when you're struggling with something and not many people are there to help. If we had something on our faces when getting ready for school, she would lick her finger and gently wipe our skin clean. Sometimes she would finish work early and pick us up from school, and it was so nice to see her waiting for us with Gina in her pram. On the walk home, if she had a few spare pennies in her purse, she would buy us cakes from the local bakery, then when we got in, we would watch children's TV as a family, and these are some of my fondest memories.

On the weekends, we sometimes visited Auntie Pauline's house to spend the day, or even sleep over, and we played with our cousins. As I've said, Auntie Pauline was a big figure in our lives because of the bond she and mum had, and they always seemed to be together, which made sense, as my auntie was pretty much raising her daughters, my cousins, by herself. Sometimes, we would all be in my auntie's house eating bakes – yep, fried flour and water – but it didn't matter that we didn't have much, because we were all in it together and that felt like love.

Looking back on my childhood now, I realise my mum is my hero. She gave up her life so that we could have ours, and no matter how dark things got, she always made sure we were looked after and loved. Watching her and my Auntie Pauline struggle throughout my childhood, I realise I have the utmost respect for single mothers – for all mothers – who go through more trials and tribulations than I could ever imagine, constantly putting themselves and their needs last.

When it was winter and the electricity had run out, we would all be sat in the kitchen with the gas cooker on, because the gas still had a little money in the meter, heating that one room. I watched as mum conjured meals from hardly any ingredients, and when there wasn't enough for a solid meal each, she shared out whatever there was evenly between me, Gina and Richard. As for mum, she ate any dregs that were left over in the pot, so that we didn't go hungry.

Sometimes I would catch her standing still or sitting down in the midst of all the mayhem we created as kids, and saw a look of troubled introspection and worry on her face. I guess she was constantly figuring out how we would survive another day. I sometimes ask myself, if put in her shoes, could I have done what she and so many other mothers have had to do? The truth is, I don't know, and my dad certainly couldn't have done it. You're my hero, mum – you're my mother and my father. You've lived your whole life in service to us, and it hasn't gone unnoticed!

THE STAINLESS STEEL SHAFT

My adolescent years were some of the most testing of my life. When I was around 12, we moved from a two bedroom council flat to a three bedroom house, which gave us the additional room we needed, and mum was so happy. I didn't realise what a sense of achievement it was to apply for a mortgage, see it get approved and then buy the property you wanted until many years later, when I purchased an apartment of my own.

The new house was in the same borough of Walthamstow, which made the transition a lot easier and meant that we could all continue going to the same schools. I had recently started secondary school at the Holy Family College, and it was there that I had my first glimpse of just how mean teenagers could be to one another. I was, and still am, absolutely useless at football, which has never interested me, but I nevertheless found myself playing in a game. I suppose I was trying to make friends and establish a social circle for myself at school, and the teams were the first yearers versus the second yearers.

In the UK secondary school system, the first year students are twelve to thirteen years old, and the second year students are thirteen to fourteen years old, and I was playing with the first yearers. During the game, there was a moment when I had possession of the ball, and as I fumbled around with my two left feet, not having a clue what I was doing, one of the second year boys told me to pass him the ball. Obviously, I thought he was joking, because we were clearly on different teams, but after managing to pass the ball to another player in my team, I turned around to see this tall second year boy coming for me. His face distorted with rage, he clamped his hands either side of my head, squeezed it tightly and lifted me up, so that my feet were dangling above the ground.

"Next time I tell you to pass me the ball, pass it to me!" he shouted, plonking me down when he was done threatening me, and darting off to get involved in the game again.

All eyes were on me, I tried desperately to stay strong and hold the tears back, but they sprang from my eyes and streamed down my face. He was a lot taller than me, and I had never had a physical conflict with anyone up to this point, apart from the beatings my mum imparted, which were very one-sided. But this … this felt a lot more personal. It was the first time I had seen the world as a cruel, harsh place, and I felt alone and embarrassed. I spent the rest of the game running around sheepishly, trying not to get the ball passed to me out of fear of getting beaten up or embarrassed in front of everyone.

It didn't take me long to realise that a lot of the kids at school came from rough neighbourhoods and were a lot more battle hardened than I was, so to speak. I put this down to us hardly ever being allowed out to play unsupervised, whereas other kids hit the streets until all sorts of hours into the night. Mum was pretty strict when it came to what we got up to outside of her control, and it wasn't until I got older that I understood where she was coming from. Far from wanting to deprive us of a social life, she just wanted to keep us safe in a volatile society, at a time when any number of things could happen at any given moment. As I hit puberty, I became increasingly aware of a sensitivity in my nipples, which became swollen and enlarged. They became one of my biggest insecurities. I was so embarrassed by them that whenever it was time for P.E. and we had to change into our sports gear, I glanced around anxiously in the changing rooms, waiting for the right moment, with the least amount of people looking in my direction, to whip my shirt off. Then, as quickly as humanly possible, I would pull my sports top over my head and torso.

For the most part, it worked well, but the world being what it is, and quite cruel at times, one day I wasn't quick enough and another boy saw what I had been hiding.

"Oh shit, what's going on with your nipples?" he asked loudly. "Why have you got tits?"

Everybody's attention was suddenly focussed on me. The other kids started to point and laugh at me, and I felt my eyes welling up again. Knowing that crying would invite more ridicule, I held tears back and quickly finished putting my T-shirt on … but the berating had yet to conclude. "So when you're with your girlfriend, who sucks on whose titties? Does she suck yours too?" mocked another boy.

I had never had a girlfriend at this point, nor had I met any girls who had shown any interest in me, but his words still stung – as did others imparted by other pupils keen to get in on the act. I had no father around to ask whether what I was experiencing with my nipples was normal, and whether he had gone through the same thing as a kid. Eventually, I went to my mum and told her about them, and how much I hated their appearance. She told me not to worry and that it would pass.

"It's probably just your body changing," she added, but I begged her to see if there was anything that we could do about it. I guess mum's take on it was: I was her son, she loved me regardless of my transforming body and didn't see it as a big thing, but she wasn't the one who was having to deal with constant ridicule at school; and eventually, seeing how distressed I was, she agreed to take me to the doctors. A few days later, I found myself being examined by a doctor, after being asked to remove my T-shirt. After touching and prodding my nipples and the
 surrounding area, he told me I had something called gynecomastia, which is an increase in the amount of breast gland tissue in boys or men, caused by an imbalance of the hormones oestrogen and testosterone.

He told me not to worry about it and that it would most likely go away in time. Mum was happy with this and agreed with him, but I was devastated. I had gone there thinking that there would be some kind of magic pill, medicine or treatment to take to cure my problem, but clearly I was stuck with it. The doctor suggested taking up weightlifting to build up the chest area, to try and camouflage my gynecomastia, but I was 14 years old, I knew nothing about weightlifting, going to the gym, or how one would even go about joining one. The gynecomastia was a problem that would stay with me for many years, but we'll get back to that.

Having man breasts wasn't the only thing I got bullied for at school. Things were still quite tough at home, so when me and my brother needed some trainers for P.E., mum took us to a sports shop she had found. As soon as we got there, I knew this wasn't the sort of place my friends from school got their trainers from. This shop sold shoes and trainers for the poor, and instead of being neatly presented on shelves, they were bundled up in baskets and scattered all over the floor.

We tried to find the best trainers out of a bad bunch, and I ended up with some trainers called Rebels, while my brother got a pair of Golas – cheap and cheerful brands that we both knew were going to bring us a whole world of hurt at school. My trainers looked like they had been sewn together with offcuts from other styles, were predominantly black, with a horrible bright green logo on them, had an assortment of other, random colours all over them, and they looked extremely long and flat. Yes, mum made us wear them to school and yes, we got bullied and were the butt of many jokes because of them.

Just when we thought it couldn't get any worse, mum bought some Wahl hair clippers and started cutting our hair, because going to the barber was an unjustifiable cost for a household struggling to put food on the table. One day, walking back from school, Richard and I saw that the corner shop was looking for kids to do paper rounds, so once we had okayed it with mum, we went and spoke to the shop keeper and, luckily, both of us got our first ever jobs as paper boys. It paid about fourteen pounds a week, and I couldn't believe I had my own money. We could afford to go to the barbers and get a proper haircut, and even helped mum out sometimes by buying small items of food for the house, such as corned beef, bread, rice and sugar.

Towards the end of my fourth year at school, I popped out to a shop around fifteen minutes away from where we lived. It was there that I saw the most beautiful girl I had ever seen walking towards the shop – a golden skinned, beautiful bodied girl with a T-Boz style haircut. We caught each other's eyes, and I said hello to her and asked where she lived, because I had never seen her before. She told me her family had recently moved to the area, I felt a little vibe whilst we were talking, and it so happened to be national kissing day, which I had heard other students talking about at school.

Even though I had never spoken to a girl in that way before, and was feeling all kinds of nervousness, I asked her if she knew that it was national kissing day. She smiled, as if knowing what I was getting at, stepped towards me and we kissed. I couldn't believe it; I had never really spoken to a girl before, and there I was, kissing the most beautiful girl I had ever seen. She told me her name, but it didn't matter, for I would always call her golden because of her skin. Walking to school one morning with Richard and Gina, I saw her again, except this time she was with her two younger brothers and wore the uniform from a neighbouring school. I couldn't believe it when she told me she was in year eight, the first year of secondary school, as she looked so much older. From then on, we would always see each other in the mornings and walk to school together.

Over the course of the next year, we grew very close and I came to love Golden very much; but I was still very awkward when it came to talking to girls, especially those I liked. I had no father around to show me how to talk to women, nor an older brother who could pass down any pearls of wisdom, like some of the kids at school did. Me and Golden never got together during our teenage years, even though it was something I badly wanted, and feeling awkward around the fairer sex was something that would remain with me for many more years.

During my last year at school, whilst preparing for my exams, a few of us went to my friend Simon's house during study leave, but instead of studying, we sat in his bedroom smoking weed. For the record, I would just like to say that I never liked weed. It did nothing for me, I didn't like the feeling it gave me and I didn't like how it gave me the munchies, but I did it because everyone else did and I wanted to fit in.

Simon had a York weights bench in his room, with a silver barbell, loaded with two 10kg concrete weighted plates, resting on a rack. One by one, each of them got on it and pushed out a few reps, and while watching, I remember thinking quietly to myself that they were the same age as me, and that if they could lift it, I must be able to, even though I had never lifted a weight in my life. When it got around to my turn, I laid on the bench, gripped the bar and used everything I had in me to lift it off the rack; but as soon as I got it over my chest, I realised I had absolutely nothing left, and it came crashing down on top of my chest. I lay they struggling and grimacing, feeling stupid. Everyone laughed as a couple of them helped me lift it off my chest, and that day I promised myself that I would never, ever be the weakest man in any room ever again. Shortly after, I saved up enough money from my paper round to buy my own York weights bench.

By the time my last year at school came around, I had made some enemies in teenage boys from another school. When I look back on it now, and the sheer stupidity of how the following events started, it disappoints me; and I feel even more disappointed at the fact that to this day, street wars and lifelong enemies are still being created by the same pathetic, unproductive school of thought that is: "What are you looking at?"

My first set of enemies took a dislike to me because I had stared at them in the street, but the crazy thing is, I was only staring at them because they were staring at me. Sometimes I saw them walking on the street whilst I was on the bus, and with outstretched arms they shouted: "What the fuck are you looking at?!" I hated confrontations, and still do to this day, so I tried to pretend I hadn't seen them and looked away.

Once my final year had concluded, mum somehow managed to get enough money together to take us to Saint Michael in Barbados, where she was born. A beautiful island, I got to meet some of my Bajan relatives, and it was nice to get away from

Walthamstow and the ever- escalating situation with this group of boys that without a doubt would become violent very soon.

Getting back to my bitch tits, during the holiday we went to the beach, but I didn't dare take my top off, despite the intense heat. The beach was packed with people, and the last thing I wanted was for anyone to see these horrendous female-like breasts of mine and be subjected to additional ridicule. So, instead of being at the beach bare chested, like pretty much every other male there, I fried in a T-shirt or vest. At this age, I truly hated my body. Not only did I have female breasts to contend with, I also had braces fitted because my teeth were completely out of control, and orthopaedic insoles in my shoes because I had hideously flat feet.

Needless to say, I have some very uncomfortable memories from my teenage years, but little did I know that being ridiculed at school for the shortfalls in my physical appearance, DIY haircuts from my mum and generally just being poor would be the least of my worries. Soon enough, I would find out what it was like to have enemies who wanted to do me real physical harm.

After leaving school, I joined a youth training scheme at Ford in Dagenham to become an electrician. I loved learning about how electricity worked, how to wire up a house, the fuse board, lighting system, the ring main, other domestic circuits, how to calculate electrical diversity and what size cable to use for different circuits. Mum was very proud of me and how I had found an honest, respectable trade straight after leaving school, even though my GCSE grades had been appalling. I even ended up re-wiring mum's house some time later, when I was eighteen years old.

One evening, on my way back from Dagenham, I was walking to Walthamstow Central bus station when I saw two of the boys I was having this ongoing staring competition with, along with a girl who knew all of us. I was alone, but they had already seen me and pride prevented me from taking another route. As we drew closer to one another, the two boys parted, so that I had to walk between them, and as I did they both barged into me and turned around. I could see that they clearly wanted a fight, so I said: "Do you think, cos I'm by myself, that I won't fight you?" The truth is, I really didn't want to fight. I had never had one, I was outnumbered and scared, but I swung first to try and get the edge over them. I caught one of them, who ducked down; and, as I was trying my best to batter him with everything I had, the other sucker punched me perfectly from the side. As his fist struck me, I saw a flash of light in my left eye, stumbled back, and as I looked up, there was a bus station full of people watching.

"Come on, let's go," the guy who had hit me told his friend.

I had lost the fight and now had a black eye, tears were streaming down my face, and I looked at the girl before running off, saying: "I'm gonna fucking stab them the next time I see them!" The truth is, I wasn't going to stab anyone. I was just scared, humiliated and hurt, so that empty threat was all I had left to give.

As I moved through the various modules in the youth training scheme, I managed to get a placement after a manager from an electrical company came to the youth training centre and held interviews for two potential apprentices. Me and another guy got the two positions on offer and I loved going to work every day, with only one day a week spent at the training centre. I was out in the real world installing real electrics. The only thing I was missing was tools, and the electrician I was attached to told me I couldn't keep using his.

The youth training scheme had a budget allowance for individual students to select and order tools that they would need once successfully selected to go on a placement. I ordered an assortment of insulated screwdrivers, a hammer, a cropper to cut cables, pliers and an axe that was actually described as a stainless steel shaft. Once they finally came, it was such a relief to not have to constantly ask to borrow tools. However, there were still a few things I was missing, so one evening me and my good friend Clinton went to Homebase, a DIY store where you could buy all sorts of hardware and tradesman tools.

I was wearing my big blue puffer jacket, and at this point had quite a big Afro. It wasn't braided at that time, so I wore a woolly hat to cover it and went into the store. It was dark outside, so Clinton sat on the other side of some fencing in the garden section of the store. I walked through the store, innocently pushing a trolly, and as I made my way up and down the aisles, I selected an electrical multimeter, a cordless power drill and a machete. I slowly strolled into the garden area with my trolly full of the items I had selected and mooched around, looking at small plants and trees.

Making my way to where my friend was sat on the other side, I had a quick look to ensure there weren't too many people around, then began to throw the items over the fence. Once my friend had stuffed them in a rucksack he had brought with him, I then threw my blue puffer jacket over, put my woolly hat in my pocket and combed out my Afro. I left the trolley in the garden section, casually walked back into the main store, then made my exit after strolling past its security guard with no problems. By now, my friend had already left, and we met further up the road before walking home.

In my mind, I knew it was stealing, but I didn't think it was that bad. I justified it by telling myself and Clinton that it was okay, because unlike other thieves and criminals, I had only temporarily borrowed these tools so that I could put something back into the community by going to work and doing a good job … but it definitely wasn't borrowing, I never returned them to the store, nor did I ever offer it any compensatory money.

I taped the machete I stole to my thigh whilst out and about, doing day to day stuff. On the days I went to work, I carried my toolbox and had the axe tucked down my right trouser leg, with the blade of it resting just above the waistline of my jeans, and hidden under my T-shirt and jacket. I hoped to God that I would never have to use them, because I didn't know how to knife fight and, I suspect, neither did my teenage enemies … which meant one thing: that if we ever used weapons on each other, it would have been a very, very messy affair, with the swinging of blades and God knows what other types of weapons teenagers carry around with them. Even if I was to win, I would almost certainly get injured.

As I excelled in my placement, I began going to college for one day a week, instead of the youth training scheme in Dagenham. On the days I went to college, I carried an extendable police baton, bought from a shop in Forest Gate, on the inside pocket of my jacket, because knowing my luck, I would probably bump into these guys when I was least expecting it.

One college day, just as I had predicted, I popped into a shop nearby and guess who walked in? It was none other than Mark, the main guy I had a problem with. He saw me and smiled, then left the shop first. After purchasing a few items, I walked out of the shop, but didn't even have time to plant my feet on the ground properly before I saw him in front of me with something in his hand. I couldn't tell what it was, but as he lifted it in the direction of my face, I heard a hissing noise consistent with a spray – CS gas, as it turned out, though the wind must have been blowing in the opposite direction to my face, so I only got hit with a little of it. It burnt a little, robbed me of breath for a short while and made me cough.

Rage took hold of me, I pulled out my baton, extended it and swung for Mark, but he dodged it and ran towards the college entrance. I chased him all the way, screaming: "Next time I see you, I'm gonna fuck you up!" I couldn't believe he was going to the same college as me, and the following week, I came out of class during the lunch break and walked to the shop with some friends who were attending the same electrical course as me.

"Let me know if you see anyone acting suspiciously or coming towards me," I asked, but before they could respond, I looked over my shoulder – a horrible habit to have, but a necessary one, in case I was being attacked from behind – and there was Mark, along with a couple of other guys. One of them had a crutch in his hand, the other had his hands in his pants, as if clutching a machete (which was all the rage in those days – everyone seemed to be carrying one), while the main guy, who had previously gassed me, had a Jack knife.

I absolutely shat myself, as all I had was a baton, so I nervously crossed the road whilst looking back … but it was too late – they had seen that I was trying to get away, and I heard one of them shout: "Let's fucking get him!" I realised a man's voice can be very menacing and disturbing when used aggressively, and it's a truly scary thing to be outnumbered, especially in a situation where you're being shouted at and chased by people who have weapons. I don't believe I have ever run as fast again in my entire life as I ran that day. I was running that fast, I nearly tripped up on my own feet … and I knew that if I fell or they had caught up with me, I would be in serious trouble.

I think that a lot of the time, teenage boys only want to badly injure their adversaries, but when there's a few of them and they get caught up in the moment, that's when murders occur, and I definitely didn't want that to happen to me. As I was from the area, I knew where I was going, and as the college was very close to my old school, I ran towards it and kicked the double doors of the entrance open as I ran through them. I knew this building, they didn't, but I could hear them screaming to each other: "Fuck him up!"

There were students everywhere, on their break, and screams rang out as they jumped aside to get out of the way. I made it to the rear playground and then out of the car park gates, and while they were still chasing me, they were never going to catch me at this point. I ran onto the main road and jumped on a bus that was just about to pull away.

On the bus, I was in an uncontrollable state of fear, and when I got home, I phoned my brother, Kiyan, who my dad had had with another woman, and who was a year older than me. We met a few years earlier, when dad saw fit to introduce us all to each other after years of us asking him, on the few occasions we were blessed enough to see him, if we could meet our half brothers and sister, of which there were five – two only child boys, Kiyan in London, and Ramon back in Jamaica, who was the eldest of us all; and then two brothers and a sister from his relationship with Julie.

Getting back to the matter in hand, after calling Kiyan, I also rang a couple of friends for help dealing with the trio and any of their clan. In those days, we called this back-up, though God knows what the ever-changing street slang is for it now. They all arrived at my house and one of them, a guy called Ivan who had been in the year above me at school, had a car, while the other, Joseph, a former classmate, also had a personal conflict with this group of boys.

Hidden in the attic, unbeknown to mum, was a .38 special revolver that Richard had managed to acquire from a contact.

Neither of us wanted to actually have to use it, but guns were becoming more prevalent and we wanted to use it as a deterrent to those we were having skirmishes with. I handed the gun, which contained no bullets, to Kiyan, packed my stainless steel shaft in my Moschino jeans trouser leg, and gave Joseph my police baton before we all climbed into Ivan's car. Parking in the car park of a hospital that was close to the college, the plan was that I would sit on a wall in front of the car by myself, in the hope that if they were around and saw me, they would think that I was alone.

We sat there, me on the wall and the others in the car, for maybe half an hour to an hour. I started to think that maybe we wouldn't see them, and wondered what I would do about going into college the following week by myself, with everything up in the air like this. Well, just as I was about to give up on my plan, a car screeched to a halt, which caught me completely off guard, as I had been expecting to see them coming for me by foot.

Mark jumped out with a bright green stoplock, a metal mechanism used for deterring car thieves, and he was so close to me that I had to jump off the wall and run a little in order to create some space between us, so that I could pull my axe out from down my trouser leg (I hadn't anticipated how difficult it would be to pull it out whilst on the run). Holding it in my hand, I turned around and watched him stop dead in his tracks.

I partly chose an axe as a weapon with which to defend myself because of the psychological advantage it afforded over someone you are about to fight. I imagine that staring at an axe, with daylight reflecting off its blade, would intimidate an enemy enough that a fight wouldn't ensue; that they would run off … and if they didn't run, well, then you had bigger problems than you thought, you would be in a fight with a psychopath, and God only knows how that story finishes.

I stood there with my axe while my back-up jumped out of the car with an assortment of weapons.

"Let's fucking go, then!" I screamed at Mark, as Joseph came into his line of sight whilst extending the baton.

Now it was a startled Mark's turn to run, as Joseph swung for him, missing him by mere centimetres. Mark managed to gain some speed, but Kiyan and Ivan jumped out in front of him, my brother swung at him and clipped him in the face with the gun butt, and he began to lose his footing. God must have been on his side this day, because not only did he manage to regain his footing, but as I chased him into the road and lunged at him with the blade of the axe, I missed him by a matter of inches.

When I look back on this moment now, I see Mark running into the road and loads of students and pedestrians stood around, watching this horrendous spectacle of humanity; and realise I was caught up in the moment, trying to show off and to demonstrate to Mark that I was just as willing as him to do serious harm, which is why I lunged at him with the blade of the axe. When I originally left the house to pursue my revenge, I made a conscious decision that if I saw him, I was only going to beat him with the spine of the blade and not the blade itself.

Thinking about it now, I see that whether you call it God, the universe or the powers that be, something or someone was looking out for both of us that day, because it could have changed our lives forever, with one of us badly wounding or killing the other, and ending up in prison.

Anyway, Mark escaped, the car and driver that he had turned up with sped off, and we got back in Ivan's car and made our way back to my house.

Whilst all of this madness was ongoing on a daily basis, I was still living at my mum's, and from time to time I continued to give her reason to discipline me with the odd beating. Even though I had been lifting weights for a year or so, was taller than her, bigger than her and definitely stronger than her, she would still let me know who was boss. One day, during my morning routine, as I was getting ready for work, mum called me downstairs for breakfast. Mum followed me into the living room with a cup of hot tea that she had made for me. I don't remember exactly what was said, but I think I showed her some attitude that she wasn't in the mood for.

I was older now, I had a job and was earning money, and I must have felt brave, so I spoke back to her for the first time ever. Up until then, I had never, ever argued with my mum out of respect, and the fact that we had been taught never to talk back to adults or give them any lip; but on this morning, I ran my mouth and mum was enraged. I saw her face change immediately, she threw the tea in my face and, my God, it was so hot! As the tea ran down my face and I gasped for air, I saw that she was about to follow it up with a slap, so braced myself so that when her hand connected with my face, my head barely moved.

As mum withdrew her hand and silent tears fell down my face, I could see that she had definitely felt it too. Her hand hung down by her side and she rubbed it on her leg, and stroked the inside of her palm with her fingers. Her hand was clearly stinging, and I imagine it had hurt her as much as it had hurt me. That was the last time my mum ever beat me, and I vowed it would be the last time I ever cried.

During this period of time, a new family moved into the area, about a five minute walk away from mum's house. Richard and I saw the two brothers from this family on a daily basis and instead of saying hello, talking to each other and becoming friends, we stared at each other and, before we knew it, we had made some brand new enemies – awesome, just what we needed and, even better, they were just around the corner from where we lived with my mum and little sister.

I would walk Golden home sometimes after she had come to visit me at my mum's, and we cut through the estate where these two boys lived. Whenever I saw them, we stared each other out, it was such an uncomfortable feeling, and confrontation seemed inevitable. One night, me, Richard and Clinton were cutting through the estate and the brothers were there with a gang of others. Straight away, I knew that this wasn't going to end well, but they had already seen us and we were committed, so we confidently tried to walk through them. They stared at us, some words were exchanged and a fight broke out.

Richard fought with the younger brother, and me with the elder. Richard stuck an awesome headbutt on the one he was fighting, whilst I found myself in more of a push and tussle. "Do you know where I'm from, blood? I'm from fucking Finsbury Park!" shouted the elder brother.

A borough in north London, it meant nothing to me, and we eventually agreed to let go of each other, walking on whilst they issued a barrage of threats about the next time we saw each other. All I remember thinking was: 'Brilliant, now we have a war on two fronts: the guys who had chased me through my old school, and these new ones, who live just around the corner'.

A few days later, Golden came to visit me and, without her knowing, before I walked her home, I went to the back of my wardrobe, where I kept all my weapons, and put my machete in my trouser leg. We set off, and just as we started to cut through the estate, I saw the brother I fought with.

"Walk on," he yelled. "I wanna chat to this girl."

There was no chance of that happening. He didn't even know her, he was trying to purposely disrespect me in front of one of the most important people in my life, and a few words were exchanged.

"Don't ever walk through this estate again," he snarled. "If you do, I'm gonna fucking batter you!"

I walked Golden back to her house and we said our goodbyes. Then, just as I was about to take the long route back home, so as to avoid making my way through the estate, a wave of rage, fear and frustration washed over me and I thought to myself: 'Fuck this, I have a machete in my pants – I'm gonna show him just who the fuck I am!' Only now that I'm older, a lot more honest with myself, and maybe a little wiser, can I actually admit to myself that I was scared – very scared.

Regardless of my inner turmoil, I walked back to the estate, imagining how the next few moments of my life would unfold; talking and swearing to myself whilst I rehearsed what I was going to say. When I reached the estate, I saw a girl who knew us both, and the beef between us.

"You should go – quickly – before he comes back out," she said. But this time, I had come looking for him and wasn't leaving. And it wasn't long before my latest enemy reappeared.

"I told you not to come through here!" he hollered, screwfacing me. "You fucking …!" "Fuck you! If you wanna go, lets fucking go, then!" I shouted back at him, cutting him short.

Striding purposefully towards him, while mouthing off obscenities, I don't think he had expected to see me in such a headstrong state … that I was offering to fight outside his front door.

He paused for a moment, then told me, whilst walking back into his house, that he was going to get the 'beast' – street talk, back then, for a gun. I started walking home, trying not to let the fear of what had just been said overwhelm me. By now, it was dark and the street lights had just come on. As I got to about twenty meters away from the estate, I heard the pattering of footsteps and heavy breathing behind me, and as I turned around, I saw him about to lunge at me with what looked like a Jack knife.

Running into the middle of the road, whilst pulling out the machete from my trouser leg, I was sure that somebody would see what was happening and call the police, or that a car would stop and break it up … but the truth, in situations like that, is that nobody wants to get involved, and I don't blame them. I paced backwards into the middle of the road as he walked towards me, keeping his distance. I could see curtains shifting from inside the houses that lined the street, and people staring out of them to see what all the commotion was about; and as I looked down, I could see the street lights glistening off the blade of my machete. It looked ominous, though God knows I didn't want to actually have to use it.

"You have no idea how close I came to putting the clip in my gun, you little pussy'ole – the next time I see you, you're dead! You better hope you don't see me again!"

He walked back to his house, I kept pacing backwards a little longer, keeping my eyes on him, then put my machete away and walked home. Over the next few years, I was like a ninja, selecting my routes to and from work in order to avoid my two different groups of enemies. Every now and then, we would bump into one of them and have little skirmishes.

There was a time when things had gotten so out of hand again that Richard and I decided to steal a car and runover the oldest of the brothers, the one we were having the biggest problems with. We called some friends who were willing to back the idea, and went out at night to look for a car.

I had never stolen a car before, but some friends told me how easy it was to pilfer older style models, and that all I needed was a flathead screwdriver. We found a little Citroen hatchback, and some of my friends kept lookout whilst I pulled out a red emergency window hammer, the type that had a hard, sharp tungsten steel hammer head. I stole it from a bus to add to my arsenal of weapons, which by now was plentiful and very diverse – I had all sorts, including a taser, purchased in America on a holiday mum and my auntie managed to take us on, and a samurai sword, which I got in Spain, when a friend and I drove there.

I broke the window, then me and one other got in and started to rip off the steering wheel housing to get to the wires and black box that I would stick the screwdriver into, and turn, to start the engine. Once we got the steering wheel housing off, I tried starting the engine, but it wouldn't go and I had no idea what to do – my friends hadn't given me any advice on problem shooting cars that wouldn't start whilst you're trying to steal them. And then I heard a lookout shouting: "Feds! The Feds are coming!"

Somebody had seen that we were up to no good and called the police, or Feds as we called them. I panicked as we jumped out of the car and saw a police van arriving. Everyone scattered in different directions, but one of my friends got caught and arrested. I tried to call him all night to see what had happened, but didn't hear from him until the next day, when he explained that he had been questioned about an attempted car theft. He said nothing and denied being there, and because the police had nothing else to go on and hadn't caught anyone else involved, they had to let him go.

In hindsight, when I look back on this now, I feel very reckless and irresponsible for asking my friends to get involved in something so ridiculously stupid that it could have potentially ruined their lives for a very long time and left them with a criminal record. Eventually, this would all start spinning out of control. Richard and I couldn't go out with our mum or sister for fear of bumping into one of these two groups, knowing full well that these teenagers had absolutely no respect for the parents or family members of their so called enemies. Anything could have happened, and we couldn't be putting mum or Gina in that kind of danger.

One day, on top of all the ducking and diving, selective route planning and refusing to go out with mum, I got a phone call from the youth training centre, telling me that they would like to see me in Dagenham the next day, which was strange, because I hadn't been there in ages and I was supposed to be on site, working. When I got there, I was told I would be having a progress meeting with my electrician mentor and the manager of the company with which I had been working. As I sat in a classroom, awaiting the meeting with my mentor, something felt off and I didn't have a good vibe about what was about to happen.

Eventually, the manager opened the door and entered the room. We began speaking and I was told that the firm had decided to move forward with only one apprentice, and unfortunately it wasn't me. I was gutted, and didn't understand what I had done wrong, but before the meeting drew to a close, the manager asked me, with a baffled look on his face, if I had been taking an axe to work. I immediately knew what this meeting had really been about. The truth is that I used to travel into work every morning with my toolbox in my hand and stainless steel shaft hidden in my jean leg, then once I got there, I put the shaft in a centrally located, padlocked container where we kept valuable electrical fixings and tools … and it appears that someone had seen me removing the axe from my pants and hiding it there.

I tried to explain the situation I was in with these boys, and how I had to protect myself with something if I saw them on my way home, but I could tell that he wasn't interested from the befuddled expression on his face. The situation I had just explained seemed completely foreign to him, and it was too late: the decision had been made, and rightfully so – why would an electrical company want an employee working for them who carried around an axe in his pants?

I think it was about this time in my teenage years that I first experienced what I've come to call psychotic thoughts. I would be talking to somebody – a family member, stranger or friend – and whenever it was a conversation or moment that seemed perfect, maybe filled with love from family members, building a really good rapport with someone I had only just met, or even just hanging out with friends, a vision in my head would play out of me doing something outrageous, like sucker punching the person I was in the moment with.

It would only happen in moments that I would describe as perfect, as if I was being shown that, while the moment was perfect, there was an alternative that could see me completely ruin it and turn it into the worst possible moment ever. I don't know where these thoughts came from or why I was even having them. It would make me feel guilty to the point that I didn't actually hear what was being said in the moment anymore. Instead, I would be engaged in a conversation with myself, screensaver face on, asking myself: 'why am I thinking this?', while trying my hardest to get these destructive thoughts out of my head.

This is something that, since it first happened, has never left me. Sometimes, the thoughts have been a lot more violent than just sucker punching someone, and sometimes they would be acts of violence against myself. I take pleasure in knowing that I have never acted on any of these thoughts, and know that I never will. I'm no psychologist, but think this is the difference between those who have psychotic thoughts and those who act on them.

I think we all get psychotic thoughts once in a while, but only a true psychopath would act them out.

A few months after being sacked, I started working as a labourer with a builder who had recently done some work at my auntie's house. When he saw that I could fix electrics, he started using me to bring in electrical jobs. I would do the first and second fix of extensions we built, and fault find for individual customers who reported electrical faults. He would always get a qualified electrician to carry out the required testing and certification once I had finished.

After working with him for a couple years, he took on a business partner. He was quite a funny guy who told me he used to be in the Royal Green Jackets territorial army, and shared some of his experiences with them. Listening to him telling his stories, I considered giving it a go. I thought it could be fun, so I roped four of my friends into it, and off we went to Davies Street in the West End, where the TA centre was. They told us to come back at the weekend, when they would give all new joiners a brief, so that's what we did.

Upon arriving at the centre, we were introduced to the different personalities and ranks present – a mixture of regular servicemen (soldiers drafted there for a specific amount of time) and TA ranks, or part timers. They sat us in a room with a TV, put on a DVD of Saving Private Ryan, and after the first 20 minutes or so of the famous beach landing scene, I was sold – I wanted in, and I wanted to go to war then and there. After the beach scene had finished, they spoke to us for a while, asking us why we wanted to join. They wanted to get a feel for us and what we were about, and during this conversation they told me that I would need to cut my braids off. Surprisingly, I had absolutely no issues with it, as I was convinced it would be more rewarding to become part of something bigger than myself.

We were then shown an SA80 rifle, the weapon of choice for the British army. They knew exactly what they were doing, showing young men war movies and letting us get a feel for the rifle, so of course we were going to join. We filled out some paperwork and were told to return the following Tuesday. We attended every Tuesday and some weekends, when we had overnight exercises in the field, though my friends eventually dropped out, saying it wasn't for them. I don't think they liked taking orders or getting shouted at, but for me it was fascinating and a momentary escape from all the dramas I was having with my two different groups of enemies. In addition, I didn't have the slightest clue as to what I was going to do career wise, as my dream of becoming an electrician had failed miserably.

Then on the day of September 11 2001, when I was at work labouring, there was an unusual amount of excitement on the radio channel we were listening to. We began to get inundated with unscheduled news reports of a terrible incident that had just occurred in New York, America, which left everybody stunned. Amid the fallout from the 9/11 terrorist attacks, and details of who was responsible for the atrocity began to emerge, I knew exactly what I wanted to do – I was going to join the army full time.

During a Christmas party at the TA centre later that year, a friend of one of the part time ranks came along, and I got talking to him. He was a Royal Marine Commando, but I had never even heard of them. He told me he had just passed out of training, achieving his green beret, how hard he was trained, and having to march 30 miles in eight hours with 40lbs of kit on. I was absolutely amazed and wasn't even aware that men could do such things. I had absolutely no exposure to the armed forces before going the TA, and there was clearly so much more that I had to learn.

In that moment, I knew it was the Royal Marines that I wanted to join, with the added advantage of removing me from the ambitionless path I found myself on and the drama I was having with my enemies. I told mum that I was going to join the Royal Marine Corps and that I had booked an appointment at the local careers office, but I don't think she was onboard with my plan.

"There's no place for a black man in a white man's army," she warned.

"Oh, and you know this from all your extensive years of service in the military?" I responded.

I respected and appreciated where mum was coming from. She had come to the UK in the seventies and experienced racial abuse, though I was going to write my own story and my mind was set. Although she may not have wanted me to join the Marines, she accompanied me to the careers office and was there every step of the way, giving me her full support. I suppose deep down she was just sacred and worried for me, especially considering everything that was going on in Afghanistan at the time.

I completed my aptitude tests and one on one interview with a Warrant Officer, second class Sergeant Major, in which I was successful; and a few weeks later, a letter arrived with a date and instructions for me to attend a Potential Royal Marines Course (PRMC), down at the Commando Training Centre Royal Marines (CTCRM) in Lympstone, Devon.

Over the next few months, I went running four times a week so that I would be able to achieve the three mile run in twenty one minutes requirement. I would also have to undergo a personal fitness test, a bottom field acquaint, where a lot of the physical training was to be carried out, a bleep test in the gym, followed by as many push-ups as you could do in two minutes, as many sit-ups as you could do in two minutes, a swimming test and numerous classroom periods.

As well as focusing on my running in the build-up to the PRMC, I practiced doing as many push- ups and sit-ups as I could within the time limit, though I wasn't too bothered about the swimming because I had seen it loads on TV, and how hard could it be anyway? It was just some water.

When I arrived at the Commando Training Centre, me and the other potential candidates were ushered into forming a line by drill leaders who were there to meet us. I had grown this little moustache that I was quite proud of, but as the Training Corporal arrived in front of me, after slowly walking past the line of candidates, humorously insulting as many as he could, even for things such as being ginger, he saw me and immediately asked: "Why the fuck do you have a dead ferret on your lip? That's going to have to go – it's fucking Chad (Chad is Marine slang for cringeworthy)!"

I enjoyed the PRMC, even though it was all very foreign to me. Some lads said it was like being in a rugby or football club, which I had never experienced, but I got stuck in and gave it my all. I passed the three mile run with time to spare, found the bleep test, push-up and sit-up requirements fairly easy to reach, but then came the swimming.

All that was required of us was to jump into an Olympic-sized pool from a diving board, swim half way across it, turn around and swim back, then tread water for three minutes. Whilst I waited in line, I watched all the other guys jump in and complete it. It looked so easy that in my mind I had already passed. When it got to my turn, I climbed up the ladder to the diving board and jumped in, but once my head was above water level, I began to breaststroke and couldn't stay afloat.

I began to sink, and wondered whether I wasn't swimming fast enough, but the harder I tried, the deeper and faster I sunk – in fact, I couldn't really call it sinking anymore … I was blatantly drowning. Feeling something hitting me on the side of my head, I grabbed onto it and was pulled up and over to the edge of the pool, where the Personal Training instructor stood looking at me. As I coughed my lungs up, gasping for air, he said: "Fucking hell, you're going to have to learn how to swim before you come back here, fella!"

At the end of the course, when the three days were over, we were debriefed, individually interviewed, and told whether we had been successful or not. I was over the moon to be told that I had passed, despite my complete lack of swimming aptitude. I was so proud to have succeeded. I had hope again.

A few months later, I received a letter with a start date for the extensive training that would determine whether or not I would become a Royal Marine. I had mixed feelings about leaving London. While I was excited about the possibility of a completely new life, a part of me felt like I was running away and leaving my brother and friends to deal with our enemies. It honestly felt like I was the cause of the problems between us and our two sets of enemies, and I thought that if I took myself out of the equation, things might quieten down. maybe they wouldn't have to deal with the confrontations, random moments of violence, and just the complete bullshit of the drama anymore. A lot of my actions during this time came from a place of fear – fear of being hurt, fear of looking weak, and fear of admitting to myself that I was feeling fear at all.

WET SOCKS

I was never the best soldier – not by any stretch of the imagination. I wasn't even a very good one. I hated the field, the rain, the cold and, most of all, I hated having wet socks.

I joined CTCRM on 4 March 2002, when I began my thirty weeks' Royal Marines Commando training. I was in 827 troop and there were about sixty of us, ranging from the ages of fifteen and three quarters right the way up to twenty eight years of age; though this number would dwindle away massively over the course of the next thirty weeks.

The first two weeks in foundation block were a complete shock to the system for me. It was the beginning of the transitioning from civilian life to military life, and all sixty of us recruits lived in one massive dormitory. During this phase, we were taught everything from scratch, including how to fold clothes perfectly so that they were no bigger than a piece of A4 paper – any bigger and you would fail locker inspections. We were taught how to shower our bodies, how to pull back the foreskin of your penis and make sure it was cleaned, and why maintaining hygiene was so important.

It was explained to us that if you went down with an illness, the chances were that your bivvie (slang for a bivouac shelter or improvised campsite) partner would go down; if your bivvie partner went down, your section went down; if your section went down, the troop went down; and if your troop went down, the company went down, etc … to the very exaggerated point that the entire British armed forces could go down due to one bloke not staying on top of his personal hygiene. This is why it's such an essential part of military life.

I had never been in a communal shower, nor had I ever seen so many naked men before, and it was intimidating. There I was, with this embarrassing body of mine, and there was no way of hiding it. I would either try to be the very first one to wake up in the morning and shower, or wait until pretty much everyone had finished and get in there, quickly washing myself before our first timing of the morning.

We had fitness tests, map reading lessons, gym sessions, weapon practice periods, weapon handling tests, corps history lessons and much more besides, and there was very little time in between periods. Clock time was precious, and we had to use the time in between periods carefully. You had to ensure that you were immaculately dressed and in the correct rig – marine slang for military attire – for the next period. We had to be out on the road, in front of the block, stood in file and at ease, five minutes before the designated timing, as a good Marine is always five minutes early.

Week after week, training got progressively harder. Without even knowing it, I had become physically fitter than I had ever been, I was passing my swimming tests and could even tread water … though in truth it was more a case of me fighting for my life, to keep my head above the water line. When the struggling got too much, I would take a deep breath, allow myself to sink for a little bit, then push off the bottom of the pool, making my way to the top again so that I could continue the struggle.

This would go on for the entire three minutes, and I occasionally glanced at the other lads bobbing around effortlessly, talking to each other and laughing, taking it all in their stride. I, on the other hand, would be in the fight of my life, swallowing and coughing up swimming pool water. I would get out after the three minutes and just be grateful that I hadn't embarrassed myself by downing – not that what I was doing was much more graceful.

Over the coming months, the troop got increasingly smaller. Some lads would quit because the training and general lifestyle had become too much, and they just wanted to go home and feel some love and affection from their mothers. Other lads were failing rope climbs, map reading, field craft or some other aspect of training, and would quit or get back trooped so that they could be retaught the skill or theory behind whatever subject it was that they had failed.

I felt like quitting every single day. I absolutely hated the field, which is what soldiering is pretty much all about. During one exercise, called hunters' moon if I remember correctly, we were given a field craft lesson on 'wet and dry'. We were taught that whilst out in the field, there could be all sorts of adverse weather conditions, or rivers that may have to be crossed in order to obtain the mission objective, and that the correct way to administrate yourself after such an endeavour was: upon reaching the troop harbour and completing all harbour routines, change into your dry clothes that you had waterproofed and packed in your bergan. The wet clothes that you took off were to be rung dry and laid out on top of your roll mat, but under your sleeping bag, the theory being that your body heat would hopefully dry them out overnight.

The thing is, when you're in a harbour, you have to get up at all kinds of crazy hours in the night to go on sentry duty, and guess what? You're not allowed to do that in your dry clothes because if it rains, then you would have two sets of wet clothes, which wouldn't be very good field craft. So, the idea was that you changed back into your wet clothes, packed your sleeping bag away and went on sentry. Just before last light, the training team took the troop to a little pond type pool of water, and as soon as I saw it, I knew that it was going to completely ruin my day.

They made us hold our rifles above our heads and wade through the pool of water, which was just below our necks, and we had to squat under the water for a few seconds so as to insure we were completely soaked. As we got out of the pool and patrolled back to the harbour, I felt water squelching out of my boots with every step I took. I was cold and soaking wet, and all I could think was: 'this is not for me'. When we got back to the harbour to carry out the wet and dry drill, I removed my soaking wet rig as fast as humanly possible, then put my dry rig on. I rung out the wet stuff and placed it in between my sleeping bag and roll mat.

At some ungodly hour in the middle of the night I got a shake, which signalled it was my turn to go on sentry, so I got up, sat on top of my sleeping bag and began to strip my dry clothes off. I don't know how many of you reading this have had the luxury of putting wet clothes back on, which admittedly doesn't sound like that much of a thing, but let me tell you, it most definitely is. As I sat there, having stripped off my perfectly dry trousers and socks, while holding onto my still very much wet, previously worn uniform, I struggled to accept what it was that I had to do. Eventually, I managed to first gather up the minerals to put my socks on. I had rung them dry and they were mostly just damp, being such a small item. Then came my trousers, which were still soaked through, despite having been rung out earlier, and while it wasn't a nice feeling, my legs could take it … once I removed my dry shirt and put the wet one back on, however, it was a whole different ball game.

The wet material clung tightly to my skin, and there wasn't much cloud cover, so it was a very cold night. The wind was blowing quite softly, but just hard enough to send a horribly cold chill right through my wet clothes and into the very core of my body. I got up with my weapon, walked over to the sentry position, and when I got there, I laid down in prone position, observing my arch's over the lens of my SUSAT (sight unit small arms trilux – a scope, basically). As the cold wind blew and the chill cut deep into my body, I lay there thinking: 'how the hell has my life come to this?'

I just wanted to kill people, not be cold and wet, sleeping in the woods. I promised myself that I would put my chit, the equivalent of a resignation letter, in the very next day. The next day came and I didn't quit, the exercise ended and we went back to camp. There were many more exercises just like that, and every time we went out in the field, I promised myself that it would be my last time, that I would quit … but the truth is: I didn't have the balls. It would have been like admitting to myself that I was weak and a failure, and I would have had to go home and deal with my enemies; plus, they would have blacked out my face with a permanent marker on the troop photo that was kept in our block, and I really didn't want to join the many others who had already met that fate.

During training, I was blessed to meet Ethan, a fellow recruit who would become one of my closest, lifelong friends. Anyone who has ever been in the military will know and understand that it is a community where you will meet some, if not all, of your closest friends for life. In brotherhoods like these, you develop such camaraderie that it would be hard to imagine a day when you no longer talk to the comrades you met there. There's something to be said when you've seen each other naked, have witnessed each other in your worst moments, have confided in each other about personal hardships, and have seen each other's weaknesses, whether it be out in the field, map reading periods, PT or up on the thirty foot ropes. All of this serves to bring you closer and develops strong, lifelong bonds. This is what I grew to have with Ethan and a small group of others, who I consider my brothers.

I passed out of training in November 2002 after successfully completing the thirty weeks' course. My mum and many more of my family members came to watch my passing out parade, a ceremony in which recruits officially graduate to Royal Marine status. My dad even made an appearance, looking very proud every time he introduced himself to the other families as my father. My family got to see me and the rest of my troop dressed in our Lovetts during the awarding of prestigious honours achieved during training, and the presentation of a green beret to each marine.

They got to see us, in our best blues, elegantly march around the drill hall executing arms drill movements at the halt and on the march, in synchronicity to the sound of the Royal Marines' band playing The Last of the Mohicans. For those who've never seen it, it's quite a thing to behold. The troop is inspected by a high ranking guest of honour, and upon completion of the ceremony, the final command you hear given is: "Royal Marines, to your duties! Quick march!"

I got drafted to 45 Commando Royal Marines up in Scotland, where I joined nine troop Yankee Company. Early the following year, around February 2003, nine troop was attached to Zulu company force protection and we deployed to the Kuwaiti desert, where we acclimatised to the Middle Eastern weather and prepared to cross the border.

I couldn't believe it. I had only had my green beret for two minutes and I was already at war, which is exactly what I had joined for. I was in a desert for the very first time in a foreign country I had never been to.

During the acclimatisation period, we trained every day. We practiced section attacks and radio communication drills, we had first aid practice periods, there were rehearsals at night time with helicopters and coalition troops … the training didn't stop.

Whenever Iraq launched a scud missile that had shown up on detection equipment somewhere, we would hear the beeping of military vehicle horns or the clanging together of mess tins, which worked as an alarm system, giving us early warning that there could be incoming, indirect fire. Since there was a threat of chemical capabilities, we had to don our respirators immediately every time this happened. We had to kneel down, get the respirator out of its sack and pull it on, over our heads, confirming with a finger check that the seal around the face was complete, and then shout "Gas gas gas!", alerting anyone else in the vicinity who maybe hadn't heard. We then made our way to the trenches we had dug and waited for the all clear.

Eventually, the day came when coalition forces crossed the border to invade Iraq. The night before, I remember hearing jets flying over our heads and dropping payloads on carefully selected targets, dominating the air space and gaining air superiority. In the morning, I saw thick, dark dust clouds that covered the entire area, and by now the spearhead units of the coalition forces had crossed the border and there were troops on the ground. We received intelligence reports and objective updates throughout the day, and the following night, before crossing the border ourselves, when far in the distance I saw what appeared to be a massive contact.

There was red tracer, a round that has phosphorus burning on the back as a means of target indication, which was being fired from right to left by Western forces; and then I saw green tracer rounds firing from left to right by enemy forces. The whole thing was very surreal. I had watched so many war movies by this point and now I was actually in one, albeit I didn't actually do much, as the troop I was with weren't there as an integral part of the main war effort.

Nevertheless I was there, and I was fascinated.

The official war period lasted just over a month, though for many of the years that followed, troops and close protection operators who were deployed over there would experience some of the worst conflicts Iraq had seen. My troop returned to the UK in May and re-joined Yankee company, where we began pre-deployment training for a Northern Ireland peacekeeping deployment.

Once beat up training was complete, the whole unit was sent home on pre-deployment leave for a few weeks. Just before returning home, I had applied for a credit card with a three thousand pound limit, and once it was approved, and I was back at mum's house in London, I began researching the best places to go and get my gynecomastia dealt with. I found a private doctor's surgery in Harley Street, where I went for an initial consultation.

The procedure was explained to me and I was told that it would cost two thousand pounds. I was more than happy to pay that and thought it was a bargain. In fact, I would have paid any amount to get this embarrassing bane of my life removed. My mum tried to talk me out of it, saying I didn't need it and telling stories of how many people had gone under for surgeries and never woken up, but none of this mattered to me, as I wanted these man breasts gone.

The day of the operation arrived, and when I went in for surgery I was handed a gown to wear and shown to a room. Once all of the preparation was done, I was taken to the operating theatre, where an IV drip was attached. The doctor then asked me how many pints of beers I could drink, and I jovially told him ten, which was definitely a wild stretch of the imagination at that point. I was a lightweight in comparison to some of the other lads I had met in the Marines, who had clearly declared war on their livers.

He told me to count backwards from ten down to one, but I don't even remember making it to six. The next thing I remember is waking up in a private room with my mum sat there keeping me company. These are the sort of things I love about my mum and am so grateful for. The doctor came to see me once I was awake, and actually showed me the breast tissue he had cut out. I was so happy to see it there in a petri dish and no longer a part of my body. I left the surgery the same day, with my mum accompanying me home. They bandaged up my chest, told me to take it easy, to avoid strenuous activity, and that I should be fully recovered after a couple of weeks.

During my time at home, I would see my old enemies from up the road from time to time. We stared at each other, and while we stayed out of each other's way, there was still clearly a lot of bad blood there between us. The rest of my leave passed by uneventfully, and when it was over, I returned to 45 Commando up in Scotland, and we deployed to Northern Ireland.

Yankee company was split over a few different locations. I spent time at Aughnacloy, Aldergrove, Dungannon, Ballykinlar and Clogher over the six month period we were deployed there. We would be on a six day rotation of either day patrols, night patrols or camp security. During the day and night patrols, we would go out in multiples – sometimes on foot and sometimes in vehicles – always providing mutual support to each other.

For example, there was Alpha to Hotel (names we used for checkpoints, so that we never had to name actual locations or grids unnecessarily on the net, which safeguarded against being ambushed), locations where we would set up vehicle checkpoints and stop and talk to the road users. There would be 'the chatter upper' talking to them. The military variant of a Land Rover, called a snatch, would be parked in such a way that they boxed the vehicles in once we pulled them over, and the cut offs had stingers or caltrops. I was mostly one of the cut offs, laid in a ditch at the side of the road, holding onto the caltrops or stingers, and my job was to deploy them if a vehicle ever broke through the checkpoint.

It was a winter deployment, so it was cold, wet and miserable. It was grim, and we laid there soaking wet for what seemed like forever. During the camp security rotations, we were on a six hours on/six hours off sentry routine. Sangers are fortified enclosures, and in this case were big metal boxes with reinforced glass windows, where we conducted our sentries and watched our arcs. There were multiple sangers and one super sanger on camp. Most sangers were just above the top of the protective fence line that surrounded the camp, but the super sanger was massive, affording us 360 degrees of archs and a clear view of most things in the surrounding area.

When you have time to sit in a sanger by yourself for two hours, before moving onto the next one, only to crack exactly the same detail, things can get dark very quickly, so you have to try and find ways to occupy yourself. You can do this by carrying out radio checks with the other sentry positions, which is over in a matter of seconds; you can imagine what you will do when you win the lottery, even though you probably don't play it, which was a favourite of mine; and you can clock watch, but I promise that if you do this, they will be some of the longest hours and days of your life. I done it all, and when I looked at my watch only fifteen minutes had passed.

I don't know why, but I began writing poems from the thoughts circulating in my mind. I found it killed time and kept my mind occupied. Back then, I had no idea why my poems were so deep – sanger duty was dire, but not to the extent of the content I was writing.

Why so many questions?
Death inevitably comes to us all so …
How will I die? When will I die?
How and when will the ones I love and care about die? How will those of you reading this die? Who will be murdered? You? Me? Who will come into some sort of depression and take their own life? What will be engraved on your gravestone? What will we have engraved on our parents' gravestones? What families will bring murderers, rapists into this world? Yours? Mine?
What makes murderers, rapists and all those alike do what they do? Does it really take all sorts to make the world go round? Is it selfish to want to die before the ones you love and care about, so we don't have to feel the pain when they go?
What is there after death? Is there an afterlife? Is God a woman or a man? Is there a God? I mean, is there really a God? If so, what is he/she doing against all the evil in the world? Is there a Devil? Is there more evil in this world than there is good?
Will you have children? If so, what will they do? Does the Bible answer all these questions? What makes someone's faith to their religion so strong? Is it something that's happened or is it a security thing? Do people feel more secure and confident if they believe there is something or

*someone watching over us? What are we living for? What is the aim to
life? What is the reason for our existence? To reproduce? To make as
much money as we can before we die? To be poor? Why are some people
so rich and spend so much money on so many unneeded luxuries? Why
are some people so poor and can't even afford food? Are we all just
victims to some sort of super being who is conducting an experiment? Is
it really what you know or is it just who you know? Do we make our
own destinies or are they already mapped out for us? Are some of us
just meant to have shitty lives?*

As we got close to finishing the tour of Northern Ireland, I was
told that there was a big chance I was going to get pinged for a
signals course and go down the communications branch of the
corps, which didn't really scream out at me as something I
wanted to do. Instead, I decided to leave the corps, but that I
would first put in a request to join the Motor Transport Branch
and get my driver's license out of it.

We completed the tour of Northern Ireland in March 2004,
returning to 45 Commando before going home on post-
deployment leave. Whilst at home on leave, the situation with the
two brothers who lived up the road started to escalate again, and
my brother told me there had been a few altercations on the
street between him, our friends and these guys whilst I had been
away. I felt bad, like I had abandoned Richard and our friends.
One day, there was a knock at the door and, after checking the
spyhole first, I couldn't see anyone, so went into the kitchen and
looked through the window to see if anyone was there.

Two boys stood there at the edge of the drive, and I recognised
them as youths who were always with the main brother I was
having this problem with, and who sold drugs for him. At this
time, these types of boys were called youngers – slang for boys
or young men who were below the legal age of what's considered

manhood, which meant they were classed as juveniles. A lot of the time, these youngers would carry out the work for their olders, knowing that if they got caught, they would do less time because of their age.

So, I saw these youngers stood outside the front of my mum's house, wearing hoodies with the hoods pulled up over their heads and scowling, not really looking like they had come to have a laugh.

"What's the problem?" I asked, leaving the house.

"One of your boys saw us on the street and disrespected us, man," the louder, more aggressive of the pair scowled, telling me his name and where he lived.

"If you know who he is and where he lives, what are you doing at my house?" I asked.

"Who the fuck are you talking to?" he snarled, whilst half pulling out the handle of gun that he was concealing in his hoodie.

At this point, I had seen many guns, rifles, weapons and arms in general, so it didn't particularly bother me. Only around a couple of metres away from me, I stepped towards him. My plan was to grab hold of his wrist with my right hand before he had a chance to completely pull out the gun, and punch his face in with my left; but at that point, the guy he had come with, who was stood even further away, started reaching down his trouser leg to pull out what I assumed was another gun, so I stopped my advance. The house door flew open and my brother and two friends, who had been inside, emerged with the three samurai swords we kept indoors. "Leave it, man, he's got a beast," said Richard, while ushering me backwards.

As we were retreating in front of our own house, the youngers became increasingly irate, clearly growing in confidence. It wasn't how I wanted things to go, especially with my little sister, who had seen all of this unfolding, being indoors. By now, Richard had gotten rid of the .38 special we had hidden in the attic, which turned out to be a really good thing because in the hype of that moment, all I was thinking was that if we still had it there, I would have gone and got it, and shot this guy dead from the bathroom window.

Because it wasn't just Richard and I who lived at the house – there was our mum and little sister to think about too – and I would be returning to work soon, I decided to go against everything I grew up believing, which was never tell the police anything. So, after justifying it to myself, I called the police and reported that two gunmen were outside our house. The two youngers decided to leave after shouting their mouths off at the front of the house, as neighbours' curtains twitched and parted to observe the goings on.

I couldn't believe that it took the police fifteen minutes to show up and, of course, by the time they did, the two young men were long gone. There was a police helicopter up in the air, assisting the ground police in the search for people fitting the description I had given, but they were never found. The next day, two high ranking police officers came to the house and left us with a panic alarm that we were to use in the event that the pair ever returned. I felt very weak for calling the police, and even worse at having a panic alarm fitted, but told myself that it was the right decision – the only decision – as my mum and sister's safety came before anything else.

A few days later, Gina came back from the shop in a very tearful state, having seen the brother who had an issue with us.

"He gave me his mobile number, and told me to tell you to call him," she said. "He said: 'Your brothers think they're bad, but if they carry on, I'll see them one day and lick off their head tops!'"

Slang for shooting someone in the head, I was enraged that he had spoken to my sister like that. In fact, I was enraged that he had spoken to her at all.

"it's alright," I told her. "You don't have to cry or worry. No one's going to get shot." I took the number from her and called it. As soon as he answered, I told him it was me; and before he had the chance to say anything, I told him: "My sister's got nothing to do with this, so don't be approaching her on the street."

"Look, I'd never do anything to her. She has nothing to do with it and I think she's cute," he answered. "I'm vexed at my youngers for coming to your house with guns, but if you and that brother of yours keep acting like you're badmen, you're gonna get merked (slang for killing somebody) when you least expect it. I'll see you outside of the manor and lick off your head tops. Let's squash the beef between us. We live too close to one another, and there are others to think about – our families – who've got nothing to do with any of this."

I agreed, of course. I had never wanted any of this in the first place and hated confrontations, and as my leave was soon to be over and I would return to my unit up in Scotland, leaving my family at the house, I would be unable to help or retaliate if anything was to happen. As much as I was glad that we had negotiated a truce, during our phone call I had also heard a threat that me or Richard could be away from our neighbourhood one day and be shot dead. I was scared for my brother, knowing that I wouldn't be there much longer, so in that moment I decided I was going to kill him. I mean, how hard could it be? I was a Royal Marine Commando now, a trained killer, a steely-eyed dealer of death, so I could kill him, no dramas.

My leave came to an end and I went back to Scotland, where I started working on my plan. I decided to give it a year or so before I made my move, so that hopefully nobody would suspect me, and ordered black tactical combat trousers and a shirt online. My plan was that when the year had passed, I would travel down to London without telling anyone, not even my brother. I would set up an observation post in the allotments across the road from this guy's house to surveil him, and when the opportunity presented itself, I would come up from behind him and cut his throat open.

It most definitely wasn't the prettiest plan, and would be very messy, but in training we had been taught the mnemonic K.I.S.S., or Keep It Simple Stupid. This essentially meant maintaining the simplest version of your plan, because the more elaborate you make it, the bigger the scope for failure. So of all my plans, of which there were many, I decided to go with this one, as it was simple, straight to the point, and he also had quite a few enemies, so no one would have been able to decisively say who had done it.

The Depths Of Depression

From the depths of my depression my anger is fuelled
So cold and bitter and full of hatred it's brewed
There's torment and frustration in every arc that I view
Every day that goes by my morale loses the duel
To the rest of my feelings that have already surrendered to the gloom
If I could just take a minute, a moment or two, to put into perspective my depression for you
The dark grey clouds on a wet, miserable day
The ones I have loved who haven't loved me the same way
Orders I hate but still must obey
Getting up to work on a cold winter's day
Role models of mine that evil has had slain
Unfortunate lives of which illness has claimed
Innocent children brutally murdered and maimed

The daily struggles and stress that burden the brain
Visions that haunt you and won't let you sleep
Brings you to your knees and makes a strong person weak
For these are the foundations to the depths of my depression
The tip of an iceberg, the scratch on a surface
The step to a stairwell that leads to hundreds

On returning to 45 Commando after leave, the majority of the unit deployed to Tampa Bay, America, for an exercise. I was put on rare party (common at times like Christmas, Easter and summer leave, this means remaining in camp to maintain its security, defence and integrity) to conduct guard duties whilst awaiting my upcoming driver's course.

During this time, I discovered how easy it was to borrow money from banks. I already had the two thousand pound debt from my boob job, which I was paying back via my credit card each month, and now I decided to take out a loan to buy a car for when I completed my driver's course. I couldn't believe how easy it was to borrow money. I only had to apply for credit cards and loans, and I got them, especially as I was in the military. The money lenders knew that I had a stable job and that they could bleed me dry for years, especially as I was young, financially unwise and not wanting any advice from anybody.

A good friend of mine, another Marine in the same troop, had a Grand Jeep Cherokee that he was trying to sell, and I loved big four wheel drives, which I thought all real men should sit behind the wheel of. I had ten thousand pounds from the loan, and he wanted seven thousand for the Jeep. My mum told me she didn't know much about cars, but that she thought I should get it checked by a mechanic to ensure it was in good condition. I wasn't really interested in hearing this, because I was buying it from a good friend and I knew he wouldn't rip me off, so I told her not to worry and that I knew what I was doing.

After buying the Jeep, I parked it on camp and occasionally drove it around, even though I didn't have a driving license at this point. Within the first week of purchasing it, I noticed that it pulled to the right a little, but around the two or three week mark, it was obvious that something was seriously wrong with it. I took it to a garage to get it looked at, and the mechanic said that the drive shaft was badly damaged, had been for some time, and because the vehicle had most likely been driven around like that for a while, it had caused various other problems. He told me that it wasn't something you could fix, and that a whole new drive shaft was required, plus some other parts; and that it wasn't economically viable for a Jeep of this age. He told me that he would do it, but he wanted to be honest with me.

I messaged my friend, who was in America on exercise, and relayed what I had been told. He promised me there had been nothing wrong with it, and that he would get his dad, who was in the country, to call and help me out. His dad called, and while I was expecting help – some sort of compensation to help fix it, or even a fraction of the money I had paid returned to me, as I had been sold a non-roadworthy vehicle – what he actually said was: "I'm sorry, but it was sold as seen."

I was devastated, not only because of the money, but because he had been my close friend, and I would never have dreamt that he would have done this to me. When the time came to go to Leconfield, York, where my driver's course was to be held, I got the Jeep towed there, not having a clue what to do with it.

Whilst I was on this course, I bumped into Ethan one day. He had recently been posted there to do the same course, and it was so good to see him again and catch up with him. He arrived with a guy called Aaron, who would soon become another of my closest, lifelong friends.

One of the lads on my course had heard about my Jeep drama, and offered me a thousand pounds for it. To pay just a grand for such a vehicle, even though he had to get the drive shaft fixed, was probably a bargain for him; though it made me feel sick, thinking about how much money I had lost on it. By now, I had completed the Category B part of the driving course, so had a driver's license and still really wanted a car. I found a car dealership not too far from camp and went in to speak to the people there, despite not having any money to buy anything. After showing me the various vehicles on offer, we went into an office and the sales rep brought up some options on his computer. They offered me finance, and amazingly I passed the credit check and drove away with a Ford Focus that cost seven thousand odd pounds.

By now, I had spent what had been left over from the ten thousand pounds loan, and had also increased my credit card limit on two cards, issued by different banks. I had only been in the corps approximately two and a half years, so my monthly wage left a lot to be desired, especially for someone who had multiple direct debits coming out monthly from more companies than I can possibly remember, and I was constantly overdrawn. I remember thinking how lucky I was to be in the military and have my food taken care of – all I had to do was go to the galley on camp every meal time.

I started getting letters from the banks about being in arrears, some of them titled in red ink, which I knew only too well about from having seen them arrive at my mum's house over the years. When I actually sat down one day and looked at how much I actually owed, it scared me. I had amassed over twenty thousand pounds' worth of debt and I was barely twenty three years old. One of the lads, Kevin, had a good laugh when I told him about it.

"You'll never pay that off, you'll never own a house, find a woman or have a family – you're fucked!" he said.

Kevin was a good guy, and we actually became good friends, but in that moment his words were most unhelpful. I hadn't even thought about it that deeply, but he was right. What woman in her right mind would get involved with a man who was in so much debt? What he said changed my whole state of being, and it was the first time I ever thought about committing suicide. Deeply depressed, I laid in bed at night in the barracks, listening to the lads talking and laughing, sounding like they didn't have a care in the world; while I laid there, trying to think of the easiest, least painful way to take my own life. I mostly thought about jumping off buildings, which I imagined to be a quick, clinical death, as long as I picked the right building.

I wished I had listened to my mum when she had given me financial advice, because if I had, I most probably wouldn't have found myself in such a situation … but one thing I have come to learn about myself is that no matter what, I will always choose the hard way. Regardless of how many people try to help me or point me in a better direction, I never learn.

A Quick One Before I Depart

The pain is unreal but it's too late for second thoughts
The water's turning red and my wrists are sliced apart
The pain is unreal but it's now coming to pass
My eyes begin to close and my life's about to depart
The pain was unreal but now I find peace within the dark

After several weeks of being marooned in some of the deepest depths of depression I have ever known, one of the lads told me about consolidation loans. By doing that, I could pay off all of my current debts, eliminating all monthly direct debits, apart from one, to whichever provider issued the loan. It felt like there was hope again.

I went into my bank and applied for a consolidation loan; one big enough to cover all of my current existing ones and, as had been the case before, it was awarded to me. I borrowed another twenty odd thousand pounds, but over the ten year course of the loan, interest included, the total repayment amount would be thirty thousand pounds. It felt like I was just sinking deeper and deeper into debt, but I agreed and signed for it.

It was probably the best way that I could have dealt with my situation once it had gotten so bad, and my monthly payments were manageable, falling to around three hundred pounds. I had money in my pocket again, I could go out with the lads, and I no longer wanted to kill myself. There aren't many things that have made me want to take my own life, but of the few that there have been, money was most definitely front and centre.

Now that I was in this horrendous amount of debt, my plans changed drastically. I couldn't leave the corps as I had a thirty grand loan to pay off, and it felt as if I would be staying in service for the rest of my life.

After completing the driver's course, I was drafted to motor transport troop at Stone House barracks in Plymouth. Shortly after, Ethan and Aaron were drafted there too, which was pretty awesome. We would go out at night to all of the bars on Union Street and met Danny, a tall Viking looking guy who was also based at Stone House. There was Dan, based just up the road at the Citadel, who was in the Army and was the brother of my good friend, Dave, who I met at 45 Commando. Last but not least, I met Richie, who was based at 42 Commando, not far from Stone House barracks. I was the only Londoner in the group, and the other guys were from Liverpool and Manchester, with strange accents. We were always together, going ashore (Marine slang for going out) at the weekend.

At this point, I was in the gym every day, as were most of the guys I hung around with. We did either weightlifting or cardio, but as I hated cardio I stuck to the weights, whereas guys like Ethan would absolutely annihilate themselves doing cardio. Ethan was a beast in the gym and smashed all of our physical assessments.

My thinking was that, to my knowledge, no woman has ever approached a skinny man on the beach, grabbed his wrist and said: "Oh my god, your resting heart rate is amazing!" It just doesn't happen, but women do stop men to complement them on their muscles, and that was where I was with my reasoning. It didn't demonstrate any depth of character, or even a decent level of maturity, but that's where I was in my life back then.

Despite going to the gym every day, I still wasn't the size I wanted to be, which bothered me; but luckily, I knew a guy who knew a guy, and just like that, I started taking steroids. I began by using Deca by itself, which anybody who knows about steroids will tell you never to do, because when you take it by itself, you will most definitely have some very, very embarrassing moments in the bedroom. I experienced 'Deca dick', or losing an erection, but didn't know that the Deca was responsible. It gave me a complex, because now I thought I couldn't function sexually, and had to face some very awkward moments, especially with one night stands – it was no good spending all night telling somebody how awesome you are, only to get back to the bedroom and not be able to back any of it up.

After watching a few online videos and Googling it, I realised that the sexual dysfunction was down to using Deca by itself, so I added some Sustanon to it, which eliminated my bedroom problems immediately, and I felt like a man again. I managed to gain some decent muscle over the next few months and began to get much stronger than I had ever been before.

In late 2005, after completing an exercise in Senegal, Africa, we sailed back through the Canary Islands and docked at Santa Cruz, where we were allowed shore leave. Many lads went to Playa de Las Americas and had an amazing time there, but I stayed more locally and went out with a different group of friends than I normally did. These guys found a place where many beautiful professional lovemakers worked. I don't particularly like the word prostitute, or any of the other colourful words used to label the women who work in this industry, so you'll always hear me refer to them as lovemakers, and this is mostly due to the lady I had the privilege of meeting at this location.

We got two taxis and made our way to the location, a mansion with a massive electric gate at the front that retracted to let us in. We pulled up outside the front entrance of the property, and there was a massive bouncer stood there, dressed all in black wearing a bandana that covered some of his facial features. This was all very new to me; I mean, by this time I'd already been with a few lovemakers, but never somewhere so fancy. He let us in and we were shown to a part of the property that had a bar, which was good for me, as I got to drink a little to settle my nerves. This was a little outside of my comfort zone, and at this point in my life I would never have had the balls to find such a place, actually go there and pay for an experience by myself.

After one drink, the host brought the ladies in, of which there were four; but the lads I was with told them we weren't ready yet. We played a game called spoof between us, to establish the pecking order, and I came in third place. Once we had completed the game, the host called the ladies back in, this time there were six of them, and I had already seen the woman I wanted to pick. She was beautiful, with olive coloured skin and a firm thickness to the shape of her body. She wore glass type, transparent high heels and a yellow silk robe with white lingerie, and I was hoping that none of the guys higher up the pecking order would pick her, as I wanted her badly. When it finally came to my turn, the lady that I wanted was still there, so I picked her immediately. Once we had all chosen, the ladies left the room, returning moments later with what looked like a makeup bag and fresh towels. We were taken to different rooms, and the lady I was with, who had the most beautiful accent, told me her name was Sabrina. She gave me a towel and signalled at me to get undressed. It was clear by now that there was a language barrier – she spoke Spanish and knew absolutely no English, whereas I spoke English and knew absolutely no Spanish.

It didn't matter, though, because as creepy as this might sound, it felt like there was a connection between us, even though we couldn't really communicate with each other. I get that most people reading this will say: "Of course she made you feel that way – it's her profession," but by now I had been with a few lovemakers and they definitely didn't all make me feel connected. We went back into the bedroom after showering, disrobed and got onto the bed. We knelt on the bed, staring at each other with these shy grins and expressions on our faces. I already knew exactly how I wanted to start. She was so beautiful, I just wanted to taste every inch of her, so I laid her down and that's exactly what I did. There's something that feels so good about being able to pleasure a woman and see that she's truly enjoying it. Again, some of you might think that she was acting, but all I can tell you is that I've been with women who I haven't been able to please, and I've been with women who've been acting.

The experience I had with Sabrina felt very honest, and after we had finished being intimate with each other, we lay there on the bed. She caressed my face and smoothly ran her hands down my arm. There was something that felt so caring and nurturing about how she was touching me and, as weird as it might seem, she made me feel seen.

I think that my desire to be with lovemakers grew because of this particular experience, and they were definitely not all as caring or nurturing as Sabrina, but some of them showed me it's possible for someone in that profession to show care and affection to the person they are providing the service to. Of the whole expedition, sailing to Africa through Madeira, then back to the United Kingdom via the Canary Islands, Sabrina was the best thing that happened.

It was late 2005 when I returned from Africa, and my plan to sneak home unannounced and assassinate the guy from up the road had taken a bit of a back seat. That said, it was still one of the top priorities in my mind, although my brother told me everything was good; that there had been no more altercations with the brothers and his crew since making the truce. But I still held a deep-seated grudge towards him and wanted him dead. Work, however, was quite busy at this point, and by the time it got to 2006, the situation in Afghanistan had been escalating again and we were told that the whole brigade was going to deploy there for the winter.

Motor transport troop was split up and we were individually sent to different troops, some going to 42 Commando and some amongst India Company, Stone House. Before deploying to Afghanistan in September 2006 for six months, me and one of the lads, Duffy, became engaged in a typically banterful, testosterone-fuelled conversation about who was more of an alpha male. Well, it was obviously me … I was in the gym every day and was on steroids – how do you get more alpha than that? He obviously didn't agree, so we came up with a bet that went along the lines of: once we deployed to Afghanistan, if either of us were to get killed or injured, the one who took his death or injury in the least emotional manner would be the most alpha male. Once we were deployed, the war became an eye opener for me, because people I knew and had friendships with were getting killed and seriously injured.

We were based in Lashkar Gah, southwestern Afghanistan, the capital of Helmand province, while some of my friends who had been sent to 42 Commando were based in Sangin Valley. I was able to stay in touch with them through blueys, a forces free air letter service. There were also internet and satellite phones which we had to book in advance and use with iridium cards, which had a twenty minute allowance per week for phoning home.

Most days, Op Minimise, the suspension of all personal telecommunication between personnel deployed in theatre and the outside world, was called. It typically happens when someone has been killed or very seriously injured, and the MOD are endeavouring to ensure no sensitive information is divulged before the individual's family and close relatives are informed. I can't imagine anything worse than a mother, wife, child or close relative finding out that they've lost a family member through hearsay or social media.

I had friends who had been killed in battle, friends who had been killed by Improvised Explosive Devices and friends who had stepped on mines, leaving them seriously disfigured. It was all very surreal, getting information through that someone you knew or had met during military service had been dealt such a tough hand. It was an awakening, and it was sad.

Whilst based at Lashkar Gah camp, we rotated through guard duties, hearts and mind patrols in the local villages, and moved as small, mobile operating groups in a district called Garmsir, which was located in the southern part of Helmand province and shared a border with Pakistan, where many insurgents crossed over to join the Taliban war effort.

Whilst out on our hearts and minds patrols, we would interact with some of the locals and ask what the needs of their communities were. There were programmes in motion where engineers were building schools for them, and we gave the children water, footballs, white boards, dry line marker pens and other bits of stationery. During one of these patrols, the troop boss and some other team members were out on foot interacting with the locals. I was driving one of the three WMIK Land Rovers that were slowly creeping up the centre of the village track in support of the lads out on foot.

A cute little girl, who couldn't have been more than around nine or ten years of age, approached my vehicle. I signalled for her to come over and gave her a packet of these apple flavoured sweets that came with the ten man rations packs back at camp. These sweets were hard to come by – the minute they were put out in the galley, they got ravaged – and she took them and walked away. As we kept crept forward, I noticed in the mirror that she was stood by the edge of the road, overlooking a small cliff, unwrapping the sweets one by one and throwing them over the edge. I didn't understand why she would do that, as these sweets were awesome, so when she came back over to the vehicle, I gestured at her, as if to say: why did you throw them away?

She started talking to the lads up on top cover, whilst pointing at me. No one understood what she was saying, since none of us spoke Pashto. We called the interpreter over, and after speaking with her, he told us that she had been asking the white guys up top why they had brought 'this' black man – me! – to her country. It was then that I understood where she was going with it, and why she had thrown the sweets away. By now, she was pretty much shouting at me, and other kids had started gathering to see what all the commotion was.

They were all laughing, along with my team mates and interpreter, and the only response I could conjure was to say: "Durka durka, Stan," the racial piss-taking bit from the film Team America. She certainly didn't find it funny, grabbing her bottom lip and stretching it out, conveying the old joke about black people having big lips. She started to flick her lip whilst allowing the sound to come out of her mouth, like people do in front of a baby to try and get them to laugh, though the message behind her version of it was very different.

She had all the kids who had just arrived doing it too, it was like a chorus of flapping lips, and she had the entire village in hysterics. I had absolutely no comebacks and, just as I thought it might be over, she pointed at the vehicle tyre, which was obviously black, then pointed at me, as if to demonstrate the similarity between the colour of the tyre and me. I had just been absolutely destroyed by this ten year old child, and even I was laughing at this point. Finally, the savage berating drew to a conclusion and we continued on our patrol.

In mid-January 2007, my multiple moved down to Garmsir, Forward Operating Base (FOB) Delhi, on our mobile operations group rotation, and on the twentieth of the month, we went out on patrol to JTAC Hill. A defensive position that had been built up on the top of a hill that the Afghanistan national police manned, coalition forces went up there most days to provide support and get eyes on the ground towards the south and the Pakistan border. Upon our arrival, we immediately came under fire from insurgents who had taken up fire positions from the camouflage provided by the wealth of bush and plant life south of the hill.

We immediately returned fire, shots flying back and forth until there was a lull in the battle. Using the time to reload empty magazines, whilst the multiple commander sent situation reports and updates over the net, we were generally in high spirits, as it wasn't anything new to come under fire whilst out on patrol. When the insurgents opened fire again a little while later, we could hear the crack of the rounds as they whistled past us, overhead and through our position. I had already swapped positions with one of the lads and was on the GPMG (General Purpose Machine Gun), which fired 7.62mm calibre and provided seventy percent of the section's firepower.

As we returned fire, I saw a plume of smoke that I had learnt about in training. As soldiers, we clean our weapons and apply oil to lubricate all metal-on-metal surfaces, to prevent against rust, or soldiers' gold as we call it, before reassembling them. Applying too much oil dictates that the next time it's fired, the firing pin strikes the primer, igniting the gunpowder … and the chances are that the oil will ignite too, creating a plume of smoke that, under fire, will give your position away.

So, after seeing this, I gave a target indication and concentrated a heavy weight of GPMG fire in the direction of the smoke cloud. With no return of fire from that position, I was quite pleased with myself, thinking I may have killed someone. Then, out of nowhere, the next thing I knew, I was stretched out flat on the ground, with no idea how I had got there. My team mate, Goz, who was on the same position as me, looked at me as if to say: "What are you doing?" I had absolutely no idea, I was so confused, and as I looked at the GPMG and it was lying against the sandbags all skewwhiff, I tried to get up, but couldn't. I then thought that maybe I didn't have enough mussel clearance (ensuring the mussel of your weapon has space around it when you fire, as when this doesn't occur, it can affect the bullet's trajectory or create a breach of the mussel) when I fired and had shot myself, but that couldn't be it, because at such a close range, the round would have ripped some of my body off.

As I lay there completely befuddled, with Goz shouting at me to get back on the gun, I heard the crack of rounds flying just above my head. Someone from a south easterly position had opened up on us. I think at that point, it dawned on both me and Goz that I had been shot. I'm not sure why it took so long to figure out – it's not like it was rocket science, we were in the middle of a gun fight, and now I was lying on the floor, unable to move.

Looking back, it was pretty obvious to see what had happened. The only explanation I have for the delay in realising this is that you go out on the ground every day, never thinking it's going to be you. Why would you, when you're surrounded by other lads? I used to think that if something bad happened, it would be one of the lads beside me who got hit – not me. As far as I was concerned, the chances of me becoming injured were way too small. I believe every soldier has to think like that, or you would never go out, for fear of being the one who gets shot, who steps on a mine, who gets hit by a suicide bomber or IED, or who doesn't make it back home to his family.

As Goz pulled me out by my feet from the position we were in, I heard the bullets whizzing overhead, tear through a blue plastic chair that the ANP (Afghanistan National Police) used to sit on, and into the bund (Built Up Natural Defence) line (a mound of mud or earth that provides cover from incoming enemy fire) of the hill. In the military, people describe flying bullets as 'lead wasps', and rightly so. I had my head turned so far to the left, it was almost digging into the ground as Goz pulled me out on my back by my legs, screaming out that I had been shot. I remember thinking, just one round, a few inches lower, is all it would take to completely ruin my day, whilst watching the blue chair rattling around from the impact of the rounds.

Once he had pulled me far enough away from exposure to the incoming enemy fire, he ran off to get help and came back with the Corporal, who asked me where I had been shot. At first I thought it was my back, then my shoulder, but as I looked at the latter, there wasn't any blood, so I told him I hadn't been shot. He and Goz lifted me up into a seated position, removed my body armour and cut my rig off … and then I heard Goz shouting that I had indeed been shot.

I couldn't believe it, and was like a dog chasing its tail as I turned around to try and see what they were talking about, but my upper body didn't want to respond to me. Then Goz reached into my pocket to get my morphine out and administer it to me, but in that moment, I remembered the bet I had made with Duffy.

"Nah, I don't want any morphine," I told Goz. "And tell Duffy I took it non-emotionally."

This wasn't entirely true because as I started remembering the event, the moment I had been shot actually came back to me. I realised that it had felt like I had been hit in my back by a sledgehammer, and that I had screamed out … well, maybe less of a scream and more of a yell… a war cry even; yes, an alpha male recognition of pain – that's what it was.

What I found strange is that I had always imagined being shot to feel like an intense burning sensation, when it was more like a dull thud that completely knocks the wind out of you, and renders you momentarily disoriented and bewildered as to what's gone on. That's how it was for me, anyway.

The doctor arrived and requested that I be escorted back to the FOB. The lads wanted to carry me but, still thinking about my bet with Duffy, I said that I would walk. I made it to the vehicle at the bottom of JTAC hill and, once back at base, was assisted straight into the doctor's office, which was actually more of a derelict room in an abandoned building. The FOB had been repurposed as a home to troops whilst in Garmsir, and defensively built up as a fairly strong fortified position.

The doctor laid me down on my front, whilst tending to my back, and told me to keep me calm, which I thought I was. I was actually quite proud at how I'd handled the situation, but then my body started shaking involuntarily. I didn't understand what was happening, and started questioning if I was dying. The doctor told me that it was shock, which surprised me, because up until now I had always assumed that shock only happened if you panicked or got the fear … that it was something you got from being weak in the moment, and being unable to accept what was happening. It turns out that I was very wrong – shock is a chemical reaction your body can have as a response to a traumatic event, regardless of your state of mind or how tough you think you are.

The Immediate Response Team (IRT) arrived on a Chinnuck helicopter that would come in under fire carrying a section of Royal Marines, who would fan out immediately upon landing and take up defensive positions around the Chinnuck, whilst the onboard medical team retrieved the casualty and escorted them onto it.

We arrived at camp, and I was carried on a stretcher straight into the operating room, where there were around five to seven doctors, none of whom had a rank lower than Lieutenant Colonel, if I remember correctly.

They were a highly spirited group of banterful surgeons. At this point, I had only had one operation – the one for my gynecomastia – so it was fairly new to me and I really needed to use the toilet.

"I don't want to be on the operating table under anaesthetic, pissing everywhere, and all over you guys," I told them.

"Here you go, then," one of them said, handing me a vase type looking thing. "You can piss in that."

I felt a little bit shy to go pee pee in front of all these doctors, and I think they sensed it. "Are you sure you're a Royal Marine Commando?" one of them teased. "I thought Royal Marines were tough and confident?"

They knew I would respond to that type of goading, and they were right. I was representing the whole corps and couldn't be letting the side down, so I peed in the vase in front of them. A couple of them started laughing.

"I thought all black men were supposed to be big? Well, that's clearly not the truth in your case," smiled another.

I found them really funny and couldn't stop laughing. "I've just been shot and now I'm getting small dick jokes thrown at me. Talk about kicking a man when he's down!"

This was the sort of banter I had grown to love – light-hearted, harmless ribbing that made moments like this more bearable. Cheerfulness under adversity is a core ethos of the corps and, I imagine, one that all cap badges hold – how else could we do the job that we do and keep going back for more?

After my operation, the doctors told me I had been very lucky, as the round had entered via my left shoulder at a diagonal angle and exited through my left mid-back area. They said it was a miracle that the bullet had missed all bone structure in the shoulder area and not hit the lungs, which are positioned much higher up in the body than most people think.

I stayed in the field hospital for a week or so recuperating, and the Navy nursing staff were amazing – I owe a great debt of gratitude to them and the surgeons. Whilst I was there, the doctor who had been down in Garmsir with us came to see me, handing me the cutting of my combat 95 shirt, where the bullet had pierced and entered my shoulder, and the bullet itself. It was all in one piece, found in between the ballistic mesh and inside face of the rear body armour plate. I was told that because of the way the round had travelled through me, and the fact that it remained complete, meant it had most likely been at the end of its trajectory when it hit me. To this day, I still have the round I was shot with and the cutting of the shirt, though the dried blood around the entrance hole has now turned a yellowish colour.

I was able to leave the hospital and return to Lashkar Gah camp for a few weeks before my multiple was due rest and recuperation (R&R). I was put on light duties as I could barely lift my left arm, so worked in the ops room on radio watch and had physiotherapy every day, which really helped with my recovery.

When our R&R was due, I went home for two weeks, which was a culture shock – I went from being in a war zone to being back at home with the family within a day. Going out with some friends one day, we were waiting at a bus stop when a car drove by and the exhaust backfired.

Acting instinctively, I took cover immediately, which greatly amused my friends, who couldn't stop laughing. In Garmsir, receiving indirect fire and diving on the deck to take cover was a regular occurrence, and had become muscle memory.

When I redeployed back out to Afghanistan a couple weeks later, I went straight onto radio watch again, until I could have a physical assessment from the doctor and physio stating that I was fit to rejoin my multiple. We only had a few weeks left of the tour at that point and, once I was back in my multiple, we were told we would probably go back down to Garmsir for a few days' rotation. When I heard this, something in me didn't like the idea very much. It was almost a feeling that now I knew that bad things could happen to me too, there was a chance they would finish me off. It seemed personal somehow, which it clearly wasn't, but the mind can generate some crazy thoughts at times, as I knew all too well by now. Fortunately, we didn't end up going back down there before heading back to the UK.

Sometime after returning, I heard that the guy up the road who I had had so many issues with had died from a heart attack. I was so relieved, happy and glad that he was dead, as I wouldn't have to go through with my crazy plan, and didn't have to worry about him ever making trouble again for my family or friends. It's quite a cold, dark thing to feel happiness over the death of someone, but that was definitely how I felt at the time.

The Tunnel of Darkness

If I could shut my eyes and just be dead, no tears of anger should you shed
For from this life I have fled, no more torment and frustration inside of my head
And it is I that should shed tears of anger for you,
For in this cold bitter world you still await your doom
But I am now gone and free of my gloom
From the tunnel of darkness in which we are all consumed
So cry for me not but feel sorry for your souls
As the tunnel of darkness will swallow them whole

After being shot, something changed in me. I would constantly think: 'what if I had just moved a couple of inches to the left whilst firing the GPMG?' The round that had dropped in through my left shoulder may very well have entered through my head instead, changing everything, and I started to think that if I was going to get shot and truly risk my life, I should at least be getting paid more for it.

By 2008, loads of lads had left, and plenty more were handing their notices in, including Ethan and Aaron, to go and work in

Iraq and Afghanistan, as close protection operators earning what seemed like crazy amounts of money. I really wanted to join them and put my notice in, but was scared that the time to leave would come and I wouldn't be able to find a job, which would have put me in a very bad situation, considering I still had a thirty thousand pound loan to pay off … and I definitely didn't want to have to start thinking about killing myself again.

This is part of the trap that lads create for themselves as young soldiers. It's so easy to get into debt and then feel trapped by not being able to leave a stable job, such as being in the military; and then you get older guys, who've never been a civilian, telling you that the grass isn't always greener … which could definitely be true in some cases, but what would they know, when all they've ever experienced, workwise, is a lifetime in the military? Maybe some actually had the minerals to leave at some point, failed miserably at civilian life, and saw no other way but to return to their comfort zone and the only life they had ever really known.

I stayed in the corps until 2012, when I left after ten years of service. During my time in the Royal Marines, I had travelled the world, had the opportunity to see places such as Norway, train in cold weather warfare and be involved in brigade size exercises. I had been on Navy ships and sailed to Africa on exercise, deployed to two different wars, trained in the Belize jungle and made an advert for the Corps in the Brunei jungle. I had been drafted to Diego Garcia in British Indian Ocean territory, a draft that is in such high demand, but one that only a handful of lads will ever get … and the list goes on.

I had met lifelong friends in the corps who I trust with my life. I had a whole newfound respect for water, and how on one hand it's the elixir of life, but on the other, it could totally zap the morale right out of you in the form of rain or a river crossing. I had met guys who were true born soldiers, who loved their profession and were happier being in the field than camp. They could push themselves to levels that far exceeded mine, and I have a level of respect for these guys that is second to none. I loved my time in the Royal Marines, and wouldn't change it for the world.

HEARTBREAK

In 2009, I met Heartbreak in Manchester at an event that Dave and another friend, Foley, had organised, called Hidden Agenda. She physically embodied everything I was looking for in a woman, with long brown, wavy hair and an entICingly beautiful, curvaceous body. I found her absolutely stunning and was instantly attracted to her. Luckily, she came with a mutual friend of ours, which made it easier to conjure up a reason to talk to her, which was hard enough, given we were in a nightclub with music blaring out. I didn't manage to get her phone number that night, but the following evening a few of us went out again, and there she was, looking absolutely amazing.

We began to talk, and there was clearly a connection there. Stood side by side in this nightclub, we leant into each other to try and hear each other a bit better over the music, and almost every time we did this, our lips nearly touched. I had never had that happen before, and we apologised to each other every time it happened; but the truth was: I liked it, and it was happening naturally. Obviously, this wasn't the ideal place to try to get to know each other, and I could barely hear her over the music, but managed to ask for her number and she gave it to me.

Over the next few days, we messaged each other frequently. It was exciting to be in that phase of getting to know someone, when both of your interests are peaked; waking up every day, looking forward to speaking to that person, with a feeling that anything is possible … that this person might even be the one.

During the first couple weeks of talking, she told me that she had a boyfriend, but that he was in prison, which got thinking: why would she have even started speaking to me if she was committed to someone, and unavailable? There had to be something there … I could feel it. We spoke for weeks, and the whole time I grew increasingly attracted to her. One day, she told me that she had ended things with her boyfriend. I was so happy. A woman I had chosen had also chosen me, which was a good thing, because by now I only had eyes for her – other women didn't exist.

She came to visit me on camp on the west coast of Scotland one weekend, which was the first time we had seen each other since Manchester. When I picked her up at the train station, I was a little nervous, although I told her I wasn't. I think I was trying to come across as a confident alpha male, and you can't do that by being nervous and lacking in confidence. She looked so beautiful, I almost couldn't believe that she was really there, stood right in front of me. We cuddled and our embrace was filled with warmth. Feeling her body, although fully clothed, against mine, and in my arms, was a feeling that brought me so much happiness and joy, I thought to myself: 'this has to be the girl' … that she was the one.

After almost kissing countless times in the club in Manchester months before, it finally happened. I kissed her again and again, and each time I did, she kissed me back. We spent the weekend getting to know each other even better in person, sharing more of our life stories.

Heartbreak told me that she was half Greek and half Scottish, and that her mum had sadly passed away a few years earlier. That weekend was the first time we had sex together, and even though I was trying to play the role of an alpha male, which I have come to realise I most certainly am not, I don't think I actually lasted longer than two minutes. Out of pure embarrassment, I think I even used the line: "I'm so sorry, it's just that you're so beautiful." I cringe profoundly at myself every time I think of this now.

The weekend flew by and, unfortunately, she had to leave, but we grew closer and closer, constantly messaging and talking to each other. I had recently bought my first apartment in Manchester, so invited her to come and visit me one weekend when I had driven back home from work, which she said yes to. On the day she arrived, just before I left to pick her up at the train station, I ran a bath with bath salts, I set candles out on each corner of the bath, and deflowered into it two bouquets worth of red and pink roses that I had bought earlier.

I picked her up at the station, and it was exactly the same as when I last saw her: a strong desire to be with her in every way, for her to be my girlfriend, and to head to wherever that would take us. When we got back to my apartment, I told her she could take a bath if she wanted, as she had been travelling a little while. As she entered the bathroom, I heard a little gasp and she came back out looking very surprised. She said she loved it, and that no one had done that for her before.

I had never done that for anyone before either, but as a massive fan of chick flicks and a hopeless romantic, I thought this was one of the best ways to demonstrate to a woman what she truly means to you. She invited me to bathe with her and, looking back on it, it was quite the picture. I had left an assortment of grapes and strawberries out on a little table beside the bath, which we ate together, and once we had finished bathing, we went to the bedroom. As we had sex, I found myself telling her that I loved her, which was true, though I certainly hadn't planned on telling her … but I didn't have to worry about it long, because she said it back to me.

She wasn't the first woman I had felt this way about, but she was the first woman I had ever said "I love you" to their face, and the first women who had ever said it back to me. It took sex to another level, telling someone you love them and then hearing them say it back to you – I mean, wow! Who knew that sex when in love was an entirely different type of beast when compared to just fucking, and this time I lasted long enough to be able to appreciate it.

It was perfect, apart from one thing that felt a little weird to me: that she hadn't gone down on me. It was the second time we had met and it had all been so intense, but on both occasions it seemed she hadn't wanted to do it. I hadn't said anything last time, and didn't say anything this time, but it did make me think. I loved giving her oral sex, and couldn't work out why she didn't want to do it to me.

We met whenever possible, but I soon sensed a change in things between us. I had asked her to be with me, to be my girlfriend, but for whatever reason she didn't feel ready to have another relationship just yet.

"I find you predictable," she began. "I can text you whenever I want and know that you'll immediately message me back."

"I thought that was a good thing," I said. "It shows that you matter and are high on my priorities."

"But I never asked you to make me a priority," she continued. "Do you know, you're nothing like what you look like."

At the time, I was in my late twenties, heavily tattooed, quite muscular and full of steroids, and this wasn't the first time she had told me that. It made me begin to question some of the things I had come to pride myself on, like not being an angry, aggressive, stereotypical wannabe 'road man' bad boy. Was that really the sort of image I needed to portray to be able to get the girl I wanted? I had seen plenty of men of that kind get everything they wanted, especially when it came to women.

Even though Heartbreak was probably just being honest, it hurt when she said those things to me, because if I couldn't be myself and get the girl I wanted, then who was I supposed to be? Who was it I needed to be?

As I mentioned earlier, I had no real father figure around, so there hadn't been anyone to show me how to be with women, and there was no older brother to show me the ropes. I was the older brother, yet couldn't seem to learn, and even my younger brother was better with women than I was.

We continued to see each other when possible, but it became increasingly difficult to get a firm date in the diary. I get that my job was probably very different to those held by men she might normally have met, as I was in the military and based up in Scotland, so it wasn't like we could see each other every day … but it felt like there was more to it than that. We had sex again on one of the few occasions we hooked up, but she still didn't go down on me and, again, I didn't say anything.

By the time I was back at work, it was constantly on my mind, so I asked her over a text. Her reply was something to the effect of: she does do it, but that she just hadn't done it with me yet. I asked her if she used to do it with her ex-boyfriend, and she said yes, which made it feel even stranger; but she came across as if there was nothing to it and that it would probably happen in time, so I put it out of my mind.

As August 2010 arrived, I got drafted to Diego Garcia for a year, which impacted things between us massively. She came to see me in London, just before I was deployed, and we spent the day and night together. Heartbreak even cried at the fact that I had to go, which was a little confusing because I had been getting the feeling that she wasn't that interested in me anymore. We left things open, with no expectations, but said that we would stay in touch.

During my year away, things started off well. We spoke fairly frequently for two people who were separated by thousands of miles, but as time got on it grew harder and harder to get hold of her. Often, when I called, her phone would ring out, which I found really hard. I think that while we had said no expectations, I had this big hope that there would be a massive romantic connection between us, and that distance would make the heart grow fonder – it definitely made mine grow fonder, anyway.

As the year went on, our relationship didn't make any headway, which was understandable – I wasn't there, we weren't together and Heartbreak didn't owe me anything. Once I got back to the United Kingdom in 2011, we were still in communication and I had been drafted down to the southwest, based in a small town called Yeovil, which wasn't far from where she lived. I was still keen to see her and explore what we could be together, but at this point I got the feeling that she could take it or leave it … that she wasn't really bothered.

I had been asking her constantly if we could meet, until one day she eventually agreed; but she said that as she had been on her feet, working all day, she didn't want to go out, so I met her at her house. It was really nice to see her again, but the spark that had been there between us was missing, and I was eager to recapture it. We watched a movie and, as it got late, I asked if I could stay and head back in the morning, to which she said yes.

In bed later on that night, I sure as hell didn't get the feeling that she wanted to have sex, and the thought wasn't even on my mind … well, it was – it's always on my mind; I'm a man and I love sex

– but I wasn't trying to coax or talk her into it. We hadn't seen each other in over a year, and she wasn't someone I just wanted to have sex with. It was nice just to be in bed with her, to be in the presence of this woman who I had grown to feel such a yearning for. I asked her if I could cuddle her, and she said yes. It was so nice to have her in my arms again, although there was a little awkwardness to it … almost like we were strangers again. As I cuddled her, she kissed me on my cheek and said goodnight. I kissed her on her forehead and before I knew it, we were kissing on the lips. Much to my surprise, we had sex that night. I hadn't seen that coming in my wildest of dreams, it just hadn't felt like it was that sort of party or that there had been any sort of desire from her to be intimate like that; and while she still wouldn't go down on me, I didn't make anything of it. Over the next year, we saw each other from time to time. Some nights, I would drive an hour or so to hers, then get up early and drive back.

By early 2012, I was more confused than ever about what was going on between me and Heartbreak. She still didn't want to be in a relationship with me, and she still wouldn't go down on me, which made me self-conscious – was there something repulsive about me that I wasn't aware of? Was there something weird about me, or did I smell strangely? I'd stare at myself naked in the mirror, questioning the way I looked, but nothing overly hideous stood out, at least not to me. My body wasn't where I wanted it to be, and never had been, but I didn't think it was that grotesque that it would put her off from doing things with me that she had done with other sexual partners in the past.

As time went on, we continued to see each other, only less frequently, and Heartbreak seemed even less bothered about how the things she said or did affected me. We had planned to see each other in Manchester, she was going to come and stay with me for a few days, but when the day came, I heard nothing from her. Once it got close to the time she was supposed to arrive, I messaged her, to which her reply was: 'I missed the coach'.

She said that she would come the following day, but then the same thing happened, albeit with a different excuse. In total, she cancelled on me the following six days and, looking back on this now, I realise it was my fault – only an idiot allows someone to cancel on them six times in a row, with all sorts of different excuses each time, and still go back for more. Eventually, we had a text conversation (she wouldn't speak to me, claiming to be too busy), and I tried to explain everything that had been bothering me. I asked her why she never went down on me, that it felt personal, and she said it was because I had asked her to, and made a thing out of it in doing so.

'We were never actually together, you know', she added. 'You do know that we were never boyfriend and girlfriend?'

Her words felt particularly mean, as I wasn't deluded. I knew we had never officially been together, that she had never been my girlfriend, but then I wrote something that I've since sworn to never, ever repeat, no matter what the circumstances: 'You're breaking my heart'. 'Are you a victim?' she texted me back. 'If we had organised a date and you cancelled on me, I would have organised a date with someone else. I wouldn't let it affect me like that. I know that you're mine, that I can have you anytime I want'.

It was true – all she had to do was click her fingers and I would've come running – though I hadn't realised it was such a bad thing to make yourself so readily available to someone you're trying to be with, and for the first time I clearly understood the old adage: 'the thrill of the chase is more exciting than the kill'. Everything she had been saying and doing was clearly her expressing I wasn't the man for her. There was no real excitement between us anymore, and I had left no curiosity to pique her attention, because I had bared it all, and way too early.

The school of thought I used to operate on back then was that if I truly liked someone, if I truly loved someone, the best thing to do was get past all of the juvenile basics that you experience when first meeting someone – the playing hard to get, the not replying to messages for hours or even days, the not making yourself as available as possible for that person. I have always thought life was too short, and that bypassing the basic pushing and pulling away dynamic at the start of any relationship meant that there would be more time to truly explore life with someone I wanted to be with … someone that there was a chance of having a future with. You could travel and see the world together, and truly and honestly enjoy each other's company, without the facade of pretending to be someone or something you're not, but I was wrong. I saw her a few more times after that, but ultimately it came to an end, as I later realised it was always destined to.

There are very few things that hurt more than the resounding truth of realising you're in pursuit of somebody or something that you just can't have. This 'somethingship' I had with Heartbreak, as I came to call it, gave me some of my biggest insecurities, which I then took into future relationships and experiences I would have with other women who came into my life.

I think that I had come to love the idea of me and her … of us. Looking back on my somethingship with Heartbreak, I think a lot of men – maybe even women too – could read this and think how silly I was to carry myself the way I did, and the manner in which I dealt with things. They would be justified in asking: "Why would you want to be with someone who doesn't want to be with you?"

If the woman I desire doesn't want to be with me, she clearly isn't the one I'm meant to be with. It's such a simple thing to understand, and who would want to be in a relationship like that anyway? I see it so clearly now, but that's what hindsight does, and it's a lesson that would take me many more years to learn and truly understand.

LIFE ON THE OCEAN WAVES

I spent some of my last year of service applying for jobs and going to civilian transition workshops that the military has in place for those leaving. At this time, there had been a massive boom in the maritime security industry, which is what the majority of lads were leaving the corps to go and do. There was a lot of money in it – definitely more money than the average soldier could ever earn in the military – and on top of that, you worked when you wanted to, so there was a lot more freedom and flexibility.

I had been in constant communication with lads who had already left, and landed jobs with some of the companies operating in the industry. A lot of them advised me on what I had to do if I wanted to enter the industry, so with the learning credits I was given from the military to help transition me into my new life, I booked myself onto the various courses needed to get into the maritime world.

I had to do a STCW95 (Standards of Training Certification and Watchkeeping), which demonstrates that an individual has achieved the standard of safety training required to work on a commercial vessel. The course entailed different modules:

personal safety and social responsibilities, fire prevention, firefighting, elementary first aid and personal survival techniques; and I had to complete an ENG1 medical, which showed that I was fit to work on a commercial vessel. I also had to apply for a seaman's discharge book which, about the same size as a passport, keeps a comprehensive record of a seaman's career, experience and every ship they have ever been on. Last but not least, I had to do a MFCC, or Maritime Firearms Competency Course, which is a licence proving that I had successfully completed a civilian recognised rifle handling and shooting package.

After I had all of these courses under my belt, it was nearing the end of my one year's notice to leave period. One of the companies I applied to replied to me fairly quickly, and while I had received other responses, this was the company I wanted to contract for. A part of me couldn't believe it – I had been invited to an induction day after they had shortlisted the CVs they wanted and completed background checks. I'm sure most people can understand the fear of leaving a job without having found another, especially given I still had bills to pay, not to mention thirty thousand pounds' worth of debt hovering over me, resting squarely and, might I say, quite heavily on my shoulders during my every waking thought.

I went to the open day and everything seemed so positive. The majority of lads there on the induction day were all ex-Marines or currently serving their year's notice to leave, just like me. The company management team were all either ex-Marines or ex-Army, with both owners also former Marines. It's such a relief to be surrounded by likeminded people when adapting to a new environment … people who, for the most part, generally get you and you get them.

A week later, I received an email stating that I had been successful, and enquiring about my availability. I told them I was available immediately, even though that wasn't completely true, as my TX, or leaving, date wasn't for a month or so; but when I showed my OC (Officer in Command) the email, and evidence that I had a possible transit tasking with this company, he allowed me to start my terminal leave early.

Within a week of providing my new employer with my availability, I was out on a task in my new role as maritime security operator. The first tasking I did was a transit from the Suez Canal, Egypt, to Galle, Sri Lanka. I flew from London Heathrow to Colombo, Sri Lanka, which took thirteen hours – the longest time I've spent on a plane to date – but I loved the idea of flying to work. Even though I would only be in Sri Lanka a day or so before boarding the vessel, I would still get to see some of Sri Lanka, a country I had never been to and never thought I would visit. I met Craig, the team leader of the task, at London Heathrow, and liked him straight away. We just got on, and it was easy to be around him. Craig was from Sandbach, a small town in Cheshire, and had served as an Army Commando in 29 Commando Plymouth. I found him to be quite a switched on, organised and very easy-going team leader, which was perfect for me. He had dreams of making enough money to get out of the industry, start his own business and spend more time with his family.

Once we arrived at Colombo, we were met by a driver who worked for the company. I always loved arriving in new countries and getting to see the happenings of day to day life whilst en route to whatever location I was headed to. After a thirteen hour flight, however, it was a challenge just trying to stay awake, never mind appreciate the beauty and exotic wonders of a foreign country. I awoke as we drew closer to the hotel where we would be staying, and it was a hive of activity. There were tuk-tuk taxis and people everywhere, I saw people riding elephants and, amid this entirely new cultural experience, I noticed something a little more familiar: a KFC.

After a journey of around two hours, we arrived at the hotel. It was a beautiful location, palm trees were dotted about, the sun was out and it was hard to believe that just a little over fifteen hours before I had been in London, such was the difference in scenery. We spent the night in the hotel and, in the morning, moved down to the harbour, at which there was an armoury where the company paid to keep some of its weapons for transits. We collected the peli boxes with all our equipment, which included binoculars, night vision kit, rounds for the rifles, bore sight calibrators rules for use of force cards, satellite phones and a chart of the Indian Ocean. Once we had checked all the kit and signed for it, we loaded it onto the pilot boat that then took us out to sea to board the vessel we were going to be embarked on. When reaching the vessel, the crew on board lowered us ropes, to which we tied our equipment so that they could hoist it up. Once the kit was on board, we followed suit by climbing a rope ladder.

We were then introduced to the captain and his crew, we read and signed the necessary paperwork for joining the vessel, then secured weapons in the armoury, which is where they stayed until we reached the HRA (High Risk Area). We were shown around the ship, the galley, the common areas and our rooms, then walked around the rest of the vessel with the chief to assess its defences. The ship had quite a high freeboard and travelled at a speed of about twenty knots per hour, which helped decrease the possibility of being successfully boarded by pirates.

There were hoses secured to the handrails, which ran the whole way along the port and starboard sides of the ship; and there was also razor wire wrapped around the handrail astern, which would make it even harder to board the vessel – can you imagine trying to board a ship boasting a seventeen metre freeboard, with only a grappling hook, a rope or a long pole with a hook on the end, whilst the vessel's travelling at twenty knots and a barrage of water is being sprayed in your face? Not only that, but you'd have to contend with armed maritime security operators doing their job from a much more stable platform, afforded to them by the bridge wings, or even getting caught up in the razor wire at the rear.

It just wouldn't be worth it, especially for those planning on having a long, prosperous career in the piracy industry. It would be much easier to wait for another ship that didn't have all of the built up, anti-boarding counter measures or armed security, comprising ex-soldiers, most likely with experience in highly hostile environments.

I had been warned by lads on the maritime circuit that gyms on ships were few and far between, and that even when there was one, it would be very, very basic. When I discovered that the ship I was on didn't have a gym, it definitely affected me, depriving me of the ability to maintain my exercise regimen.

After setting sail, it wasn't long before we entered the HRA, a zone where piracy was much more prevalent. When I started this job in 2012, the high risk boundaries were much bigger than they are today, covering a great mass of the Indian Ocean and incorporating the Red Sea, much of the east coast of Africa, the gulf of Oman, the Persian gulf, countries such as India, Pakistan, the Maldives and many more.

On this particular transit, we were bound for the Suez Canal. Craig explained that a little before seventy eight degrees East, we would prepare the weapons, bore sight zero them (effectively synchronising the weapon's optical sight with the barrel), then put them back in the box with the padlock on. Once we reached the western boundary of the high risk area, we would take weapons up to the bridge and keep them secured in their peli box. The duty watch routine was dictated by the type of ship we were on, the height of the freeboard and the speed at which it travelled, so for this ship and the measures it had in place, our watch duration lasted from first to last light.

Other ships with lesser measures, or an inability to travel at high speeds, required a three man team on board, and that the watch would continue around the clock, with a four hours on/eight hours off rotation. On my first transit, we were able to do a three hours on/three hours off routine, and only had to keep it running through daylight hours. During our off time, we were always on immediate notice to move if anything happened, so we would be in our rooms, in the galley or on the main deck, but always on standby with our radios.

The ship and its crew were Italian, which I came to learn was a very good thing, mostly because of food. We ate in the officer's mess, but dishes that I was used to having together were served separately. After eating bread with olive oil poured onto it, we had a plate each of spaghetti and herbs, which at first looked a little bland but tasted delicious, followed by a bowl of meatballs. I was confused as to why the meatballs hadn't been served with the spaghetti, and one of the officers explained that real Italian food isn't necessary prepared or served as it is in the United Kingdom.

"It's like that in the UK because the British like an oilier, creamier dish. It's always the way with the British. They like the unhealthiest version of other countries' recipes," he added, which brought a smile to my face, recognising that what he was saying was true.

Duty watch was easy, and because Craig and I got on so well, we stayed on watch most of the day together, while maintaining eyes on our arcs, scanning the ocean water – near, middle and distant – for any potential threats, and observing the ship's radar.

The transit was over quickly and had been the perfect voyage – safe and uneventful. It took about two weeks to arrive in Egypt, at which point we disembarked; but before flying back to the United Kingdom, Craig was emailed by the operations room asking for both of our availabilities, as there was another vessel inbound in the next couple days. As we were already in the country, we were asked if we wanted to man it, and the answer was a keen yes from both of us. It became a regular pattern, which is how we managed to stay together for most of our transits.

At this time, whenever I had leave I would stay in my apartment in Manchester, with my good friends Ethan and Richie – who were both by now also working in the maritime industry, but for different companies – living relatively close by in Liverpool, which was just over an hour away; while Aaron lived in north Manchester and Dave, Dan and their brother, Ben, were about a fifteen minute walk away from where I lived. We arranged nights out together, and were joined by many other friends, including Foley – guys who were and remain big parts of my life. We had fun, and it was so good to be able to party with friends who for the most part shared a military background. I have so many good memories from this era, and it always puts a smile of my face when I think about them.

Even though I was having such a good time with my friends and the new job, it started to feel like something was missing. Heartbreak was still on the scene at this point, but I had lost hope that we would become a couple. When nights out with my friends drew to a close, I went home alone, not having met anybody I could spend time with or saw a future with. I started to feel lonely, something I most definitely didn't want to admit to myself, let alone ever mention to anybody else.

It was as if my friends always had someone around, someone they could be with – a girlfriend, a lover or female friend – but I couldn't emulate them because I continued to be quite awkward when it came to talking to women. It was definitely something I was aware of, so maybe they picked up on it too. I had my own place and a lot more freedom than I ever had in the corps, but I couldn't meet anyone. I found my yearning for a relationship quite odd, because as a teenager before I'd ever even had sex, I thought all I ever wanted was to sexually be with as many women in the world as possible, and never settle down. But I was older now, and wanted a bit more out of life.

During one of my leaves, at the start of my maritime security career, my dad called me and told me that he had been diagnosed with leukaemia. He seemed positive about it, like it wasn't a big thing, and it appeared as if it had been caught in time.

"You'll be alright, dad – leukaemia's for kids," I said; or something stupid to that effect. "Yeah, I'll be fine," dad chuckled, and I put the matter to the back of my mind.

Meanwhile, back on the ships, I was getting to see so much more of the world – Mauritius, Durban, Seychelles, Madagascar, Maldives, Dubai, Reunion Islands, and so many more. In some countries, like India and Pakistan, we weren't allowed to disembark and explore, due to visa requirements. On the ships, I got to see some of the strained race relations around the world – for instance, between Pakistan and India, and Filipinos and Indians, with the latter seemingly more jovial, but I'm not well educated enough to even begin to comment on it. I don't know what it's like on land, but out on the water, these warring factions provided me with so much amusement.

In the quiet hours of the night, listening to the international distress channel, VHF channel sixteen, I heard them continually berate each other. I couldn't believe the savage putdowns they sent back and forth. I heard somebody sing a tune with the words "Filipinooo mooonkey" being repeated, and on other occasions they wouldn't even sing, whistling the melody instead, but I knew straight away what it was. Another voice would then pop up on the channel, first making a sniffing sound, before saying: "Indian boy, I smell curry – why don't you wash?" And on it went, making the nightshifts a little more entertaining.

By the end of the first year, I was well accustomed to flying all over the place to board these vessels, and found the long plane journeys tiring. Ethan told me he took sleeping tablets for the flights, so the next time I was in Sri Lanka, I went into a pharmacy and bought five hundred benzodiazepine tablets for next to nothing – around fifty pounds, if I remember correctly, and I didn't need a prescription. I'd pop three tablets before long flights and be out cold before we even took off.

I loved them, and it got to the point that when I was on transits outside of the high risk area for a few days or so, or we were anchored in national waters for days on end, with weapons locked away and sealed in the armoury, I would wake up for breakfast and, if there was no movement planned, take three or four tablets and fast-forward time to the next day ... which was awesome, especially on the ships that had no gyms or were crawling with cockroaches. The contrast between vessels was vast – those with great accommodation and facilities, and varied, quality food, making me feel like I was on a luxury cruise; while in stark contrast, others were so poorly equipped that they just felt dirty.

Food wise, I'm pretty adventurous and will try anything once, but some of the menus on the ships were somewhat of an eye opener. One of the most noteworthy culinary delights I had the pleasure of sampling was chicken foot soup, which was cool, but I think it was the thought and feeling of having something's claw in my mouth that made it a dish I doubt I'll ever be queuing up to eat again.

Another was cow tongue, which I already knew I didn't like, because dad cooked it for us on one of the few days he turned up in our lives. This, though, was something else – a massive section of tongue stretched out on a plate, with what looked like hairs sticking out of it. As I sat staring at this cow's tongue, with its taste buds as clear as day to see, I knew I definitely wouldn't be polishing it off. I ate as much as I thought would allow me to say that I was full, so that I wouldn't offend any of the ship's officers sat around the table; who, by the way, couldn't seem to get enough of it, finding it delicious.

As time went on and I boarded more and more vessels, I started to lose passion for the job. One of the things that really started getting to me was being on a ship with team members I didn't resonate with. There were normally only around twenty two crew members on board a ship, and that meant seeing the same people day in day out, which could be for months. I'm moaning here, but I was the creator of my own prison, as I needed the money, so would always stay on longer if possible.

I had no girlfriend and no children, so there wasn't any need to rush home just to be alone … well, more alone than I had started to feel on the ships, but without earning money. The other thing that really bothered me was the lack of a gym, or the basic facilities on offer if there was one. I lost so much weight that it played on my mind. I couldn't eat as much as I needed to, and had stopped taking steroids, which had become quite a big part of my life. So even though I needed the money, the job started to grate on me and I started thinking of alternatives.

Just before the end of 2012, I had gone home on leave, at a time when my dad was in and out of hospital undergoing chemotherapy, and sometimes spending short spells in the cancer ward. When I went to visit him one day, he had made a friend in the ward he was temporarily on, and they both sneaked outside to smoke, even though they had been told not to by the staff, for obvious reasons.

Heading outside with him, he was very upbeat, smiling, laughing and talking about his plans to visit Jamaica once he was done with all the hospital business. I spent an hour or so with him, then left as I wasn't in London long. It was nice to see him in high spirits and spend some time with him. In spite of all that had gone on during my childhood, and his lack of support, he was still my father and I didn't want him to be suffering from leukaemia. It honestly seemed to me like something he was going to just walk off.

In early 2013, I was on a transit with Craig again. By now a close, valued friend of mine, he said something that influenced my life more than I could ever have imagined.

"Let me tell you something: I always dreamed of going to Cuba and learning Spanish, but have a beautiful family now and my dreams have changed. But, mate, as a young, single man, the world's your oyster."

I had never thought about it like that before, as I had been too busy trying to win Heartbreak over. The only thing that I knew about Latin America at this point was that there were beautiful women there, because whenever I watched porn I always searched 'hot latina', and there was no shortage of physically gifted, full bodied, voluptuous Latina goddesses. It wasn't the best reason to travel all the way to Cuba, but all I can do is be honest, and that was my initial motivation … oh, along with wanting to experience the culture, which came a close second.

I started researching Cuba, looking at where would be a good city to go and study Spanish. There was a Spanish learning programme available to foreigners in the University of Havana, so I dug a little deeper and discovered that it enrolled students onto its courses on a monthly basis. Because of the flexibility of my job, I felt it would be most rewarding to attend a course for a couple of months. After booking my place for the surprisingly cheap cost of around two hundred pounds per month, I then had to think about accommodation.

On the verge of booking a room at the Iberostar Parque Central hotel, which stood out amongst the others I considered, I received an email from the administrator handling my enrolment onto the Spanish language course. She suggested I could live at a 'casa particular' which, she explained, was someone's home, in which you rent a room – similar to a bed and breakfast, only a lot more personal. I had never stayed in the home of a complete stranger and couldn't speak the language, and they most likely didn't speak mine, so I wasn't itching to proceed.

The email explained that the casa particular would be the home of a married couple, and that if I was truly serious about learning Spanish, it was the best option, as I would be living with native Spanish speakers and my learning would excel rapidly – a lot quicker than if I were to stay at a hotel by myself. After digesting the email and deliberating what to do, I decided to go for it. I had promised myself that I would force myself out of my comfort zone whenever possible, so this was a perfect opportunity to honour my pledge; plus it was a lot cheaper than staying at a hotel for two months.

I decided to stay at the Iberostar Parque Central for a few days at the start of May, before moving to the casa particular the night before my course started. Once it was all booked, I told Craig, who sounded surprised that I had taken his advice and gone ahead with his suggestion, telling me it was awesome that I was actually doing it.

Flying into Jose Marti international airport, I caught a taxi outside, which the Cubans called a maquina. 1950s-style American-made cars, they were everywhere I looked, coming in a variety of bright, vibrant colours and, I learnt, are a massive part of Cuba's culture. I arrived at the Iberostar Parque Central, a massive building with quaint, elegant architecture, and immediately felt assured that I had chosen the right hotel to stay in. I soon discovered that the hotel was a safe zone for me, by which I mean that everyone who worked there spoke English, but a couple days into my stay there, I decided to venture out and eat somewhere different.

I found a restaurant not far from the hotel, and entered without even thinking about the language barrier. As it hadn't been an issue in the hotel, it had lured me into a false sense of security, and as soon as I stepped inside, a waitress came over to welcome me, spouting out something in Spanish that I didn't have a hope in hell of understanding. All of a sudden, it dawned on me that maybe everyone didn't speak English outside of the hotel. It hadn't even crossed my mind, and I felt naive in assuming that I'd be able to converse in my native tongue. Not handling situations like this very well, I started to sweat and felt that everyone was looking at me. Before I could even try and say anything, she said something else – something else I couldn't understand – and by now other workers were making their way over. I tried to reply by apologising and explaining that I didn't speak Spanish, and think I even stuttered a little, as for me, this situation was intense. I felt like a fool, even though the waitress and her co-workers all seemed as polite as could be, standing there looking beautiful and smiling. In my nervousness, I told them in English that I would be back in a minute, which obviously they didn't understand, and then pretty much ran off – I just wanted to get away from that moment of sheer awkwardness, which was to be the first of many during my time in Cuba.

After that experience, I decided I would only eat in the hotel, until it was time to go to the casa particular. After checking out of the hotel, I caught a taxi, showing the driver the address on my phone to avoid language barrier problems. For the entire journey there, I couldn't help but think about what I was about to do. I would soon be moving into the house of a complete stranger and living there for two months. I was sure that there would be difficulties communicating with them, and was more nervous than I had ever been.

When the taxi arrived in the residential area of Vedado, where I would be staying, the driver pulled up outside the property where my host lived. I got my bag, rang the bell of the property's outer gate, and a man and woman came out. Smiling warmly, they seemed naturally full of joy and greeted me in English … and my entire being felt a sense of relief. Both doctors, the man's name was Ricardo, his wife was called Dulce, and I was so happy to have made the right choice by staying at this casa particular.

We sat down, and Dulce made us a cup of 'café', or coffee, which I soon came to realise was a big part of Cuban culture. Over there, it's standard to drink a Cuban coffee multiple times a day, and definitely after each meal, and while tea had always been my thing, I was willing to experiment. Whilst drinking our coffee, Ricardo explained the rules to me – I wasn't allowed to put toilet paper down the toilet (it had to go in a small bin by the side of the toilet); I wasn't allowed to bring any girls back, especially lovemakers; and that while breakfast was included in the cost of the room, I could pay a small fee to eat lunch and dinner with them, if I wanted to.

Ricardo then took me outside to show me what I had to do in the mornings in order to get to the university. He walked me down to the main road, Avenida de Maceo, and told me that I would have to hold my hand out to signal a maquina. All I had to say, he explained, was "sube por M?" which basically means "do you drive up the road M?" M is the name of one of the roads out there, which have been constructed as a grid system like the roads in America. This too was a new concept to me, as we don't have anything like this in the UK. After that, we walked back to the house and I settled into my room, before going to bed.

In the morning, Dulce prepared breakfast and a café, and after saying my goodbyes and asking Ricardo one more time what it was I had to say, I headed down to Avenida de Maceo. It was only around a six minute walk, but all the way there I repeated what it was that I had to say: "Sube por M, sube por M, sube por M …" When I reached the main road, I held my hand out, and in no time at all a maquina pulled over. To my shock and horror, there were people already in it – I hadn't realised that most of the maquinas were more like public transport for many people, so now had to repeat the phrase Ricardo taught me in front of the others in the car, who for the most part weren't even looking at me, most likely thinking about their day and minding their own business.

The maquina driver leaned over towards the window and looked at me, as if to say: "Where are you going?" I quickly blurted out, amid an ever growing state of discomfort: "Sube por M." I was even a little proud of myself that I had remembered it, although from the driver's reaction, I hadn't remembered it well enough or pronounced it correctly, as he looked confused and said something to me in Spanish. I had absolutely no idea what he meant, so I reluctantly repeated it, even though my entire being wished that I didn't have to. But it was too late now, I was committed, and again, he didn't understand me … but now people inside the maquina were looking.

One of them wound down a window to, I guess, ask where I needed to go. People sat on the other side of the vehicle leaned over to see what was going on and, just like in the restaurant, I felt heated and awkward. By now, it felt like I had been stood on the roadside, having this awkward interaction with the driver and his passengers, for a lifetime, although our exchanges probably didn't last longer than a minute or so. In my state of embarrassment and awkwardness, I signalled with my hand that I would walk instead, and with that, the maquina drove off.

I had no idea where the university was located in relation to where I was, or how to even go about getting there, but I knew one thing for sure: I wasn't going to hail another taxi and go through that again anytime soon. I took my phone out of my pocket and switched on data roaming, which I knew would be very expensive, but I didn't care, as the alternative of calling another maquina over was even worse and scared me stiff.

It took me just over an hour to get there, so despite leaving the house in plenty of time to arrive early, I was now late; and not only was I late, I was dripping in sweat, and that was how I met everybody on the first day of my language course. I imagine I made a very smelly, sweaty first impression.

The university was massive, not that I had any kind of reference point as to what a small or large university was, never having gone to one myself. It displayed beautifully impressive architecture, with steps leading from street level all the way up to the campus, and just before reaching the top, there was a bronze statue of a seated lady wearing a gown, her arms outstretched, with the Latin words 'Alma Mater', which means nourishing mother, inscribed in bronze just below. Beyond that, there were these massive columns that made up the main entrance, and which were so imposing that they could be seen when stood at street level.

Luckily, there were signs in English, directing foreign students to the language course classrooms. The university was packed, and once I found the classroom I needed, I was showed into a room, where everyone enrolling that day was sitting a test that would determine the level of Spanish they would be taught. I don't know why I even bothered sitting the test, as I could have told them immediately that I knew nothing.

I had been practicing with a Spanish learning CD whilst on transits ever since I decided I was going to study the language in Cuba, but clearly whatever I thought I had already learnt counted for nothing out here, in a nation full of Spanish speakers. I was able to answer the question 'What is your name?' but after that things got really tricky, and I sat in that classroom completely nonplussed. One of the teachers must have seen me sat there, staring at the paper and slyly trying to look at what the Russian girl next to me had written, which was pretty crazy, because if I had managed to cheat and gone to a level that exceeded my virtually non-existent Spanish, it would have meant one thing for me – yes, more embarrassing moments.

The teacher asked me a few things in Spanish, and saw immediately that I didn't have the slightest clue as to what was going on. She took my paper, and gestured to me that I could wait outside. Soon enough, the other students started finishing and came out one by one. They told us we could have a quick break, and that once they had marked all the test papers, we would be given our entrance grades and classrooms. During the break, I just hovered around the classroom area, as did most of the students who had just arrived. There were people there from all over the world speaking all kinds of different languages, but I couldn't identify any Brits.

After a little while, the teachers came out and put the test results on a notice board. When I found my name, I saw that I had been put into 'principiante', which means beginner. In my class, there were four other students: a Korean lady, a German guy and two Chinese guys. It was a nice, small, intimate class, which for me as a beginner worked just fine. During our first day, we were introduced to the Spanish language, and learnt some of the basic meet and greets. We had breaks throughout the day, and got to talk with others from different classes, which is when I noticed that the vast majority could speak English, their own language, obviously, and were now learning their third or fourth. Some could speak even more, it was so impressive, and there I was, only able to speak English.

It made me feel quite ignorant, especially when people chopped and changed between languages, returning to English for my sake. I was whisked back to my schooldays, and found myself wishing that I had paid more attention during German class, instead of being a nuisance and acting like the class clown.

The classes ran from Monday to Friday, starting at nine o'clock in the morning and finishing at one in the afternoon. Luckily for me, I saw that private taxis occasionally drove past the university, so for the first few days I waited at the bottom of its steps. Sometimes, I would get lucky and a taxi would come by pretty quickly. Other times, it would be ages before one came by, though I preferred to wait rather than hail a maquina.

Whenever I managed to get a taxi to stop for me, I said the one thing that I knew they would understand: "Hotel Parque Central." Whilst I wasn't staying there anymore, I felt comfortable going there for food. It was well out of the way, but I knew I wouldn't be subjected to any awkward moments there, and as a creature of habit, I'll always return to my safest, most familiar surroundings. I could have paid to eat with my hosts, but was still getting used to being in someone else's home, so decided to take it one step at a time. Obviously, this became quite expensive, as I was going there for lunch and dinner, and it was also a lot of travelling back and forth.

One afternoon after class, I was walking down to the main road, where there was a taxi rank, and saw this little restaurant on the corner called Waoo! It just shone, and looked very different to the other restaurants I had seen. There were steps leading up to a door, all of the windows were open and, as I looked in, I could see waiters and waitresses all wearing yellow T-shirts with the logo Waoo! embroidered on them. For some reason, I went up the stairs to this restaurant and stepped inside, feeling that it would most likely go wrong and that I would end up feeling silly. A lady came to greet me at the door, she was stunning, and I was immediately taken aback. She had blonde hair, a beautiful facial structure and a very warm, friendly smile. The epitome of beauty, I felt intimidated at having to talk to such an attractive woman, and before I had a chance to snap out of the daze I had fallen into at the sheer presence of this woman, she spoke to me. Just as I imagined, I didn't understand a word she said, so I said: "Lo siento, solo hablo inglés," a phrase I had learnt in Spanish class, meaning: "Sorry, I only speak English."

The moment hadn't actually been that awkward or embarrassing, and I felt it had been worth it, if nothing more than to treat my eyes and senses to the sight and presence of such a beautiful specimen of the female race. Then, just before I was about to turn around and walk out, she spoke to me in English: "I can speak English, if you like?"

I couldn't believe it and felt elated, replying with all the energy and hyped up emotion of a young kid who had just walked into a shop full of sweets: "You speak English?"

"Yes," she smiled. "I'm learning."

She then asked where I would like to sit, which is probably what the waitress at the other restaurant had been asking me. In this moment, and during my time in Cuba thus far, it dawned on me how powerful and necessary it is to be able to speak another language, potentially opening the door to being able to speak to millions, maybe even billions, of other people. I chose a table and sat down, she told me her name was Yuliet and that she would be my waitress, then gave me a menu that also had English on it, which just about made my day.

The restaurant was a little pricier than the others I had seen, but as she explained to me, it was privately owned and the service was second to none, so it was well worth it. I asked her to recommend me a dish, and she suggested the steak that came with sautéed vegetables. I couldn't stop speaking to her, and when she asked what I was doing in Cuba, I explained that I was at the university trying to learn Spanish. Yuliet was so friendly, saying that she would help me, and I spoke to her the entire time I ate my meal and dessert.

I stayed there for a couple of hours, and didn't want to leave. She had bewitched me, which I'm sure she was aware of, as it must have been written all over my face. I returned every day after that, and started taking my homework in there. Yuliet and some of the other staff, who were just as friendly, helped me with it. It got to the point that Yuliet said she would only speak Spanish with me, so as to force me to converse with a native speaker, which I felt comfortable with, as it helped me improve my command of the language. During one of my many visits, I asked Yuliet if she had a boyfriend, as I would have loved to have taken her out, but she said yes. I held my chest with my hands, and jokingly told her that she had broken my heart … well, maybe not so jokingly … but she laughed and said "Aaww!" She had an amazing sense of humour, and I didn't care that she had a boyfriend, as she was the new love of my life.

Back at university, once classes finished, students gathered in different groups, having got to know one another. I managed to tag along with a group which had some of the students I was getting to know, and we sometimes lunched together. I occasionally suggested the restaurant Waoo!, which was obviously my favourite place now, and we went a couple times, although it was a little pricey for some of the students, who were doing more of a backpacking type of holiday experience, had been there a lot longer than I had, and probably still had a fair amount of time to go, so being economically cautious made absolute sense.

During one of these lunches, two girls came along who I had seen from afar, but wasn't sure where they were from; but the minute I heard them speak, I knew they were British. I was so happy, and while everyone else was really friendly and great company, sometimes it's just nice to be able to speak to someone from home, especially when you're in an unfamiliar country, can't speak the language and are way out of your comfort zone.

Over time, I became quite friendly with Roxane and Katherine, who were both twenty three years of age and could speak multiple languages. Katherine could speak French, German and Spanish, for which she was in the advanced class at the university, plus Hungarian. Roxane could speak German, a little Afrikaans and was also in the advanced Spanish class.

I was so impressed by these two young ladies. There I was, struggling to even speak English correctly at times, and these two girls, at twenty three years old, could speak six languages between them. What had I been doing my whole life? Yep, playing the class clown, trying to get people to like me, and this was the first time I wished I had done better at school. Watching Kat and Rox, as I soon came to call them, switching between languages was so impressive. They were friends from the UK who had travelled to Cuba together, and they spoke in German whenever they wanted their own little side conversation.

We started getting together at night with some of the other students, visiting different clubs. One night, we were sat on the Malecón, a broad road and sea wall that runs for a few miles along the coastline through the Vedado neighbourhood. People gathered there to drink, dance and just chill out. Well, one night a few of us went there after a club, and whilst we were sat there, chilling out and talking, a police car pulled up in front of us. Two black policemen got out and started talking to us, and specifically me, but obviously I didn't have a clue about anything that was said after "Como estás." I was trying to tell them I didn't speak Spanish, but don't think they believed me.

The one thing I did understand was "Pasaporte," which they asked me for, but I never like to carry mine around, because if I lose it or it gets stolen whilst in a foreign country, the hassle I'll face will be immense; and, on top of that, I won't be able to work again until I receive a replacement. So I didn't actually have it on me, and things were getting a little uncomfortable. They couldn't understand me and I couldn't understand them, but luckily Kat and Rox came over and spoke to them. I could only make out bits of the conversation, but they explained it all to me after. It turns out that the policemen had been asking why I was hanging around with them, and where I was from. Kat and Rox told them that I was British, and that I was studying at the university with them.

You see, as I mentioned before, I'm a black man, and in Cuba there are many black people. Sometimes, some of the black men, and other men of colour, try to hustle tourists or ask for money, so when these policemen saw me – a black man with these fairer skinned, obvious tourists – they just assumed that I was hustling them, when actually I was one of them – a tourist. This was something that became a normal occurrence for me, and at times the police, just like before, thought that I was pretending not to be able to speak Spanish, though luckily for me there was always someone around to help.

I went out with the girls a fair bit, to restaurants and nightclubs, and Rox always had a bottle of pre-mixed alcoholic drinks that packed a punch. Going to clubs wasn't really my thing because I wasn't much of a dancer, but I went wherever the group went. The only time I ever danced was when I was drunk, and even then, I felt very awkward doing it.

Everything was going well, I was learning Spanish – still at a very basic level, but nevertheless I was learning – I was in Cuba, living with a Cuban family and making friends from all over the world. I was well outside of my comfort zone, but was quietly a little proud of myself. I was making good on the promise I had made to myself.

If his schedule allowed it, Ricardo occasionally dropped me off at the university on his way to work, which I really appreciated, as it meant I didn't have to go through the embarrassing, sweat inducing nightmare of trying to catch a maquina. During the first few days of my stay with him and Dulce, I asked if there was a gym nearby, so on one of the mornings he dropped me off, he drove past one to show me where it was. Since it wasn't too far away from where we lived, my plan was to go back home after Spanish class, get changed into my gym clothes and run to the gym.

One o'clock came, I finished class, said my goodbyes to the others, and walked down to the private taxi rank, which I was doing regularly now. I didn't have to worry about anyone else other than the taxi driver hearing my bad Spanish, then when I got back to the house, I changed and ran to the gym. It took about sixteen minutes, and as I drew closer, I could see that the entrance to the gym was below street level.

As I reached the steps leading to it, I was about to head down when I saw a table just inside the entrance, and about five or six women sat around it, talking. Stopping dead in my tracks, the battle I now had was whether I could go down there and insert myself into what would most definitely have been a very awkward scene. I knew I would have to interact with somebody at the gym when paying to enter, but certainly hadn't expected a group of women to be present when doing so.

As I stood there, other gymgoers came and went, but I didn't take another step. I'm not sure how long I was there for, but at some point, one of the women looked up and saw me, and my immediate kneejerk reaction was to run off before I felt even more awkward. I ran all the way home, hating myself for being so weak and really wishing that I knew more Spanish.

When I got back, Ricardo and Dulce asked what had happened, as I hadn't been gone long. When I told them, they couldn't stop laughing, and I couldn't blame them. I had gotten all dressed up in my skimpy vest and short shorts to go to the gym, ran all the way there, seen a bunch of women, got scared and socially awkward, then immediately ran all the way back. I had been a Royal Marine for over ten years, been to war twice and been shot, but five women sat around a desk at the gym had made me nervous.

I was so frustrated with myself. How could I let such things affect me, and how was I ever going to get in the gym to train if I couldn't even get past the front door? The following day, when I got back home after finishing class, Ricardo told me that he had been to the gym, paid my fee and given them my name, and that all I had to say when I got there was: "Hola, mi nombré es en la lista, mi papá lo pagó en la mañana," which meant: "Hello, my name is on the list, my father paid for me this morning."

I was so grateful to him. The gym was a massive part of my life, and I sorely missed the routine it afforded me. Now all I had to do was remember the sentence he had told me. I set off running to the gym and, just like with the maquina debacle, kept repeating this monster of a sentence to myself: "Hola, mi nombré es en la lista …" But by the time I got to the gym, the sentence had become totally confused in my head. I approached the stairway and sneaked a little look at the desk area without being seen. There was only one person there – a man – and I was so relieved, I almost danced with joy.

I rushed down the steps quickly before my luck changed and more desk dwellers had the chance to turn up, but as I reached the man, I said something along the lines of: "En la mañana, mi nombré es mi papá, en la lista lo pagó, hola," which meant something like: "In the morning my name is my father, in the list it paid, hello." It was absolute gibberish, and the man at the desk gave me a look of bewilderment; but I think he must have been there when Ricardo paid my fee, because it was almost like something clicked, as he looked down the list, we found my name, and he gestured at me to enter the gym and work out.

I was so happy; I was finally in the gym, and wasn't too worried about being unable to speak Spanish here, because I was fluent in gym talk, which is mostly gestures and grunts, and that language is universal. I went there every day, and started seeing who all the regulars were. I saw the same faces training at the same time every day, and one of the guys I came to know as José

121

must have taken one look at me and known I was a foreigner. One day, after seeing each other in there a number of times, he asked if I wanted to train with him and his friend. He spoke English to a level that enabled us to chat, and as I knew no one in the gym, it seemed like a good idea, and another way of getting to know more people and maybe bettering my Spanish. That day, we trained legs together and talked the whole time. It turned out that he was actually from Spain and was married to a Cuban lady, and that the friend he trained with was actually his brother-in-law, Fiti. I started training with them every day, and after the gym we went running at the nearby Parque Revolución. My friendship with them grew very quickly, and although Fiti couldn't speak any English, and my Spanish was very limited, José did his best to translate any conversation between us.

They mentioned that Fiti's grandmother had moved in with them, and that they were looking for someone to rent her place, but as I was already staying with Ricardo and Dulce and liked it there, I thanked them for thinking of me, but told them that I already had somewhere to stay. By now, I had been there a little over a month, and everything was going well. I had friends at the university and at the gym, but one day, after classes, I got back home and Ricardo, who had pretty much become my adopted father out there, and Dulce asked if they could speak with me.

We sat down, and they explained that they hadn't planned on me staying so long, and that some time ago they had booked someone in to rent the room that I was using. They expressed how sorry they were, and I could see that they felt bad, so I told them not to worry and that I would find somewhere else. With a few days left until I had to leave, I asked Jose and Fiti if their grandmother's place was still available, which it was. It worked out perfectly, and before I moved out, I invited Ricardo and Dulce to my favourite restaurant, Waoo!, and introduced them to the love of my life, Yuliet. We had a lovely evening, and I was so glad I got to say goodbye to them in such a nice way.

My new home was just a stone's throw away from Ricardo and Dulce's place, and the family I was staying with invited me down for breakfast every morning. They were a really close-knit household, including Jose and Fiti, who I already knew, Dayan, Jose's wife and Fiti's sister, their mum, dad and grandmother. They all tried to speak to me and make me feel at home, which I did very quickly, although my Spanish wasn't good enough to have a full-on conversation or even understand most things. I would say there was an understanding there, one that I guess came through facial expressions and body language.

José and Fiti sometimes invited me down to the porch of the main house, where the rest of the family were. With salsa music playing, once I saw Fiti dancing with his girlfriend, some of his friends and his sister, I was spellbound. The style of dance was called 'casino rueda' whereby, as part of an interactive circle, the female partners changed partners as the dance went on. They also clapped hands at certain points and I loved it, wishing that I could dance like that.

Fiti would call me out sometimes and try to teach me some moves, but although I was working on being outside of my comfort zone as much as possible, this was a bit too much for me. I would try for a couple steps, laugh nervously, then sit down out of fear of embarrassing myself and an acute sense of awkwardness deep inside, saying "No puedo" – "I can't" – and hoping that it wouldn't offend him. I'm pretty sure it didn't, and that he could see that my reluctance to dance was down to nerves.

When June came around, I had been in Cuba well over a month, and one day Kat and Rox suggested going out for dinner. It just so happened that it was on the twenty sixth, which was a bit strange, as it was the same day as my birthday. I think that, during one of our many conversations when getting to know each other, the subject of how old we were and our birthdays came up. Well, these two amazing women, who were also by now my closest friends out there, had remembered.

I met Kat at the hostel where they stayed, but as I was a little late, she told me that Rox had gone ahead because she wanted to go to a shop first. Me and Kat got in a taxi and, as I heard Kat give directions to the driver, I realised we were going to my favourite restaurant in the entire world. I just remember thinking what an amazing gesture it was for them to do this for me. When we got there and exited the taxi, I looked at Kat pretty much elated, and she smiled back at me; then as we walked through the doors, I could see Rox sat at a table with all of the other students I had come to call friends.

A part of me felt a little shy, as I had never been one for celebrating my birthday or having people gather for my sake, but to see all of these kind-hearted people sat in my favourite place for my birthday was one of the happiest moments I've had in my life, and still is to this day.

They bought me a cake, sang happy birthday, and after we had eaten it, the restaurant staff, waiters and waitresses brought me out a cake with a candle on it, giving me another rendition of the song, this time in Spanish. The only thing that could have made it better was Yuliet being there, but it had landed on her day off. I spent most of the night with my friends from the university, until I got a message from José, asking me where I was and if I could pass by the house, so I said my goodbyes and thanked all of my friends, especially Kat and Rox. When I got to the house, José, Fiti and the rest of the family had also got a cake, and had been waiting to sing me feliz cumpleaños and celebrate with me.

They were such an amazing family, and it had been a truly joyful day.

A couple days later, when I went to Waoo! for lunch, Yuliet and Lili were there. Lili was another waitress who had shown me so much kindness, and always spoke to me whenever I went there. At the end of my meal, they gave me a desert cake with a candle in it, and wished me happy birthday. It was perfect.

After two and a half months of living there, the time came to leave Cuba. It had been such an amazing experience, I had made some lifelong friends and even managed to grasp a little of the Spanish language, moving up in class from principiante to elemental. I spent time with some of the nicest, most loving, caring people I've ever had the pleasure of meeting. I even met the girl of my dreams, though unfortunately for me, she was still in a relationship, which didn't surprise me, because she was so perfect. She wasn't just the girl of my dreams; she would clearly have been the girl of many a man's dream, and some lucky individual had actually managed to be the man she wanted to be with.

When I returned home to the United Kingdom towards the end of July, I submitted my availability to work, and a warning order came back for a job that was a ten day transit from the Suez Canal, Egypt, to Galle, Sri Lanka. I was to fly from London Heathrow to Cairo on the eighth of August, then on the fifth I received an email stating that there was going to be a seven day delay on our transit, so to be on standby. On the eighth, my mum received a phone call from Julie, who told her that my dad had been coughing up blood during the night, and had been transferred to an intensive care unit. Mum told us as we woke up, and said that she was going to visit, asking if I wanted to join her, my little brother, Ryan, and sister, Reannon, who she was taking with her.

I planned to use the day to visit friends I hadn't seen in a while, but then mum said: "You know, a lot of times people don't come out of intensive care." I honestly didn't think much of it, but said that I'd go along too. We all went up there together – mum, Ryan, Reannon, Richard, Gina and myself – and when arriving at the hospital, we went up to his room, where two of my half- brothers and my half-sister were stood with Julie. That day, from all the goings on in the hospital and the way people were speaking, I came to the realisation that he had actually been living with them for some time, but can't say it was a problem for me, as we'd learnt to survive without him.

Dad's 'other' family explained that he had woken in the night in pain, and had been coughing up blood, so the doctors put him into an induced coma. The doctors then came in and spoke to us all, but constantly referred to Julie as his wife. I was so confused as first, I quietly asked Richard if he had gotten married to her and not said anything, but he said no, he didn't think so; so I assume that's just how she had introduced herself to them at the hospital.

The doctors explained that dad had a ruptured lung, and that it wouldn't be possible to operate on him because he would most likely suffer a heart attack. We all put our ideas across, as to what they could potentially do, wondering why they wouldn't do something to help him, despite none of us having any medical expertise whatsoever, and they eventually took him away. We called another of my half-brothers, Kyian, to tell him that the situation wasn't looking good, so he should join us and have the opportunity to say his goodbyes, if this was going to be the day that dad died.

Kiyan duly arrived, and the doctors came back a couple hours later.

"I'm sorry to have to tell you that the operation has been unsuccessful," one of them began. "When we opened him up, there was a lot of internal bleeding, and more damage than we could have ever repaired. We couldn't locate the bleeds, because there was so much blood. Again, I'm very sorry to have to tell you this."

It dawned on me that dad was going to die, so I asked: "Well, can you at least wake him up? Take him out of the induced coma for a few minutes so that we can at least say goodbye to him?"

"I'm afraid that won't be possible – his heart simply won't be able to take it. I'm sorry, but there's nothing more that we can do for him."

"In that case, can you all leave the room so that my mum can have some time with him before he passes?" asked one of my half-brothers.

"Umm, excuse me, can we just take a moment to acknowledge that my mum was the only woman he was ever actually married to?!" said Gina, who had tears rolling down her face, and was clearly feeling the emotional weight of the moment, loss, deep sadness and, I imagine, a multitude of other emotions.

There was a collective, compassionate outcry at that moment from my mum, Richard and myself. "Gina," we said, understanding that this wasn't the moment to start getting into all of that, even though she was absolutely right. Gina is very sincere and leads from her heart, which was being absolutely torn apart in that moment, as I imagine all of my siblings' hearts were. I think the only two people in the room not crying were my mum and myself.

It wasn't a surprise to see mum like that, as I had never seen her cry. I knew it wasn't through any sort of hostility towards my father or the situation, and that it was more a coping mechanism.

Instead, she internalises her emotions, which manifest into other reactions that maybe don't call for such harsh responses.

For my own part, I hadn't cried since I was sixteen, and saw it as a weakness – what the hell could possibly be gained from crying? When people mourn for a loved one, the person they're crying over is still dead, so I've never seen the point of it. That's not to say that I was unaware of a sad moment in our lives, but I wasn't going to allow myself to indulge in what I thought was such a pointless display of emotion.

We all stayed in the room, and slowly but surely dad's heart slowed and faded, along with the beeping from the medical devices attached to him. Eventually, the doctors and nurses came in and told us that he was gone. One by one, my siblings all kissed him on his head, while some held his hands and said their goodbyes. I kissed him on his forehead, and whispered in his right ear: "I love you, dad, journey well," then told my mum and siblings that I had already made plans, so had to leave. I didn't see the point in hanging around the hospital anymore, dad was gone and I had genuinely made other plans.

Before leaving, I went to see little Ryan and Reannon, who had been patiently sitting in the waiting room, with all of us taking turns to be with them whilst each person said their goodbyes. They clearly knew something was wrong, having seen family coming and going from the waiting room, in different emotional states, all day. They had also developed their own little relationship with my dad over the years. He had played with them and showed them affection, and when I saw them, they were sat there with tears in their eyes, obviously very moved by the moment and whatever their six and four year old understanding of death was. I gave them both a hug and a kiss, and told them it was okay.

As I went about my day, one thing that played on my mind was that I wasn't even supposed to be in the United Kingdom that day. I should have already been on my way to Egypt to board another vessel … it's crazy how things work out.

Shortly after this, and dad's funeral, which I was lucky enough to make it back home for, the relationship we had with our half brothers and sister eroded. It's funny what death can do to a family or family members. I've seen it destroy relations between families and, unfortunately, a lot of the time it's irreparable. It wasn't the way I wanted things to go, and I held my dad responsible for this for many years.

I truly love all of my brothers and sisters, and hope that my half-sister never has to suffer the pain that my mum had to go through because of the actions of her mother, my dad not being innocent at all, and being the biggest part of the problem that has caused my mum so much pain.

I would just like to take a moment to say that while I use the term half-brother and half-sister in this book, the truth is that I see all of my brothers and sisters as the same. The 'half' is only used here to paint the picture, set the scene and make it easier to identify my different siblings.

At this point, my desire to be on the ships had faded, just as the daily rate of pay had. Craig had left to start his own CrossFit gym, and I didn't want to be away at sea for days on end, on the bridge wings by myself, alone with my thoughts; feeling lonelier by the day, or on a transit with some guy who I had nothing in common with. I spoke to Ethan, who was now in Afghanistan on the close protection circuit, whenever I got the chance, and he told me he had the contact details for the recruiter of a private security company operating out in Iraq. He said that I should send them my CV, and see if I could enter the close protection circuit.

During this period of my life, I found a whole new respect for those who come to the UK with no command of the language and throw themselves out there on the front line, trying to converse with native speakers. That might be in whatever job they have secured, or simply on the street asking for directions, but it takes balls, and I hadn't understood that until being that person out there in Cuba, trying to learn Spanish. It can be a challenging, scary and completely out of the comfort zone experience to put yourself through.

Cuba showed me that there are good people with kind hearts all over the world, ready to help in whatever way they can. What may seem like a little thing for the person helping can actually be a massive thing for the person receiving that help. It can change someone's entire perspective of the experience they're having in whatever country, city, town or situation they're in. Each and every one of us are ambassadors for our nations.

JOY

To this day, this woman remains one of the most beautiful human beings I have ever had the pleasure of meeting and sharing time, space and energy with. Just as I was about to start my new career as a Close Protection Operator (CPO), I was introduced to the beautiful Joy by a close friend of mine. Dave, whose girlfriend was good friends with Joy, gave me her phone number, saying: "Phone this woman. I've told her all about you, and she said she would love to meet you."

I was intrigued not only at the opportunity of meeting this lady, who he had recommended very highly, but also about what he may have told her that could have possibly made her want to meet me. By now, I had decided that I wanted to live in South America, so the timing of this made me feel a little unsure – was I to call this lady and possibly start something that was destined to fail, which in turn could result in me hurting her? Dave told me that I was overthinking it, and that all I had to do was have a chat with her and see where it led, so I did.

I started speaking to Joy in February 2014, sending her a WhatsApp message saying hello, introducing myself and asking how she was. She replied, and we began this back and forth of constant communication, getting to know each other, asking questions, sharing likes and dislikes, dreams and aspirations. She told me that Dave had explained to her that I had just left maritime security, and was beginning a new career in Iraq as a CPO. I explained that I had intentions to move to South America at some point, and her response was: 'Perfect, I'm not looking for anything heavy. I just want to have a laugh with someone who doesn't take themselves too seriously'.

The minute I heard that, I was in. She was this beautiful, funny, quick-witted, happy go lucky type of individual, and I loved speaking with her. She told me she was a bespoke couture dress designer, and sent me some photos of her work. Her dresses had been in famous magazines, on display in luxurious hotels and worn by celebrities at prestigious events all over the world. Her life was completely different to mine, as she was a somebody. During the time we had been getting to know each other over WhatsApp, she had been in America and I had been in the UK, awaiting a date to fly to Iraq for an induction period with the new company I would be contracting for out there.

It turned out that I would fly to Iraq two days before she would return to the UK, so we would miss each other, but it was okay. Joy was very easy-going and we made plans to see each other once I returned. We spoke every day once I arrived in Basra, Iraq, constantly texted each other, and whenever I had a break in my day, we interacted. Our video calls during the evenings lasted for hours, but they were fun and came naturally. I really enjoyed talking to her, and we spoke about what it would be like when we finally got to meet, what we would do and where we could go.

After ten days of induction, I returned to the UK, but because I'd just changed jobs and had to buy loads of kit for my new job, I was broke. I had absolutely no money, and didn't feel comfortable about meeting Joy until I had a few pounds in my pocket. I think my mum, whose house I was currently staying in, could sense that things were a bit tight financially, and said she wanted to give me some money. I didn't really want to take from mum, who was running a house and raising my little brother and sister, but she said it was okay and that she wouldn't offer if she didn't have it … which was absolutely untrue – I'd seen her go without many times in order to make sacrifices for us.

Joy, who had booked a room in a five star hotel in the centre of London, told me to make my way there, and that she would meet me there once she'd dropped her sister off at the airport. I got there and waited for her, and an hour or so later, there was a knock on the door. I opened it and Joy froze, which I totally understood. Before now, we'd just been voices or faces on the other end of a phone or internet line, whereas this was the first time we were meeting in person.

Entering the room, I tried to ease any nerviness between us by saying that we didn't need to do anything if she didn't want to, but any tension didn't last very long. We cuddled, we kissed, we touched, then one thing led to another and we had sex for the first time. At this time, I was taking a course of steroids, and had decided that it would be good to try a site injection, directly into my left tricep, but it turned out to be one of the worst ideas I've ever had. My arm swelled considerably, by the evening it was clear to see, and it was hurting. I could press on the swollen area, and it would retain the indentation of my thumb.

I was honest with Joy, telling her that I took steroids and what had happened. She was concerned for me, suggesting that we get some anti-inflammatory tablets on the way to dinner. The restaurant wasn't far away, so we got dressed and set off to get the tablets, which helped tremendously. The restaurant was called The Cut, which I'd never been to; but as soon as we arrived, I realised I had no business being there with only the sixty pounds in my pocket that my mum had given me, but decided to try and play it cool.

We were greeted at the door, ushered to a table and given a menu. Looking through it, I saw that a bowl of chips – just chips! – cost seven pounds, and then I saw the steak part of the menu. Some of the steaks on offer were valued at more than a hundred pounds, and I remember thinking that they were more expensive than the footwear I was wearing. As I searched for the cheapest thing on the menu, I even contemplated getting a plate of chips and saying I wasn't hungry.

Over the years, I had developed the belief that a man should always pay when out with lady at dinner, but I had absolutely no idea how I was going to achieve that ideal in this current situation. A little while later, a waiter arrived at the table, wearing white gloves and holding a silver tray that had three different tiers of steak on it. He began to explain the different cuts of steak, and the degree of marble that each one contained. I had never heard this in my life, and remember thinking: 'What the hell? This meat has marbles in it?', but obviously I didn't say anything, because I didn't want to look stupid.

Whilst he was explaining, I had one eye on him and the steaks, and the other on the menu, frantically trying to search for the cheapest option. Finally I found it – a small fillet cut that was priced at thirty odd pounds. Now, I thought, all I had to do was come up with a good enough reason as to why I would pick the cheapest option, after he had just explained how delicious and mouth-watering these big cuts with high degrees of marble were. When he finished explaining the various cuts on the multi-tiered tray, I asked which dish had the least fat, knowing that it would be the fillet. Once he had indeed confirmed that it was the fillet, I said something about how I was very active in the gym and was watching my diet, which drew some laughter from him and Joy …. and I was so relieved.

The food arrived, we ate, we talked and when we were finished, Joy said she had to use the bathroom. When she returned, she said: "Come on, let's go." "But we haven't paid," I said.

"I've paid already," she replied.

I didn't know what to say. I had been so worried about not having enough money, not coming across like some kind of penny pinching Scrooge, or a man who couldn't afford to go out on a date with a lady and cover the bill. I felt such a sense of warmth towards her for taking care of it, even though I did ask if I could pay something towards the bill.

"No, it's alright," Joy smiled. "There's no need to talk about money – it isn't important."

She didn't say it in a pretentious way – it was just said as a fact. Money wasn't important when we were enjoying each other's company, and sharing this moment together. We spent the rest of the night and following morning intimately together, enjoying each other's company.

Over the next few weeks, we spent a lot of time with each other. When I first went to her place, where she lived and worked, I saw some of her luxurious, bespoke dresses and they were amazing. There were tables throughout the huge open plan floor with bits of dresses, materials, Swarovski sequins, sewing machines and dress making equipment everywhere. This woman was a highly creative individual, and I had never seen anything like it, but then why would I have? I had never known anybody in this industry who would have exposed me to this sort of artistry. Her dresses were expressions of her creative spirit, they were beautiful, and Joy explained that some of them could take up to a year to make. We spent a lot of time with each other over the next few weeks, until I had to fly out to Iraq for my first rotation. I planned to use the first wage packet from my new employer to take Joy to Spain, and wanted as much as possible for it to be a surprise. During a video call, I asked her if she was free for the dates I had selected. When she said she was, I told her she would need her passport, a massive grin spread across her face and she asked excitedly: "Why? Where are we going?" I said it was a surprise, and that she would find out soon enough.

I finished my rotation, arrived back in the UK, and a few days later we flew to Spain. I took care of everything – flights, accommodation and hire car. I wanted to make sure that Joy didn't have to spend a penny after she had taken such good care of me during our first date, and many days after, whilst I had been so broke.

When we got to Spain, I picked up the hire car and we made our way to a villa that my friend's mum owned. Located at the top of a steep hill and surrounded by a mass of undulating countryside that spanned as far as the eye could see, it was an amazing villa with a swimming pool, and we had been allowed to stay there for free.

We headed into Barcelona during some of the days, and at night, and having been there before with some friends, I remembered a place we found where live sex shows were performed. I couldn't believe what I'd seen, and with Joy being quite openminded, I thought it would be funny to take her there, as no such place existed in London that I was aware of.

We arrived at the location from before, only to discover that it wasn't there anymore; but me being me, I asked around to find out where it had moved to, or if there was another such venue. A taxi driver told me he knew where one was, called Bagdad Espectacular, and after Joy said she was okay to go, we got in the cab. When we got there, it seemed very different to the place I had been to before, which had been a small cubical attached to many others, surrounding a fairly sized inner space that had a rotating circular bed in the middle of it, where the male and female talents would have sex for everyone to see.

I paid at the entrance, and we followed the stairs down to a basement type club, where there was a bar, a rotating stage and some seats in front of it. A very intimate setting, we bought some drinks and sat down. Music started playing, and the stage started spinning slowly, before a young woman emerged from behind a curtain dressed in lingerie. She began to dance to the music, and slid up and down the pole that was in the middle of the stage. When the first song was done and the second started, she took her clothes off, pulled out a vibrator and began to pleasure herself onstage.

I believe Joy was quite surprised, and whenever we looked at each other, we giggled, as if teenagers again. When the performance finished, the lady left the stage and two more women replaced her. Wearing lingerie, they danced very sensually to the music playing, stripped off and started to passionately kiss each other. Lightly touching and caressing each other, one of them laid the other down softly on the spinning stage, then began to pleasure her with her mouth and fingers, whilst her legs were spreadeagled.

I think Joy was quietly amazed and intrigued, as it's quite something to observe other people having sex. Then, much to my surprise, the women invited one of the men sat in the audience up on stage. Oh shit! This was an interactive show, and as my stomach churned, me and Joy looked at each other at the same time, in shock. Without saying a word, I knew that we were both thinking the same thing: 'Oh my God, they could call us up on stage!' The man they chose to join them was told to lie down by one of the ladies, with the other undoing his belt and pants, before both pulled his pants, then boxer shorts, down.

The guy was loving it, and I got the feeling he had been there many times before. They put a condom on him, and then one of the ladies mounted him. Looking like he was in heaven, he laid there with his mouth open, eyes closed, face twitching, with his jacket and T-shirt still on while his lower half was exposed. When the song finished and their show came to an end, they got up and sent the man back to his seat. He looked so happy with himself! Next, a woman came out alone. Beautiful and voluptuous, wearing PVC boots and scanty lingerie, she danced to her first song, and I could see that she oozed confidence and loved making eye contact with the audience. When her second song started, whilst she ripped her skimpy outfit off, the curtains flew open and a male talent stormed in rock hard, focused and ready to go. Boarding the spinning stage, she immediately began to pleasure him with her mouth. It was a sight to see; this was a lady who was clearly very passionate about her job and gave it her full, undivided focus and attention.

After a short while, she positioned herself on all fours, he entered her from behind, and went to work hard. Whilst he was pleasuring her, she jerked forward violently from the sheer force of his thrusting, and you could hear skin slapping against skin. I held Joy's hand, as if to say: "Oh my God, are you seeing this?" She squeezed my hand tightly, leant over to me and said: "Her eyes and gaze are so intense, the next time somebody asks me how many people I've had sex with, I'll have to include this woman."

I laughed, then looked at her to see what Joy meant. Not only could I see it, but I could feel it too. Her gaze was seductive, strong and deep, she met all of our eyes individually as the stage span around slowly, and it was all very provocative. For the next show, two other beautiful ladies entered. As they began to dance to their first song very seductively, this time I could feel their gaze on me and Joy, and became very anxious, as I could tell what was going to happen next. Once the second song started, they stripped and called me onto the stage, but I sat there frozen, trying to laugh it off. One of them came down from the stage, took hold of my hand, as if to pull me up on stage, and to my amazement, Joy pushed me, goading me to go up. The lady then grabbed Joy's hand, and was pulling her up too, so I joined in, saying: "Go on! If I'm going up, you're going up too!"

We both went up onto the stage, the women stood Joy and I next to each other, then began to nakedly dance directly in front of us, grinding on us. I was in shock, and didn't know where to look, as something like this had never happened to me. The women turned around to face us, placed our hands on their breasts, squeezed them and moved them around vigorously. The lady in front of me was making serious eye contact and I felt intimidated, so looked at Joy, who was looking at me whilst her hands were on the other woman's breasts. I think she was feeling the same way: overwhelmed … overwhelmingly overwhelmed.

The lady began to pull the shoulder straps of Joy's dress down until her breasts were exposed. I began to worry a little, not knowing how Joy was taking this or how far either of us were willing to go. The girl in front of me pushed my head down and placed my mouth on Joy's breast, and as I looked directly across, I saw the other lady sucking on Joy's other breast. It was unbelievably surreal, and became even more so when the woman who had been in front of me began unzipping my flies, while the one who had been hanging off Joy's other breast dropped to her knees and began lifting up her long summer dress, as if about to begin pleasuring her orally.

At this point, Joy broke free from the nervous trance both ladies had put us in, and said she couldn't do it, but that I could stay on the stage. To be honest, I was relieved because: 1) I didn't want to be with another woman in front of Joy like that, which felt disrespectful; and 2) I was so nervous and intimidated to be up on stage in that way, I don't even know if I would have managed to become erect. We left the stage, sat back down and the ladies finished their show. When we left, we smiled and said goodbye to everybody there, including the bar staff. They were all smiling and laughing with us, as it had been quite the experience, and I think they could tell. This became a frequent go to joke between me and Joy over the next couple years whilst we dated each other. Once we returned to the UK, we went back to life as normal. I continued rotating eight weeks in Iraq and coming back to the UK for four, during which time we went out for dinners, watched movies in the cinema and at her place, and generally just enjoyed spending time together. I got to meet her mum, dad and sister, who were all such beautiful people, welcoming me with great warmth. Joy met all of my family, who she loved, and they absolutely loved her, and still ask after her to this day, wanting to know how she's doing.

She would pick me up from the airport at the end of my rotations and we would make love in the car, or up against it in the car park there. It was all so much fun, and I had so much love for Joy, and felt that she had love for me too … but something niggled away at me, and it was the sense of our relationship feeling incomplete. I hated myself for this, because Joy was an amazing woman who deserved so much more.

I used to wish that she would fall pregnant, and would say: "Take out your coil and let's just see what happens." I envisaged us having a beautiful little girl who would grow up at her mother's side, learning how to make dresses. This little girl would love it whenever daddy came home from work; she would be my princess, and I would love her so much. I thought maybe that would complete me … maybe that would fill the void that wasn't allowing me to feel whole.

I realise now that some things are just not meant to be. Joy didn't take her coil out, which I absolutely understand and, looking back, it might have been a horrible thing to say – what if it made her feel that she wasn't enough? That I needed her to have a baby if I was going to stick around? I had no right asking her that, considering we were 'just dating'.

After about two years of dating, I started visiting Colombia and, as I grew to love it and visit more frequently, Joy and I began to see less of each other. I would tell myself that it was okay, because I had been honest from the start about my plans to move to South America; and that she had always said that she was only after a bit of fun.

Eventually, I told Joy that I would be spending all of my free time in Colombia, and we stopped seeing each other. She said that she understood, and that it was okay, but years later, once I got on the medicine path and started to become increasingly aware of my responsibilities to myself and others, especially those who loved me, I wondered whether I had caused her pain. To this day, although we were never officially 'together', Joy is the person with whom I have had the longest, most loving relationship.

AUNTIE JANICE

I started working in Basra, Iraq, as a close protection operator in May 2014. It was completely different to maritime security, with so many different people and, thus, personalities, on the camp where I lived. Given the rotation of eight weeks at work and four weeks' leave routine, I could plan my leave well in advance, which wasn't something you could do in maritime security. Just like maritime security, all the guys I worked with were ex-military, so were all likeminded and, most importantly, shared the same sense of humour.

The food on camp was much better than maritime, but still left a lot to be desired. It was mass produced, generic food, with a generous plethora of unhealthy meals. Most days, I tried to stick to a basic diet of rice and chicken. I felt that I couldn't go wrong with that and, at the age of thirty two, found it quite easy to remain devoted to a good diet, especially as I was on steroids and in the gym every day, which gave me motivation to make the commitment.

The team orbat, or order of battle, comprised a team leader, deputy team leader, two drivers and two vehicles. The team leader and one driver would be in the bravo vehicle, or rear vehicle, and as the deputy team leader, I would be in the front vehicle, or alpha vehicle. We would leave the camp where we lived and pick up clients at seven o'clock in the morning. It only took us around ten minutes to reach them, and we transported them from their camp to the locations at which they worked throughout the day, providing armed protection for between one to four clients per team.

On starting this new career, I was very observant to see if it would be possible to bring steroids in with me through the airports and onto the camp where I was living. The first rotation was enough to make me think that it would be possible, and justify the risk of bringing them in. I had lost a fair bit of weight and strength through working on the ships, and desperately wanted to get back into a good gym routine, and be as big and strong as I could possibly be.

I returned after my first leave back onto rotation with all the steroids I needed, and managed to make it through the airports and onto camp unnoticed and unchallenged. Some of the locals I worked with were able to get me ten milligram norditropin human growth hormone pens. Oh my God, I loved human growth hormone so much! I could sleep for two to four hours a night, and wake up feeling fully rested for the first time in my entire adult life. My complexion looked amazingly clear and healthy, and my vision improved, even though there wasn't anything wrong with it to start with. I woke up every day feeling rejuvenated. I have so much love for human growth hormone it's indescribable.

During my time on that contract, I met so many other guys who were also taking steroids. One in particular, Jason, was absolutely massive, at about seventeen stone. We spoke about steroids and the gym all the time, and became pretty good friends.

One day, he told me that he was going to run a cycle of insulin on his next rotation. I didn't know much about it, but had heard that it was one of the most powerful hormones you could take in relation to gaining weight and becoming massive in the gym. Jason had done all of his homework, and explained it to me. He said that the insulin pens we could get in Iraq were called novorapid, a fast-acting insulin that was taken subcutaneously into the fatty tissue of the stomach. It would typically begin to work after ten to twenty minutes, and last for between three to five hours.

When insulin spikes, it acts like a train that travels around your body, flushing all supplements and glucose straight into the muscle. It takes glucose from everywhere, the dangerous part being that the brain uses it for fuel, so if you don't replace the glucose being flushed into the muscles in a timely manner, your brain ends up being starved of it, which then causes all kinds of serious problems; but yes, I had already justified this to myself as an acceptable and necessary risk to get massive, and the truth is I was sold about two minutes into the conversation. I was all about strength in numbers, and wouldn't have dreamed of doing this by myself, but with Jason doing it too, I was in.

He told me that the plan was to take one IU (international unit) per 10 kilograms of lean muscle, and we needed to bring in some form of fast acting carbohydrate, with maltodextrin and vitago our top choices. We would have to take ten grams of fast acting carbohydrates per one IU of insulin to start off with, but as our bodies got used to interacting with the insulin and fast acting carbohydrates, we could lessen the amount of maltodextrin or vitago – i.e. from ten grams of carbohydrates per one IU, down to maybe seven or eight grams of carbohydrates per one IU, the aim being not to take onboard more carbohydrates than necessary, so as to keep fat gain to a minimum.

The next rotation came and we both returned to Iraq with our steroids and supplements. The plan was to start with two IUs in the morning upon waking up, then immediately drink a protein shake containing amino acids, creatine, glutamine and twenty grams of vitago. Once showered and ready for work, with the insulin already kicking in, I had porridge for breakfast, to provide a slow release of glucose throughout the morning, or at least until my next meal. This went on for a couple of days, before I raised the dosage to three IUs, then four, five, and so on.

I don't think you're supposed to increase the dosage so rapidly, but being the impatient person that I am, especially when it comes to wanting to see results, and see them quickly, by the end of the second week I was taking nine IUs in the morning and another nine after the gym in the evenings. I felt nothing, so asked Jason if it was doing anything for him, and he said he couldn't feel any sort of change. I decided to complete the cycle, but to ditch the routine beyond that, as I couldn't see any results. Then, at the end of week three, I woke up and, before I even got out of bed, I had this feeling of absolute massiveness; I glanced in the mirror and looked like I had just finished a gym session. I couldn't believe it, the insulin had begun to work, and over the next few weeks, I went from one hundred kilos to one hundred and six. Insulin had become my new best friend, although I know it wasn't solely responsible for the change, as I was taking quite the cocktail of steroids, human growth hormones and every supplement I could get my hands on.

One morning, about five weeks into what I had now decided would be a six week cycle, not the four originally planned, I woke up, injected it and went about my normal morning routine. As I did, I got a phone call from my TL, a guy called Kai, who sarcastically asked: "Are you coming to work today or not?" I had got the mission timings wrong, and while I thought I still had half an hour to go before I needed to be at work, I should already have been there. I ran to the dining facility, grabbed a packed lunch, then ran to the vehicles.

We collected our clients from their camp, then set off for the first location of the day, which was about a fifty minute drive away. By the time we arrived, I was chatting absolute shite … or for those of you who know me, I mean even more than I usually do. I had cold sweats, was unable to balance, and felt anxious. At first, I didn't understand what was happening, then realised it was because I had missed breakfast. I'd been in such a rush that I hadn't had my porridge, or any of the things I normally ate for breakfast, before going out on mission.

I was starting to feel the onset of hypoglycaemic shock, and when the penny finally dropped, I went to the back of the vehicle, found my lunch and ate the lot. I ate the white bread tuna sandwich, a packet of ready salted crisps, a piece of cake, drank two cans of coke, and it took about an hour for me to start feeling normal again. Up until that point, I had thought that all of the hype around the danger of insulin was just talk or random one-off cases, but that morning I learnt a serious lesson: double check mission times and get up earlier.

That said, I definitely wasn't going to stop taking insulin, it was awesome. I finished the cycle, and the next time I knew I was going to run a course of insulin, I made sure to buy glucose tablets and keep them in my grab bag in case of emergency.

Later that year, I went to Medellin, Colombia. I flew from London to Bogota, then caught a connecting flight to Medellin that took about 50 minutes. On the plane, I saw a number of beautiful women, but wouldn't dare try talking to any of them for a multitude of reasons. I was still dating Joy for one, at this point my Spanish still required some serious work, and the last thing I wanted was to start a conversation and be unable to understand or express myself fully in the way I wanted to. I'd already had so many of these experiences, mostly in Cuba, and found them really embarrassing.

I landed at Medellin José María Cordova international airport and got a taxi to Poblado, which was about a forty minute drive through beautiful little towns and long routes of rural greenery. As we got close to Poblado, there were a lot more buildings, a lot more people on the street, colourful, vibrant cultural architecture and beautiful weather. I saw so many physically beautiful women en route to my Airbnb that by the time we arrived, I had already fallen in love about a hundred times.

I stayed in an apartment, in a building called Nueva Alejandría. It was a really nice apartment and perfectly located, about a five minute walk away from the shopping centre, Santa Fe, which I visited frequently; and about a fifteen minute taxi drive to the university, EAFIT, which I would be attending for a two week Spanish speaking course. I found a gym immediately, of course, with it being the number one priority in my life at that moment … and wow, again I fell in love every day, seeing women in backless onesie training outfits and all other variants of eye-catching, seductive gym wear that one could imagine.

Every Sunday, the main road, Avenida Poblado, was shut down for something called the Ciclovia. Families, couples, friends and individuals gathered to walk, skate, run, cycle and otherwise enjoy Sunday mornings as a community, and I loved it. There were people on the side of the road with signs and banners saying 'abrazos gratis', or free hugs. They came up to you with massive smiles on their faces and gave you big hugs. These people were complete strangers, but it was so loving, and I remember thinking: that's what community should be like. During my two weeks there, I found a salsa academy called Dancefree, where I sometimes went in the evenings to partake in group classes teaching different levels of salsa, depending on ability: basic, intermediate and advanced. I was obviously in basic, but still asked if there was a level even lower than that that I could join. It was okay, though, and I took comfort in the fact that there were people there who were just as two left footed as I was.

I found it quite hard to make Colombian friends, and a lot of that was down to my Spanish still being quite limited. I simply wasn't able to express myself or engage in conversations, so lacked confidence when it came to attempting to talk to native speakers.

By now, I was a bit more used to travelling alone, but still didn't find it easy, mostly because of the pressure I put on myself. I went to a restaurant for dinner and ate alone, surrounded by families, couples and friends who were dining together. The little voice in my head reprimanded me: 'Look at everybody looking at you. Everyone thinks you're a loser and that you have no friends, because you're sat here all alone and can barely even speak the language, whilst everybody else has someone and can easily speak to each other'.

My little voice would tell me this all the time – at restaurants, in the gym, walking around the shopping centres, in coffee shops … and it was even worse at the salsa school, because I had to dance, making myself vulnerable, putting on a show for everyone there. Given I still couldn't dance, this was the manifestation of one of my biggest self-confidence issues, and the only respite I got from that damn voice was when I was back in the Airbnb apartment, in my comfort zone, alone.

Then one day, just like that, my two weeks were up and, just as all good things do, my time there came to an end; but Medellin had been an amazing experience, and I already knew that I would be back, and had maybe even found a place in the world where I felt a little at home … well, at least more at home than I felt anywhere else. I returned to London, my leave came to an end and I went back to Iraq.

Over the next few years, I settled into my new job and enjoyed the routine. When I was at work, I got on with the job and kept up what by now had become an obsession with the gym, even though I didn't realise this at the time. I didn't even care what women thought, which had been one of my original priorities. In fact, I had been told by a few women – friends, women on nights out and my mum – that I didn't look nice, because I was too big.

I could always tell if I had put on weight or lost some, or looked big or small, because whenever I went home on leave, as soon as I opened the door, mum would say one of two things: "Oh, son, you're looking good! You've lost some weight, you look nicer like this," which would make me feel upset, because it meant I was going in the opposite direction to the one I wanted to be heading towards. I knew what that meant: that I wasn't taking enough steroids, and that I had to take more. The second reaction was: "Oh my God! Son, what the hell are those two things sticking out of your neck? It doesn't look good – you look too big!" The things sticking out of my neck that she referred to were my traps, which pleased me greatly, as it meant I was growing and moving in the right direction … but even then, all that came to mind is: great, it's working, but I should probably take more steroids.

I think I was training with the aim of getting to a point where one day I would look in the mirror and be happy with what I saw staring back at me. At work, people would sometimes call me big man, and seemed to be impressed when they saw me in the gym lifting heavy weights … but it was never enough. I would go on leave, and whenever I went to nightclubs and bars, people would see me walking towards them and move out of my way. It made me feel good as I was being recognised for my size, but being in the job I had, and having been in the gym since I was fifteen years old, I knew that there were numerous men so much bigger and stronger than I was or could ever be.

I saw these guys in the gyms I went to and trained with them, but still had to keep going, although I knew I was never going to be the strongest or the biggest. I mean, I'm only five foot eight, so my height alone would never permit me to be able to compete with some of the guys I knew or had seen. I think the hope was that I would be the biggest, strongest version possible of myself, so I kept bringing the steroids in and taking insulin and human growth hormones.

One thing I was sure of is that I was definitely bigger than any of my school friends who had been in the bedroom that day when I failed massively, trying to lift a mere twenty kilos on that York weights bench.

I started going to Spain, visiting different cities during some of my leaves, always enrolling onto Spanish speaking courses wherever I went. Spain was nice – I especially loved Barcelona – but I had the feeling that it wasn't far enough away from home. It was another country, but still in Europe, and I had the same type of feeling I got whenever I was in the United Kingdom – the sense of not feeling at home.

At the end of 2016, what me and Joy had came to an end, so I decided to start visiting Medellin again. I would go home to my mum's house in London on leave, stay for a couple days or so, then fly out to Medellin, where I remained for most of my leave, getting back to London just a few days before flying to Iraq. I enrolled in Spanish schools in Medellin, constantly trying to better my Spanish, and also began to develop a keen fondness for Colombian lovemakers.

It wasn't something I had intentionally gone over there to do, but spending all of your time alone eventually gets lonely, and it's nice just to have someone there who appears to like you a little … someone caring who shows you some affection, someone you can sit with, watch a movie or go to dinner with, so that I wasn't constantly sat alone with that little voice telling me people were laughing at me because I had no friends.

Even if I was paying for it, it was nice. Some of these women really talked to me, telling me about their lives, aspirations and dreams, and why they were in that line of work. Some had kids, some had families, including mothers and grandparents who couldn't work – so they were out doing their best to make money and support their loved ones. Some of them weren't even from Medellin, but had travelled there from other cities, in the hope of raising enough money to pursue their real dreams.

Many people will frown upon this, but the truth is: you never know what someone else is going through or why they're doing what it is they're doing; and why the hell should we judge them anyway? In my case, I had begun to feel quite lonely outside of work, so these women provided me with company and helped me escape the solitude for a while … and obviously I paid them for it. It was reciprocity, and in my experience, they always treated me with care and affection, and I treated them the same.

I really enjoyed my trips to Medellin, and really started to think about how I could spend all of my time there. Living there also made sense from a financial perspective, because it was quite expensive paying for flights to visit every leave, and all of the travelling involved meant spending hours on planes and at airports, which ate quite a bit of the time I had off; and it was quite exhausting too. These are all first world problems, I know, but they were still problems, and they were my problems.

As 2016 drew to a close, the project I worked on was coming to an end … well, not so much coming to an end as constantly cutting the rate that it was prepared to pay for security, so I was now getting to see the ugly side of the world of close protection. It was proposed that our wages be cut by more than fifty percent, which devastated me and the rest of the lads; but the one thing you learn quickly in the security industry is that there is no security in security – every day could be your last, for any number of reasons.

Luckily, I was able to get onto another project, so in February 2017 I moved to another contract, this time up in Bagdad. Unfortunately, and quite sadly, this coincided with the death of my Auntie Janice, who had been fighting colon cancer for the past year and a half. Fortunately for me, the way things worked out meant that I was on leave and in London during the last couple of weeks of her life, so I had the opportunity to go to Whipps Cross hospital and see her.

The first time I went to see her, she was very weak, bedridden and in need of help to do most things, like going to the bathroom and washing herself. It made me feel really sad to see her like this, as Auntie Janice had always been a very strong woman who had become a single mother after her marriage failed, just like my mum and Auntie Pauline. She had been a school teacher her entire life, and for that reason, growing up I had always seen her as quite a strict woman. She knew how to deal with children, having had to control them every day of her career, was swift and stern with her discipline whenever we were up to no good, and she also gave us homework to do during the school holidays. To see her like this, lying on a hospital bed, so dependent on others, I was taken aback. She asked me how I was, and how I was getting on with work. We engaged in general chitchat for a bit, but as we spoke, I couldn't believe how frail she looked, and tried to imagine how she was feeling.

She had two sons, my cousins, the eldest of which, Ibim, had developed autism in his very early years. Once her health had degraded to this fragile state, she had asked that Ibim not be brought in to see her. She didn't want him to see her this way, I guess out of fear that he wouldn't understand what was happening to her, and that it would only cause him grief and suffering. I don't have any children, so can only imagine the deep sorrow it must bring a parent, and what sort of place they must be in, to make a decision like that.

Before entering the ward she was in, my mum and aunties asked me to ask Auntie Janice if she would let Ibim visit her, as I imagine everyone by now had realised that this wasn't something she was going to recover from; and that they had asked her and had no joy getting her to change her mind. So whilst visiting her, I asked if it would be okay if Ibim came in to see her, and she seemed surprised to know that he was there. She told me that she hadn't wanted him to see her like this. It felt to me in that moment that she had also arrived at the realisation that everything wasn't going to be alright; that the chances of her making a full recovery and walking out of hospital were very slim, or non-existent.

Auntie Janice told me I could bring him in, then said something that I have never forgotten, and something I never imagined, or had prepared myself to hear, from someone I loved so much:

"I'm scared." It was one of the closest encounters with crying that I had had since the last time I wept at sixteen years old. I held her hand, and could see the fear in her eyes. To see my Auntie Janice, who I knew as a strong, independent and strict, but very loving woman, like this was one of the most unsettling things I had ever experienced; and what's more, I had absolutely no idea how to reply to what she had said.

I resisted the urge to let tears fall, and whilst holding her hand, asked again if it was okay to bring Ibim in to see her, to which she said yes. I went to the main doors of the ward in the hospital, where the rest of the family were, and got Ibim. When we reached her bed, the way he greeted her was amazing. It was so loving and tender. He clearly knew that something was wrong, and while he didn't have the ability to express himself fully, he hugged and held her with such love and adoration. It was overwhelming to see how he stroked her face, and was calling her mum. She held him, and said: "I'm so sorry, who will look after you now?" Some other family members came in, and everyone was at her bedside until visitors had to leave.

The next time I saw her, she had been moved to a hospice, could no longer talk and wasn't conscious. She died that day, and a few days later I had to return to work, missing her funeral as we were only given compassionate leave to visit immediate family who were terminally ill, or attend their funerals when they died. I missed Auntie Janice's funeral, but I had been there for the most important part, and got to see her and talk with her before she passed away.

My new contract was amazing, and I stayed on a camp with coalition forces and supporting logistical companies. There were even more people on this camp and, most importantly, there were women – a great number of them – who without even knowing it, provided a sense of normality for me and many of the other lads too, I'm sure. I hadn't had this in Basra, and certainly not on the ships, and while to some this might not seem like something to get excited about, after being surrounded by men and the masculine school of thought, especially those who are ex-military or still in the military, for most of my life, it was so refreshing to have women in the vicinity – and I'm not talking about it from a sexual point of view.

It was nice to have both sexes of our species present, something I had come to appreciate as normal in my younger years as a civilian. I guess it was something I had taken for granted, but since leaving home to join the Marines, I only really got to experience that during my vacations, which whizzed by. I am in no way saying that there's anything wrong with men, being surrounded by them or the masculine school of thought, which is what I've known most of my life, and I believe I've flourished in that environment; but a little normality is nice too. It may even be the same for women who, for whatever reason, have been surrounded by members of their own sex for the majority of their lives.

The new camp had massive hangers with amazing gyms in them – the sort of gyms I dreamed of, especially being on steroids, and the dining facilities were a huge upgrade from the last camp I had been on. I thought I was in heaven as there was protein everywhere. I knew that I could get massive here, but it was dangerous too – for the first time in my life, there in that dining facility, I came across melted peanut butter, which soon became one of my biggest weaknesses … my Achilles heel.

There were salsa classes every Thursday that were run by some of the contractors there, and plenty of the serving coalition females, and female contractors, attended. I had already dabbled in salsa in Medellin, so thought I would give it another go. It was something to do on Thursday and Saturday evenings, and I got the opportunity to interact with people outside of my immediate work circle.

The job there was pretty easy. I started as a site security manager, reporting to my superior on the static guard side of things, periodically visiting all the guard towers that surrounded the camp, those overlooking the amber zone, which had field of arcs over the Iraq Army camp positioned right next to us, and those that faced out onto the red zone, overlooking the main road that ran parallel to the outer perimeter wall of one side of the camp. It was an easy job, but one that I grew to absolutely detest very quickly, because it was so mundane. After a few months of being there, a new contract got stood up, so I was promoted to a team leader position and was transferred to the mobile security side of the contract the company had.

This new job was so much better. I met new clients, new personalities and did more of the type of work I had expected when originally flying out to Iraq. I worked with a team of three Iraqis, all good guys who were keen to just get on with the job. It's refreshing to have a team of guys who are willing and keen to work, guys who actually take pride in what they're doing, as opposed to those who just turn up to be a bum on a seat, a payroll number and to do the bare minimum … and we had a few of them in Basra.

We picked up the clients in the mornings at about eight o'clock, briefed them, then drove them into the Amber zone to their place of work, and escorted them with weapons slung in patrol stance, which was different from the less aggressive posture and profile that was employed in Basra. After a few months, or a couple of rotations, of having been there, I got to know a broad range of people from all of the different organisations that were based on the camp, and had a little social circle.

As already stated, I started to attend salsa lessons on Thursday nights, but the few classes I'd taken in Medellin were quite a few years before, and with me not being a dancer of any type, by any stretch of the imagination, I failed awfully. The girls I was partnered with never said anything, but I knew I wasn't doing at all well, which was quite embarrassing for me.

Nonetheless, I stuck with it because it was something I wanted to get better at, as part of a promise I had made myself to force myself out of my comfort zone. I think that for a lot of people, dancing is something that comes so easily to them, but for me it's like putting all of my insecurities on display for everyone to see. I decided that on my next leave, I would return to the dance academy I visited the first time I went to Medellin, to try and improve.

Dancefree was one of the best things I have ever done in my life. I met the dance teachers, who were all really high energy, but being shy, attending a dance school and dancing on a regular basis was quite intimidating for me, especially as it wasn't something that came naturally to me. The receptionist, Karol, who soon became one of my closest friends, suggested that I book two hours – the first with a male teacher, then the second with a female teacher. That way, I could learn the steps and moves that the male teachers liked and used themselves, then for my second hour, with these amazing, beautiful female teachers, I could practice what I had been taught and see how it was received by a lady, who I would potentially be leading.

When out dancing, I found it hard to transition between moves, which felt like multitasking. I went to the same school at night time for group classes lasting for about an hour and a half, before it turned into a nightclub. People came in who weren't necessarily students there, and one of my male teachers constantly repeated: "Baile! Baile!", all but ordering me to dance with complete strangers, which at this point I really didn't have the minerals to do. This was the sort of self-work I wanted to do, to continue to tackle things that were completely outside of my comfort zone, but that's what made it so hard.

Eventually, I gathered the courage to do it one evening, asking a random girl if she would dance with me. This was my first hurdle, opening myself up to possible rejection, but in this case she said yes, which in a way was even scarier, because now I had to dance … and not only dance, but maybe even talk a little with a native speaker, using my still developing, but limited, Spanish.

Salsa clubs in Colombia are normally packed, so even just finding a space to dance, and being able to dance in it, is a skill in itself. I found a space, and started going through the sequence I had been taught and had been practicing. Quite miraculously, I think I made it through two of the steps in the sequence, before making a mistake. I tried to apologise to the girl in Spanish, and get back in rhythm with the music, but the mistakes just kept coming and it felt like everyone was watching me.

The poor girl was smiling with me, trying, I guess, to make me feel okay about the situation, but also glanced around the room, perhaps wondering when this nightmare would be over. I lost all confidence, and ended up dancing the basic step, in line, back and forth, which is very hard to mess up, but I still managed to achieve it somehow.

Now, anyone who listens to salsa knows that some of these songs can go on forever … or at least it felt that way to me, so I made this poor girl dance in line, the basic step, for almost an entire song. I was praying that the song would come to an end, whilst all around me there were guys leading women, spinning them around, making them smile and laugh, and just connecting… whilst I was there, punishing this girl for what felt like a lifetime. Finally, the song ended, the girl smiled politely and walked away, and I didn't dare dance with another woman for months, aside from the female teachers I had lessons with.

Eventually, I did get a bit better and could lead women in salsa through a song or two. This is one of only three things that I have ever been proud of myself for. The first was passing out of Royal Marines training; the second was learning to speak Spanish to a conversational level, to the point where I could converse with Colombians and all other Spanish speakers, albeit not linguistically perfect (I'm never going to be a poet, but it was still a big thing for me, as I had never been an academically driven person); and now I could also defend myself on the dance floor to a degree … well, at least with salsa anyway.

Back on rotation, one of the American soldiers I became friends with had organised a weightlifting competition that was set for a few weeks ahead. It was going to be bench press, squats and deadlifts, and you would get three attempts at each. I had never taken part in a competition before, but really wanted to win this one, so trained hard for weeks, but came to realise I knew nothing about preparing for such an event. I went to the gym every day, and pushed myself to my limits. I tried to beat my personal best every week on every exercise, thinking that was how I could best prepare, but someone later told me you're not actually supposed to go for your maximum lift, or try to beat your personal best, until the day of the actual competition, and definitely shouldn't be doing it every week.

In my mind, more is more, but I injured myself doing shoulder press with sixty kilo dumbbells, which weirdly affected my chest too, so on the day of the competition, we started with squats. I squatted one hundred and eighty kilos for my first attempt, two hundred and twenty for my second, and two hundred and sixty for my third. No one bettered me on the squats, but as we moved onto bench press, I failed on one hundred and thirty kilos, with my right arm almost non-responsive due to my injury. It just didn't want to work, and I was so annoyed with myself, but I continued and, on my second attempt, I went for it again. After what seemed like forever, trying to press this one hundred and thirty kilos, with my right arm lagging behind for the duration, I finally got it up.

When we moved onto dead lifts, I went straight for six plates, or a hundred and sixty kilos. I thought that if I set the bar so high (well, what I thought was high), others maybe wouldn't want to meet my challenge, or that I would definitely win. It turned out that two of the other guys in my weight category – and there were only four of us – both outlifted me with ease. I was devastated, but also impressed, as it's quite a thing to see such weight getting lifted.

What was even funnier is that one of the guys in my category had only just arrived that day, and heard that there was a competition going on in the gym. He was in uniform and boots, so he borrowed some trainers from someone and joined in. Even though he was taller than me, I didn't register him as a threat, but the only thing I beat him on was squats. Because I beat all three of them on squats, the points awarded got me joint second place with the guy who had just wandered into a powerlifting competition and absolutely smashed it. Even though I hadn't actually done that badly, I wished that I had performed much better, so there was only one thing to do – yes, take more steroids!

Just as I was beginning to love my job, it suddenly finished, and I ended up back on the static guard contract. I was a broken man; although I was still lucky to have a job, I absolutely hated it. The money was a lot less, and the work monotonous and mundane. I started questioning the life choices I had made that had led me to where I was, and once you start going down that road, it's a slippery slope that only gets worse. One good thing I managed to do was change my hub airport from London Heathrow to Medellin José María Cordova, so now I wouldn't have to spend my own money paying for flights back and forth between the United Kingdom and Colombia.

Back in the role of site security manager meant that I had much less time to myself, so I couldn't really go to salsa class anymore because I would be on night shift, visiting all the guard towers and giving mandatory lessons to the local national guard force. I could still go to the gym, but every session was rushed, and it felt like I was just living to work – so much so, that for the first time in my life, I considered quitting and joining the dole queue, to live off the government. Then, as I hit my lowest point, a deputy team leader position came up in Basra, and the salary was a lot more workable than what I was now earning up in Bagdad, so I accepted it. After being in Bagdad for a little over a year, I moved back down to Basra in March 2018, to work on an oil and gas project.

It was quite a hard transition at first, because I had been spoilt up north in Bagdad, with massive gyms, a wide variety of equipment, and a huge dining facility that had been open at night time for those on the graveyard shift and people whose diets required another meal then. Not having access to my beloved melted peanut butter was probably a good thing, but everything else was a massive shock to the system. The gym on my new contract was a small garage type room full of hand-me-down equipment that had definitely seen better days. I had to remind myself that I was out there to work and make money, not be salsa dancing, getting massive and eating melted peanut butter, although these were things that made me happy, and if you can't do the things that make you happy, is there any point in doing anything at all? On this contract, there were a number of guys I already knew, having worked together on my first project back in 2014, which made the transition a lot easier. One thing I started to think about a lot was that so many of us had gone to Iraq with good intentions, and a grand plan to work there for a number of years, save enough money to leave the industry and enjoy a better financial standing. For some, that might mean paying off a mortgage, getting on the property ladder if they weren't already, paying for private education for their children, or otherwise giving them some of the opportunities that weren't open to them when they were kids.

For my own part, I had originally set out to eat into the horrendous debt I accrued in the Marines, and hopefully buy another apartment, house or both, then rent them out and be able to earn a rental income sufficient enough that I too could leave the industry, maybe meet somebody to settle down with and live a better life. In truth, however, anyone who has worked out there knows that only a few ever realised their dreams, with most remaining on the circuit for many years past the date they had set themselves to leave.

I've met guys who had started on the circuit many years before, some even around the time I had just joined the Royal Marines, and I have also seen a lot of these guys reach a certain age and be forced to leave, with many of them departing with nothing or ending up worse off than when they started. Every time I saw one of these guys reach that age and have to leave, or some who were diagnosed with terminal cancer and various other crippling illnesses, I thought to myself: 'That can't be me. I can't keep giving years of my life away to this industry, then leave no better off than I started, or even just die out there in a foreign land, away from family and friends'. Yet there I was, every rotation, making excuses to justify giving my life away to the circuit.

I think the honest truth is that my inability to move on came from a place of fear, a place that I think the majority of us are familiar with. How do we change that, and find the remedy most suited to each of us? This is one of the questions that landed me on the journey that I want to share in this book.

On my new contract, I woke up at five thirty in the morning, got showered, dressed and grabbed some breakfast. Once the local nationals arrived at about six thirty, we got weapons from the armoury and drove to the client's camp, which was about a twenty minute drive away. We arrived in plenty of time to pick the clients up at eight o'clock, providing them with armed security and transporting them around the various locations they had to visit on the oilfield.

After the initial shock of adjusting to my new routine, I actually grew to like the project. It was pretty straightforward, and most days we were finished by around two o'clock in the afternoon. I would then sit in my room and do some deep soul searching, to try and find the motivation to get myself in the garage style, no frills gym that upon entry seemed to suck all of the motivation and morale right out of me.

One of the great upsides at this point was that I was now flying straight to Colombia for leave, which was a good thing, but it meant I was now beginning to see a lot less of my family. I was used to this by now, and could speak to them over video calls, but as much as I love my family, I think I was actually starting to grow apart from them. I just seemed to keep choosing jobs that took me further and further away from them, and the thing is, I was okay with it.

My mum sometimes asked me why I didn't return to England and get a security job, working in a shopping mall or something, but I couldn't imagine anything worse. I mean absolutely no disrespect to anybody who works as a security guard in a mall, but by doing that I would have been re-joining the rat race that I had experienced during my brief time as an apprentice, trying to become an electrician. It would mean that I would no longer get four months off a year from my shift schedule, I would be travelling into work on Tubes and buses, or driving, not flying through different countries into my place of work, and no more Colombia. That wasn't the life I wanted, but I know that every time mum asked me, it came from a place of love, her wanting to see more of me, and for me not to be in a place she saw as dangerous, and a constant threat to my life.

In Colombia, my social circle was developing. I had friends native to the country, and quite a few American friends, most of whom I had met through salsa school. The majority of those I met were well educated entrepreneurs with an entirely different approach to life and way of thinking than mine, which was so refreshing. Some of them organised lunches, dinners and gatherings, giving me the opportunity to meet and connect with so many other people. Some of the dancers were normally there, as well as a lot of the expats who were students at Dancefree, plus people brought friends along, so I was getting to meet plenty of new faces.

Women, however, were a different matter. I tried talking to beautiful women on the streets, and in shopping malls and coffee shops, who I was physically attracted to. When I say beautiful, I mean beautiful enough that I could imagine myself with them, but not so overwhelmingly so that it would make me feel even more intimidated than I already did talking to any woman on any given day. Chatting up women had never been one of my strengths, and I felt as if they could sense it the minute I opened my mouth.

I was trying, but didn't have much luck, even though I now spoke decent Spanish at a conversational level. As soon as I spoke, they heard my accent and asked me where I was from, and whether I lived there in Medellin. I told tell them yes, but that I worked away, they would ask what I did and where, and by the time I explained that I operated on an eight week on/four week off rotation, they lost all interest.

From what I came to understand, a lot of men go to Colombia for sex, to meet women, have fun, then leave. Many women had obviously experienced this, and had absolutely no desire to experience it again. I definitely couldn't fault them for that, but it also meant that the chance of me meeting someone became much slimmer.

All in all, I got twenty eight days' leave. It took thirty six to forty eight hours to get back to where I stayed, so let's just say that door to door it was about two days' travel. It was two days there and two days back, so when I took those four days aways from my twenty eight days' leave, I was left with twenty four days. So even if I got lucky and met a potential lover on the very first day, it meant that twenty three days later, I would be headed back to work for two months, and I quickly discovered that no woman is looking for that.

I spent a lot of my free time on rotation and, once I arrived in Colombia, on dating sites and apps like Latin American Cupid and Tinder. In my profile, I briefly explained my situation, and wrote that if somebody out there found me physically attractive, and maybe even interesting, and was open to long distance relationships, then we could go from there.

I spoke with so many women on these apps, but got absolutely nowhere with most of them. Some were almost like Spanish teachers to me, correcting my spelling or use of words, and teaching me slang words. Only three women from these sites actually turned into something, and by something, I mean actually getting to meet and go on dates, which turned into relationships. The three women were called Alejandra, Grace and Amor. Unfortunately, it didn't work out with any of them, and I actually ended up hurting them all. The story of what happened between me and Amor is something I'll explain in greater detail later in this book.

The further I got into 2019, the more I had the feeling of not understanding the point of my life, the point of our existence as humans, the point of the world, or the point of anything, for that matter. I had failed in my relationships and experiences with women. I had been hurt by a few of them, and I had also hurt a few myself. By this point, I was in an on/off relationship with Amor, which also felt like it was failing, and that was down to me. I felt lonely at work, and I felt lonely when I was back in Colombia, even though at times I would be surrounded by some of my closest, most valued friends in the world, including Amor. Back at work on rotation one day in early November 2019, a friend I worked with, who I had known from my very first contract in 2014, had just returned from leave. I won't mention his name, as there's no need, but he knows who he is and I salute him. For the purpose of this book, I'll call him Scouse. Scousers are people who come from Liverpool, a city located in northwest England.

He is probably singlehandedly the biggest, most unanticipated, external driving force responsible for triggering a change in my life that I could never have predicted, setting me off on the wildest and, at times, scariest life journey I have ever been on … a journey that I am still very much on. I went into his room to say hello and see how his time off had gone, and he said: "Lad, I had an intense experience on leave." He told me that he had smoked something called DMT, or Dimethyltryptamine, and that he had met an alien.

To most people, this probably sounds like the ramblings of a madman, or someone who had been high on drugs (which is how I would have referred to DMT at that time). The most I had ever done at this point was smoke a little weed when I was a teenager, and a little cocaine, sniffed off the beautiful bum of an amazing Colombian lovemaker. Drugs, as I had always known them to be called, had always scared me, and never called out to me; but as Scouse told me his story, there was something about that moment and the expression on his face that compelled me to believe him. I knew that what he was telling me was without a

167

doubt true, and in that moment something deep inside of me knew that I had to smoke DMT.

As soon as I got back to my room, I messaged my good friend, Charles, who I met in Colombia and had become close friends with. I asked him if he had ever heard of DMT, and whether he could get some for me. He said no, but that he would ask around. A few days later, he got back to me, and said that no one he asked had ever heard of it. I was devastated.

There weren't any other people in my life who I would have felt confident enough about posing the same question to, so I continued with my rotation, and by the end of my eight weeks I had completely forgotten about DMT.

It was mid-December when I arrived back in Medellin, and the day after, I hooked up with a really good friend of mine called Derrick, who I met at Dancefree. As we walked, he told me something that I found to be one of the craziest, serendipitous experiences I've had in my life:

"I had the most intense experience last night – I was in a DMT ceremony." As soon as the words left his mouth, I had a massive smile on my face.

AMOR

I want to start this chapter off my saying: I love you, Amor. I love you more than you could ever possibly know.

In mid-March 2019, on my first day of arriving in Medellin on leave, I met Amor at restaurant, El Cielo. Amor was a girl I met on LatinAmericanCupid.com, and we had been talking since the twenty fourth of February. She worked in a bank, and was studying English at university EAFIT, had beautiful red hair and was of a slim build. If I'm absolutely honest, she wasn't what I would normally go for, but I loved talking with her. She seemed to be a truly nice, genuine girl with hopes and ambitions.

I had to really work to keep her interested. Sometimes I sent her a message and she wouldn't reply for ages, so I would message her again, asking if everything was alright – a very needy move, I know, but I was in Iraq, mostly feeling alone, and the only thing I looked forward to was hopefully meeting someone one day, so needy became my standard operating procedure. Also, I'm not silly – I know that as a good-looking woman on a dating site, Amor could have thousands of potential men in her inbox wanting to date her, or sending her 'dick pics'. Men can be so hungry sometimes, and I knew I was one of them, desperately trying to meet somebody.

I managed to keep her interested until my leave date in mid-March, when we met on our first date. It was a Friday and I took her to El Cielo, a restaurant I loved. They didn't serve dinner or courses; they served 'experiences' and 'moments', from unique flavours and tasting menus to their 'choco-therapy', where guest washed their hands in chocolate to awaken the senses. I thought it was a really nice first date, despite being really tired, as I had pretty much just landed. I suggested we both went back my place, but Amor wasn't having any of it. I don't blame her either, even though I genuinely meant just to chill and relax … although if she had come back and there had been a chance to have sex, obviously I would have taken it. Sex is connection, which is what I was looking for.

We left the restaurant and, just before she got into her taxi, we kissed and said goodbye. Two days later, on the Sunday, we met again and went to the cinema. This time, when the movie was over, I invited Amor back, and she came. We laid on my bed kissing, undressing and caressing each other, and that night we had sex. It was really nice to be intimate with her like that. Obviously, we were only just getting to know each other, so for want of a better word, I would say that our intimacy was timid in comparison to the moments of passion we shared in the future. You see, one thing I grew to love about Amor was that she was just as sexually open and adventurous as I was, which led to many moments of intense, highly spirited lovemaking. As you already know, I worked eight weeks on and got four weeks off, so if I met someone during those four weeks, I tried to push it to its limits. I had to know if this was the girl for me, the one I was going to spend the rest of my life with, as soon as possible, because if I wasn't sure, I would be up in the air about it, then have to wait another eight weeks before I was back on leave, to continue trying to figure out if that person was the right fit or not. I was getting older, and didn't have the luxury of being able to spend leave after leave with the same woman if there was the slightest chance that she may not be the right one. I saw it as a waste of my time and a waste of theirs, as horrible as that may sound.

I was thirty six years old when I met Amor, and still had this dream of having a family, of having a beautiful little daughter that I could dote on, and who would be my little princess. I already knew I didn't want a son at this point – what could I ever offer him, and what could he offer me?! I don't need a best friend, and I certainly didn't want that relationship with a son. This had a massive effect on me, and dictated most of my encounters with would-be partners, with time feeling like it was slipping away and that life was passing me by.

So, I tried to spend a lot of time with the women I met, and that's what happened with Amor. I invited her everywhere – to dance school, where I bought her salsa lessons; to the gym I went to; to nights out and gatherings with my friends, so she met everyone; and I invited her out to other places, so that we could be together every day. As I said earlier, she worked in a bank, and in Colombia most people work six days a week. She finished work at around five, then drove home on her moped, got showered and changed, then drove to my place, and we headed out to the gym or whatever event I decided was on the cards that evening. In the mornings, she got up early, said goodbye to me, then headed to work.

When we were in the gym, I pushed her as hard as possible. I even told her about being on steroids, and in such a way as to suggest that she should give them a try too. I had this image of the sort of woman I wanted to be with, the sort of woman I deserved to be with, and the image of this woman came from

Instagram. Instagram can be an amazing tool if used correctly, but I was using it for all the wrong reasons.

Amor decided she would try some steroids, so I took her to where I got mine from: a guy whose wealth and knowledge of them is profound. I bought her a mild tablet version of a steroid, and she began taking them. This all happened within a four week period because, as I told you, I had to work fast. During the few weekends I had during my leave, we visited beautiful little towns just outside of Medellin – places like Jardin and Copacabana – and had some really amazing moments together.

We even developed a whole different way of referring to each other, and Amor taught me some words and phrases I hadn't known. She called me feo (ugly man), ogro (ogre), and although a Colombian, was quite white, so I would say ask her: "Oye, animal de monte, te has estado bronceando en la luna o que?" (Hey, mountain animal, have you been moon bathing or what?). Animal de monte was something she had taught me, while I called her pendeja (asshole) too.

One day, we were in a taxi driving back to the complex of apartments where I was home sharing with some others, and as we approached the car park gate, I wound down the window so that I could say hello and the concierge could see my face. Once we were through, Amor said: "Oye, porque bajaste la ventana, solo tienes que hacer es sacar esa mano tan fea y negro y todos van a saber quien eres tu. Eres la única gorila viviendo acá," which meant: "Hey, why did you wind down the window? All you have to do is show them your hand, so ugly and black, and they will know that it's you. You're the only gorilla living here." I was practically wetting myself with laughter. This girl had banta, and she could take it too. She was very funny and always made me laugh, and while to some this might sound harsh, it was actually endearing, and these things were said to each other with a lot of affection.

As the end of my leave approached, I had this feeling inside of me … as if I wasn't feeling the way I should about Amor. She was an amazing woman, but it didn't feel like she was the one. I told myself that I could either stay with her so as not to hurt her, and probably end up being miserable for the rest of my life, and in turn make her miserable for the rest of hers; and both end up resenting each other until our dying days … or I could be honest and tell her how I felt. I mean, after all, women say they want honesty – right?

A couple of days before I had to fly back to Iraq, when I had one hundred percent decided I was going to be honest and tell her, I took Amor for breakfast to this really nice artisanal looking café, one of very few in Medellin that actually made poached eggs, which I love. We ordered our food, and began talking like normal, and at some point, when I had gathered the balls to speak to her sincerely, I started off by telling her how nice our time had been together.

"Amor, you're an amazing, beautiful person," I went on. "But I don't feel love here, at least not to the degree that I should for someone I'm going to commit to. And if I'm going to spend the rest of my life with someone, which is what I'm looking for, I have to feel absolutely in love, or I'd be wasting your time and my time."

I pinched my leg very hard the whole time I was speaking. It was a trick I had developed to make myself focus more on the pain I felt from the pinch than the awkward, very uncomfortable moment I was in. I immediately saw a look of sadness, disappointment and maybe even a little confusion on Amor's face. I don't think it was what she had expected or wanted to hear.

"But you haven't given it a chance," she came back at me. "Love doesn't work like that!"

But in my mind, from all the chick flicks I had seen, the romantic fantasies and idyllic scenarios I had built up in my mind, I knew for sure that that was how love worked, and she wasn't going to persuade me otherwise.

I felt terrible as tears began to roll down her face. It wasn't the first time I had had to watch a woman cry due to my actions, and it certainly wouldn't be the last.

We finished breakfast in awkward, resounding silence, then went back to my place. Amor gathered her things, as she had decided that if it was over, and we had no future, it was best to leave now; though before leaving, she gave me the biggest, most loving hug, which made me feel all the worse.

A few days later, I was back out in Iraq, and we had been messaging back and forth. Amor told me she had developed really bad acne, which I had noticed during some video calls we had shared. It had come from the steroid tablets I had so selfishly convinced her to try, and I felt so guilty. Amor was actually okay with it, even though we both knew that it was me who had introduced her to that lifestyle by suggesting she try some.

We continued to talk and have video calls. It was nice, jovial and friendly, and continued in that way until about halfway through my rotation, at which point I got a message saying that she was going to have say goodbye to me, which I didn't really understand. I was still in contact with all of the women from my past, but after speaking to my Colombian friends, came to realise that most of the country's women will not speak to their exes once they've broken up. There's a deletion of all photos ever taken together, and an attempt to forget that the other person ever existed.

I had never done this, but had definitely felt the pain that could lead to such a decision. I really didn't want Amor to stop talking to me. Even though it wasn't love the way I had idealised it in my head, I definitely cared for her deeply and knew that she cared for me. I asked Amor if we could try again, as I wanted her to stay in my life, and she said that she would give it another go. The rest of my rotation passed by quickly, and then I was back in Colombia towards the end of June.

On my first night, upon entering my room in the flat I was sharing, there were balloons everywhere and a card on the bed. My thirty seventh birthday had been a couple days before, and I assumed some of the guys I lived with had done it, but when I asked, they told me that Amor had come by the day before I landed, and asked if she could decorate my room like that as a belated birthday gift. I remember thinking: what a beautiful, caring gesture.

Again, we were with each other all the time. We had some really good times together, but for me something still didn't feel right … but I definitely wasn't about to end it again at the end of my leave. I thought that maybe I could be wrong, and the feeling would change. We stayed together throughout that rotation and the next. In December 2019, I was luckily enough to have Christmas off, and Amor invited me to spend it with her and her family, which I of course said yes to. I had already met her sister, mum and grandmother, who were really nice people, so it would be an honour to spend Christmas with them.

By now, Amor had developed her own friendship with my friends, including Gerardo, a guy I met at dance school. They all loved her, and she was friends with Gerardo's girlfriend, so we all went out together to the 'alumbrando la luz', the turning on of Christmas lights in different towns, and eating traditional Colombian festive foods, buñuelos and natillas. By now, the feeling that something big was missing from this relationship was overwhelming me, and I was struggling to ignore it.

I spent Christmas Day and Boxing Day with Amor and her family, which was nice, and on Boxing Day night, we made our way back to my place and went to bed. In the morning, once we were up, I asked Amor if I could have a conversation with her. I explained how I was feeling, and that while I really didn't want to hurt her, I couldn't see it working. I didn't think that the feeling inside me would dissipate to the extent that I would be able to give her the love she truly deserved.

This time, Amor showed me her fiery side. She let me know about myself, and the type of man I was, telling me I was two different people – the person I was in Iraq over video calls; and the person I was when back in Colombia, face to face.

"Eres falso y muy grosero!" she told me, which meant I was being false by trying to present myself as somebody different, and that I was very uncouth. I hated it when she told me this, but when I actually thought about it, I could see the part about me being two different people.

There was the feeling that in Iraq, I just wanted to get back to Medellin to see Amor and spend time with her … a feeling that I did actually love this woman and wanted to be with her, and I guess that resonated through our video calls and messages whilst I was at work on rotation. But when I got back to Colombia, I felt that there were so many more options out there; that maybe I wasn't supposed to be with Amor, and that most definitely wasn't fair, or a kind way to treat somebody I cared about.

I really saw a strong side to Amor during that argument. Actually, it was less of an argument, and more a case of her giving me a reality check. She spoke to me so quickly in Spanish that by the time I had translated it in my head, then worked out the way in which I wanted to respond, then translated that from English to

Spanish, she had already moved onto another part of my personality and demeanour that was in great need of a good telling off. Once she was done giving me a severe scolding, she left, and our relationship ended the following day.

Surprisingly, we stayed in contact over the next few days. I had organised another DMT ceremony, and wanted her to come – very selfish of me again, but I felt safer venturing into the absolute unknown with Amor there by my side – and, even more surprisingly, she came. I realised that I had been 'Falso y grosero' with her; I had entered her life, and tried to change her by getting her on steroids. Amor had given her all, finishing work, then rushing all around Medellin to get changed before coming over to my place to spend time with me. She had invited me into her family life and home during Christmas, she had shown me love, and I had taken her for granted. I had caused her more pain than I ever wanted to.

I'm so disappointed in myself for the pain I caused you, Amor. Shame on me; you didn't deserve that.

Amor and I have remained in close contact over the years, and I am so grateful to her for deciding to stay in my life. I would do anything for Amor, there is a deep love for her that will never die, and I appreciate her deeply.

MY FIRST ENCOUNTER WITH DMT

I arrived back in Medellin in mid-December 2019, and my friend told me that he had had this intense experience on DMT, using the exact same words as my friend Scouse did when describing what had happened to him. Derrick explained how his trip had shown him that he hadn't respected himself very much, and that he hadn't been very kind to himself. One thing I would come to learn is that different people will experience and explain their stories through completely different senses. Scouse, for example, had explained his trip to me very visually, having seen things, while Derrick had explained his journey to me as feelings that he had experienced.

I asked him if there was any chance of him giving me the details of the guy who led the ceremony? He said he would ask and get back to me. The next day, he told me that he had spoken to the guy in question, Daniel, and that he said I could have his number. I messaged him immediately, asking if it was possible to conduct a ceremony for me and some friends at my mate Charles' girlfriend's finca, or holiday home, in Guatapé, a beautiful location of serene nature, where I was headed. He asked me whether I had ever done any psychedelics before, and I told him that no, I hadn't.

Daniel asked me to watch a documentary, DMT, the spirit molecule, by Rick Strassman M.D, on YouTube, which he sent me a link for. It was interesting, but I couldn't really comprehend it at the time; and before I knew it, I had fallen asleep watching it. Nonetheless, I was still greatly intrigued.

"Yes, I watched it," I told him when speaking the next day. "And still very much want to do it."

"Okay, but it isn't the right moment for me financially, as I can't put anything towards the weekend, so I'd prefer to do it in a few weeks' time." "Can't I just buy some off you and do it myself?" I asked. "Do you know how to do it?"

"I guess I'd roll it up like a spliff and smoke it like that," I answered.

"No, that isn't how you do it!" he laughed innocently. "You have to smoke it from a pipe."

His mention of a pipe really made me think about what I was contemplating doing, picturing a crack pipe and everything that's associated with it … though I still had a burning desire to experience DMT.

"May I invite you to the weekend and cover the costs?" I asked.

"Sure, why not?" Daniel answered after pausing for a few seconds to consider my offer.

I was so happy that he agreed, and started looking forward to the weekend ceremony. Seven of us attended – me, Amor, Charles, his girlfriend, another couple, and Daniel – and we arrived at the finca after about an hour's drive. The location was magical, enveloped by nature. There was an abundance of greenery, with trees and plants everywhere; there was the Peñol Guatapé reservoir on our doorstep, mountains in the background, and we could see the Piedra Peñol, a giant granite rock that has 700 steps you have to ascend to reach the top.

I brought my speaker, which by now had become my greatest travel companion, and we sat listening to music whilst Daniel explained the process of the ceremony and how it would unfold. It started with him blowing Rapé (a sacred tobacco that comes from the Amazon, where it's used as a powerful healing medicine) through a wooden pipe up my right nostril. The only way to explain it is that I immediately felt a burning sensation in the right side of my brain. It felt like there was a fire in my head, then he blew it again, this time up the left nostril, and my brain was completely on fire.

Daniel told me to sit and meditate, to think about what it was that I wanted to get from the medicine, and with that he played a song by Krishna Das, called Sri Argalla Stotram (Selected Verses). This song is something special, and the first I had heard in that genre. It was my introduction to the world of ceremony medicine music, which would become one of only three genres I continued to listen to. He asked if the other guys wanted some, and they all tried it, apart from Charles' girlfriend.

Charles appeared to be very sensitive to the Rapé, and suddenly came over all lightheaded and dizzy. Daniel made him remove his shoes and socks, so that he could ground himself in nature. I would come to learn that grounding is a therapeutic technique that allows humans to electrically connect to, and receive healing from, the earth. All of this was so new to me. We sat there meditating, thinking about our intentions whilst Charles grounded himself. The suspense had been killing me, but then came the time for the moment I had been waiting for.

Once Daniel had prepared the pipe and DMT, he sat me down on a yoga mat and whispered his intentions into the DMT, then gave it to me to hold over my heart and speak mine into it. I asked it: "Could you please show me what I'm supposed to be doing in life?" With that, Daniel explained that now I had to put the pipe in my mouth and inhale slowly, as if sucking through a straw, let it fill up my lungs, then hold my breath for a few seconds and let it out.

As I did this, it felt as if my soul was untethering itself from my body. Daniel then held the pipe out for me to take another hit, and as soon as I did, the effect was immediate. I felt my body slowly fall back, and I became absolutely overcome with fear. More scared than I'd ever been in my entire life, my hand shot out towards Daniel, and all I remember thinking was: 'fuck, help me please, I don't want this!' Daniel grabbed my hands and placed them both on my chest, at which point my eyes closed involuntarily. I began to hear the most frightening arrangement of harmonica sounds I had ever encountered in my life, and now know this song to be Canta de armónica by Nicolas Iosada (I still find this song scary today, but cannot stop myself from listening to it, as it's amazingly powerful).

I felt my hands dissolve into my chest, then my entire body melt away into nothing. I became aware of a thought telling me: 'I told you, you shouldn't have done this, now we're stuck here like this forever'. At this moment, I lost all sense of who I was, and didn't know how I had got to this place I now found myself in, or even where or when I was. I imagine it's like a baby being born into the world, being greeted by an overload of sensory receptors into an alien environment, not knowing how to interpret anything it's seeing, feeling or experiencing.

I then became aware of a bombardment of colours, geometrical shapes and patterns everywhere. There was no barrier between what I was perceiving and myself, whatever 'myself' was at that point. The strangest thing was that I began to remember this place … I knew this place. I was sure of nothing, aside from the fact that I had definitely been here before, amid an overwhelming feeling of familiarity … a familiarity with more depth and absoluteness than I had ever felt about anything in my entire life. A figure appeared; it was that of a shadow that took the shape of a jester. I remember seeing the outline of the jester hat, but as a whole it was a completely obscure figure. I was so scared that I began to panic, and as the intensity of my panicking grew, the jester began to grow in size and the colourful, geometrical patterns became to darken. The more I struggled, the bigger the jester grew, and I began to fall into a void of nothingness … complete and utter darkness. During this falling, which was accompanied by an acute sense of intense fear, memories started to come back to me, and I began to remember who I was and that I'd smoked something. I then recalled Daniel saying to me that if I came across any beings or anything that felt scary during my journey, I should show them love. I forced myself to stop panicking, and thought to myself: 'Love, love, love …'; and with that, my eyes opened and I was free.

I looked around and saw Amor lying in front of me, still in her experience. I looked at my friends, and the other couple who were still sat there appeared as elves. As they looked back at me, one of them whispered in the other's ear. It felt like they were talking about me; that they were saying: "He sees us," as if I had seen them in their true light for the very first time, without the veil of reality obscuring the truth of who they really were.

I looked at the garden, at all the plants and trees, with what appeared to be a strong green aura emanating from them. I looked at the reservoir, which was immensely still and glistening vibrantly, and when I looked up at the night sky, I saw star-like diamonds beaming rays of light, illuminating the stratosphere. I was so confused, and remember asking myself: "Am I still in the experience?" I looked at Daniel, and he was sat there, peacefully holding this space and smiling at me. He used his right hand to tap his heart area, as if to say: "Everything's alright. I know exactly where you're at – welcome to the other side of the veil."

I laid back, and rested in my body for a moment. I felt my heart beating, and every little sensation in my body, lying there for the next few minutes, trying to comprehend what the hell had just happened … but it just wasn't possible to even begin to understand. What I did know for sure was that it had been something very special, but simultaneously something scarier than I had ever felt.

My first encounter with DMT, which couldn't have lasted more than ten minutes in total, had changed my entire life. I now knew that there was something greater to life than I could ever have imagined possible … I just didn't know what.

MY SECOND ENCOUNTER WITH DMT

After having everything I thought I knew about life being questioned, and being unable to shake the feeling that what I had seen and felt during my first DMT experience was actually more real than anything else I had ever experienced here in what we call real life, I knew I had to do it again.

I didn't have much leave left, so asked Daniel when he was next available and how long I should wait before I did it again. He told me that I should give myself two weeks in between ceremonies, to see how I integrated with it, especially as I had never ever done anything like it before. Luckily, by the time I decided I wanted to do it again, two weeks had pretty much passed, so a couple days before I had to fly back to work, I organised the next ceremony so that I could do it at Gerardo's place.

I told one of my friends, Justin, about my plans and, having done DMT before, he said he would like to come along and try it again. On the day of the ceremony, there were a few of us, only three of whom were going to smoke; but other close friends were there too, which I found comforting as, I'm not going to lie, I was a little scared, and their support helped a lot. Amor had come along too, which made me so happy, filling me with confidence. Daniel prepared the space by burning sage and clearing the area with it. He explained to everyone that once we started, there was to be no talking; that those not partaking in DMT should observe in silence and show love; and that it was a very different environment to where we had done it last time – we were in the city now, and the energy would be very different, so if they could respect that and the person in the experience, it would be nice.

Once he was all set, he played music from the genre I have now come to know as medicine music. He gave me and the two others some Rapé which, again, blew my mind. My brain was on fire, but soon enough, just like before, once the intensity subsided, I felt pure focus and centred it on the intention I set myself. I wanted guidance, and I needed direction. Before we started, I asked Daniel whether I could play music of my choice for when I began my journey. He said yeah it was fine, but that I should try and choose something soothing, and nothing too wild.

This wasn't a problem for me, as the music I had pre-emptively selected comprised Beethoven Piano Concerto No.5, Fantasia on a Theme by Thomas Tallis, and last but most definitely not least, Maria Callas' Vissi D'arte. I love each one of these amazing pieces of music so much that it's unquantifiable. I linked my phone to the speaker, got my playlist ready and took my place on the yoga mat in front of Daniel. He gave me the pipe, which I held to my chest and spoke my intentions into it. In my mind, I asked: 'Please can I have some guidance. What is it I'm supposed to be doing here in life?'

Handing the pipe back to Daniel, he heated it up and held it to my mouth to smoke. I inhaled slowly, just as he had told me to, and held it in for ten seconds. I could already feel my soul slipping away as he told me to take another pull. I was no longer in control of my body, and if I was to try and explain it as best as I can – which, believe me, won't do it any justice at all, but I'll try – I would say it's the feeling of seeing your body there, knowing it's there, but not being connected to it.

You feel light like a balloon that's about to float away into the sky. Whatever it is that connects us to the world as we know it just slips away and takes you with it, then your body falls back, your eyes close and your body – well, whatever feeling you have left towards your body – completely dissolves. That's how it is for me, anyway.

Once my eyes were shut and my body was no more, I again found myself awoken in a realm completely alien to me. I was met by hexagons all around me, they were all that existed in this space, and inside each hexagon was a face that I initially interpreted as demonic. Each face was black, with bright white eyes and dark black pupils with such depth to them that you could lose yourself in them forever. It had black horns for cheeks that protruded away from its face, ending with a slight curve into a sharp point, and its lips were bright red. Even though I had no body at this point, I felt as if I couldn't catch my breath. It was such an overpowering feeling, being unable to differentiate between whatever it is you think you are and the perceived surroundings. The faces would bolt out of their individual hexagons toward me – one, two, three or many at a time. For some reason, during this ceremony I was able to get a bearing on who I thought I was a lot quicker, and didn't feel scared. The faces didn't seem to want to hurt me; it felt like I was almost being mirrored, as in they were showing me what I truly looked like, or at least what one aspect of my being looked like. It felt as if I knew this face. I began to think about love, and tried to emanate it from whatever my being was at the time … and soon enough, the hexagons and faces disappeared.

I found myself stood in front of a tree, but it was no ordinary tree. Its trunk was gigantic, and the top of it was out of sight, seemingly going on forever. The tree radiated a power that I could feel in my being, and I became aware of a figure standing by my left shoulder. I could see the silhouette of what I would describe as a masculine chest, but I never got to see its face. It felt like this figure, this presence, was there to accompany me. I felt protected, and couldn't shake the sensation that it was very much like the presence I felt from my dad whenever he had been around. Then, like a spoilt child, I began shouting at the tree, my arms spread wide open as if demanding answers, asking it: "When will I find true love? Am I ever going to have children? What am I supposed to be doing here? What's the point of life?" These questions were coming more from a place of anger than inquisitiveness. Then there was a voice … I don't know if I'll ever be able to explain this so that other people can understand what it is that I truly want to say, but it was as if the voice spoke to me, though not linearly with regards to time. It seemed like, in that moment, looking at the tree, it had said what it said, but at the same time, as if what it had said was superimposed over the duration of the entire experience, before I had even asked my questions and right through to the end. The voice only said it once – "But you know this, you've always known this" – and with that, my eyes opened and there was a sense of overwhelming love. It was as if I had been submerged in the raw emotion of love itself.

I laid there looking at my hands, and from my hands down to my arms, torso and legs, with a sense of: oh my God, I have a body! It felt so silly to have a body, but at the same time so special – like a precious gift – before bursting into a fit of uncontrollable laughter that came from deep within. I hadn't ever heard myself laugh like this. It took over my whole body, and I couldn't stop myself. I could taste the atmosphere, I could taste matter fizzing away on my tongue, and when I looked around, all of my friends looked like elves, with sharp noses and pointy ears, which only fuelled the laughter.

I looked at the ground and there were equations and algebraic mathematics in a brown colour floating through matter just above the tiled flooring. I looked at the lights above, which were like bright stars with rays of lights beaming out of them. I looked to the distance, and the highest buildings were like liquid metal, glistening and melting away. Then I looked at Daniel, who was sat in front of me in a seated, meditation pose, with his hands pressed together, as if praying. I noticed that there was something going on with his forehead, and as the laughter subsided for a moment, I saw that it had an ocean of waves in it. The more I paid attention, the more the waves seemed to calm, giving way to what was behind it; and as they cleared, I saw an eye emerging from his forehead. God knows what he must have thought as I stared so intensely and inquisitively at his face … but there it was, a third eye. I started to laugh again, feeling so much love for everyone there; love for my family back in the United Kingdom … love for everyone everywhere.

THE COVID PANDEMIC, ETHAN AND GOLDEN

On March 12 2020, during leave, I flew from Colombia to the UK for a first response emergency care course (FREC). It's a course that we, as close protection operators, need to refresh every three years. In the few days before I flew, there had been so much news and hype about a new virus that was sweeping through the world at an alarming rate. I didn't really watch the news, which always seemed to be nothing more than negativity and scaremongering, and the few times I had, I had never walked away feeling good, so it wasn't something I was interested in giving any of my precious time to.

I already knew how to be depressed and negative all by myself, so didn't need any help getting there, though this was different. I was aware, through word of mouth, of how scared people were around the globe, and heard talk of airports possibly closing down; but thought to myself: 'it'll be alright, I'll head back to the United Kingdom, smash out this five day course, and be back in Colombia in time for tea and stickies' … but oh, how wrong was I?

I landed back in London on the thirteenth, which was a Friday. It was nice to see my family again for the first time in quite a while, and given my course started on the Monday, it gave me a couple of days to catch up with other family members and friends I hadn't seen in some time. I thought I would also call Ethan at some point, and maybe even meet up with him somewhere if possible, as we hadn't spoken in a few months.

On Sunday night, I made my way down to Bournemouth, where the course would be held, starting the following morning, as planned. During the course of the week, however, with the constant escalation of what was now being called a pandemic, social anxiety had risen to an all-time high. I mean, people were getting banged out in supermarkets over toilet tissue, and it was like the Wild West, just trying to buy some Pot Noodles. Anyway, as the week went on, airports all over the world started shutting down, and for the first time, I began to wonder if I was going to be able to make my flight back to Colombia, which was booked for the twenty third.

Once the course finished, everyone who had attended it bomb-bursted (military talk for dispersing rapidly) as soon as possible. There was talk of curfews being put in place, and nobody wanted to be stranded somewhere far away from home and family. As I made my way back to London, there was barely anyone on the trains, as no one was travelling unless it was absolutely necessary. I got back to my mum's on the evening of Friday the twentieth and, again, it crossed my mind to call Ethan, but I was so caught up in the hype of what I was going to do if I couldn't get back to Colombia that I put it on the backburner. I don't know why, as it takes mere moments to call or text someone. I could have phoned or messaged him, then gone back to worrying, as I have always been pretty good at finding time to waste on that, but I didn't.

By the Saturday, I was getting WhatsApp messages from friends in Colombia, showing me memes of captions saying that the country had closed all of its borders. There was no movement in or out due to the pandemic, and I began to wonder whether I would even make it back to work. Sunday the twenty second came, and around evening time, I saw that I had received a message on Instagram from Ethan's younger brother, who I had never had contact with on any social media platform. Something felt wrong, with the message simply saying: 'It's Ethan's brother, can you please ring me'.

After messaging him back, I received another message immediately, and we swapped numbers.

Before we even began to speak, I felt a horrible dread come over me … a horrible dread that he was going to tell me something I really didn't want to hear. When we began to speak, he asked me if I was sitting down, and all I was thinking was: 'don't say it! Please don't say it!' He then told me that Ethan had passed away. I didn't understand, and didn't want to hear what he was telling me. He explained that Ethan had suffered a heart attack earlier that day, and that he had been trying to find me on social media, so that he could let me know.

After saying goodbye to each other, our call ended, and I felt paralysed by sadness. I sat there speechless, asking myself why the hell I hadn't called or messaged him any one of the numerous times he had come to mind. Once again, I was faced with the immortality of someone who was very close to me, but for some reason this was affecting me way more than anyone I had lost before. Ethan was like a brother, I confided in him, we had gone through Royal Marines' training together, we had seen each other at our worst and best, so how had this happened? Ethan wasn't supposed to die yet.

I went into the front room of my mum's house, and as I sat down, blurted out in disbelief: "Ethan's dead." Mum had seen him years ago during our passing out of training, and he had been to the house a couple times, while my brother Richard knew him from some of the times we had all gone out together. There was a part of me that felt so sad I almost cried, but what would have been the point of that? He was gone, I hadn't got to speak to him before he died, and no amount of tears were going to bring him back or undo the fact that we hadn't spoken. When looking back through our messages and conversations on WhatsApp, I struggled to understand and accept the fact that even though I could see and read all the messages he had sent me, and hear the tone of his voice in each and every one of them, he was now nowhere to be found on the planet. He had gone.

I went to visit Ethan once he had been moved from the hospital to the funeral parlour. I arrived at Hull station, where Anne, Ethan's girlfriend, and the mother of their eight month old son, picked me up with her sister and drove me to the parlour. The whole way there, I imagined what he was going to look like, and what I was going to say to him. I hoped that I would cry. I wanted to cry. When we arrived, I walked into the parlour, and the staff showed me where he was.

When I walked in the room, I saw him lying there, absolutely motionless and devoid of all the life and energy I had known as Ethan. It felt surreal, because there had been no build up to his death. It wasn't expected, so seeing him there like that had not been something I had expected to see so soon, not even in my most horrific nightmares.

I walked towards him and held his hand, which was cold and stiff. As I went to speak, all I managed to say was: "It wasn't supposed to be like this." I thought there might have been greater depth to what I wanted to say to him, but there was nothing I could have said that would have done my feelings any justice, as this was a feeling beyond words. I decided I would just stand there with

194

him, holding his hand in silence for a few moments. There was no need to speak.

A little while later, Dan and Richie arrived, then Ethan's mum and siblings, who had been visiting him daily. Once everyone had visited him, we all went back to Ethan and Anne's home, and sat there talking and remembering him; then his newborn son arrived with Anne's sister.

It was amazing to see that Ethan had a son, that he and his girlfriend had created this life and brought it into the world. Watching his son, who stood there shakily at eight months' old, with the help of his auntie, eyes wide open in awe of what they were perceiving, whilst smiling innocently at the happenings all around him, I couldn't help but think he was the embodiment of deep sadness and great happiness, ultimate loss and boundless joy, all at once.

It was sadness in the moment from us, and what I imagine will turn out to be delayed sadness for him in the future, when he starts to see other children out and about with their fathers; and then gets old enough to ask his mum where his father is. I imagine he may feel sadness, and a void from never knowing his father or the man he was, which I imagine could unfortunately cast a shadow over that part of his life.

I looked in his eyes, and there was joy in them. He didn't know the reason we were all gathered there, and he didn't know the reason why his father hadn't been around the last few days. In his eyes, I saw raw potential as he marvelled at the world around him. The possibilities were endless, he could be anything, do anything … he had his whole life ahead of him. Sat there, looking at him, I hoped that as he got older, myself and all who knew Ethan would always be able to be in his life, answer any questions he may have, and be able to tell him about his father and the man he was.

Ethan was cremated in Willerby, Hull, on the eighth of April 2020, but only a small number of us were allowed inside the chapel due to rules of the pandemic. Those who surpassed that number stood outside. I had asked if I could speak for a few moments at the funeral, which had been okayed. When the time came, and I was stood at the front talking, I could see everyone's faces … all of the sadness, crying and tears. It was overwhelming, and yet I still couldn't cry.

When the padre finished reflecting on Ethan's life and had led us in a final prayer, the casket was gently conveyed on the rollers that guided it into the furnace. Then, just like that, after a few of Ethan's favourite songs, not even his body was any longer of this world.

I'd like to just take a moment here for those of you who want to remember those we have loved and lost, and celebrate in their memories; celebrate the fact that the universe gave us the opportunity to have our lives touched by others, whose absences have left such voids in their wake. For someone to be able to make that much of an impact on us is truly something. I recognise a moment of reflection and celebration in the silence of their absence.

…

Once all of the curfews, rules and regulations were in full effect, it was clear that this pandemic wasn't going away anytime soon. As much as it frustrated me and robbed us of the majority of our social freedoms, there were good elements to it. For me, I got to spend time with my family, who I didn't see on a regular basis and hadn't seen in some time. I got to call and connect with friends who I hadn't spoken to in weeks, months and, in some cases, years. One of the friends I was able to speak to, and connect with, was my lifelong friend, Golden. While we hadn't seen each other in a while, we had always been in contact, I told her everything, she knew all there was to know about me, and I knew a great deal about her life too. We met up during the pandemic, in the phase when the government had decided to allow people to meet in public places. It was always such a delight to see her, and spend time with her. She's a very conscious and mindful person, her energy always resonates positivity, and it's such a gift to be around her.

Sat in the park, talking and reminiscing, I felt the urge to declare my childhood love for Golden, so I explained how I had felt towards her during our younger years. There was a part of me that now felt life was short, so what did I possibly have to lose by telling her?

"I've loved you since the moment we first met, but haven't really known how to talk to women, so never had the minerals to express myself to you in that way," I said.

"I hadn't known," she replied, a surprised look on her face. "Is it love or lust that you felt?" "Oh, it was most definitely love."

We shared a rich history together – well, at least in my head – we had inside jokes together, she had braided my hair when I was a teenager, and we had shared personal, intimate life experiences and hardships with each other. If someone asked me who in the world knew the most about me, it was her. Over the years, I had told her everything. I confided in her, and her in me, and on top of all of that, she was still as beautiful as the day we first met.

We began to see each other more frequently, going to different restaurants, which was an amazing experience, as she showed me a different way to eat. My diet had been so based around getting massive and being in the gym – nothing else had mattered – but during these moments with her, I was introduced to the world of mindful eating. We ate vegan and vegetarian food; all sorts of dishes with an amazing, exotic, mindful twist to them. In fact, there was never a moment, before or since, that I have eaten so healthy.

One night, after dinner at one of these restaurants, we stayed in a hotel, as it was quite late. That night, we were intimate with each other. It was something I had dreamed of, and imagined in my head time and time again, ever since meeting all those years ago. It was amazing, it was everything I thought it would be and, again, there was the feeling of being intimate with someone who you love, not just a quick five minute knee trembler with someone else looking for a cheap, quick thrill.

After that, we continued to see each other and share more moments of intimacy … but soon enough, a feeling that I had become all too familiar with came back to haunt me. There I was, with this beautiful woman who I had loved since school, and what seemed like the opportunity for one of the things I had wanted most in life … but now that it felt truly within my reach, I still didn't feel complete.

I now found myself faced with the gravity of a situation I had created. My very best friend, dream girl and lifelong love had shown me the one side of her I had never seen, and yet something didn't seem right. I didn't have the completeness I had always imagined would arrive when meeting the woman I was supposed to be with for the rest of my life – how could this be? Golden had everything I'd ever dreamed of in a partner, and was a profoundly beautiful woman inside and out.

As August came, the world started to return to normal, which is a word I use very loosely here, because although we were making our way back to some form of familiarity, this new version of the world was a very much more restricted and limited version of itself – way more so than the one we had known pre-pandemic. With airports beginning to open, I got an email from work saying that Iraq had opened its borders, and that they would soon start flying guys back in who had been stuck at home, and flying guys back home who had been stuck in country on camp. When I returned to Iraq at the end of August, Golden and I kept talking, but I didn't know how to address the situation. I find that I'm a very weak individual when it comes to things like that, although the root of that weakness is based in the fact that I don't want to hurt anybody; but by being weak and showing inaction, it always ends up hurting the person you're trying not to harm even more.

We finally had the conversation, and I just didn't know what to say as she unloaded on me, telling me about myself and how I had led her on. I ended up trying to hide behind the fact that we hadn't spoken about us actually being something, which further reinforced my weakness and cowardliness. I hurt her more deeply, and betrayed her trust in me, more than I could ever have imagined. I hated myself for doing that to her, and it didn't matter that none of it was intentional. Golden most definitely deserved better from me, and I wondered what kind of a monster I was, to be able to hurt her like that … my best friend, who had supported me and listened to all of my woeful stories over the years.

So now, when I ask myself again: what did I have to lose by declaring my undying love for her, the answer is: one of the greatest, most cherished and longest lasting friendships I had ever had in my life.

I had now developed a whole newfound level of dislike for myself.

SMOKING BUFO 21ST FEBRUARY 2021

During June 2021, I was on leave in Medellin, and by now had smoked NN-DMT twice. Both were amazing experiences, and the more people I spoke to in these circles who were on this journey of self-discovery, looking for answers they hadn't been able to find anywhere else, the more I heard about other medicines. One in particular that kept coming up was Bufo, which was how the people I spoke to mostly referred to the 5-MeO-DMT that is secreted by the glands of the Bufo Alvarius toad, or Sonoran Desert toad.

The way it had been explained to me was that from smoking NN-DMT, you would most likely see sacred geometrical patterns and shapes, find yourself in completely different universes and encounter other beings. From Bufo, you would experience oneness, and feel what it is to be God. These were the sort of experiences I was hearing about. The main one was that 'you die', which is the thing that gives everyone a moment of pause before going off the deep end and actually committing to smoking Bufo.

The feeling I got was that this was the one that people worked their way up to. The majority of people I met had worked with most other medicines first, and then gone on to take Bufo. I won't lie, there was a part of me that was scared from the way this medicine was described, and from the countless experiences retold to me, it didn't seem like something to take lightly. The more I spoke to people about it, the more I understood that it was an ego death, rather than a physical expiration.

At a gathering at a friend's house one evening, a few people were talking about their medicine experiences, and as I spoke about DMT, a friend of mine said: "I need to introduce you to someone." He took me over to this guy, introduced us and, as we began to talk, it transpired that he had recently smoked Bufo there in Medellin. This was how things now seemed to work: I would hear of a medicine, feel that it was something I needed to experience, then somehow someone with a connection to a facilitator or shaman that worked with that particular medicine would enter my life.

Although I had originally decided to stay away from Bufo for a little while, and build up to it, so to speak, it felt like I was being called to it. What were the chances of meeting this guy at a friend's party, that he would have smoked it recently, and have the details of a shaman who worked with that particular medicine in Medellin? It felt like it was time to smoke the toad, I got the details from him, and messaged the facilitator the very next day.

It was arranged that I would have a Bufo ceremony in two weeks' time, and the shaman sent me some information on what to expect and how the ceremony would run. The day of the ceremony was to start at ten o'clock and, as advised, I arrived on an empty stomach. The shaman, Juan Pablo, had already cleansed the area where the ceremony was to be held, freeing it of unwanted, negative energies and spirits, via the use of incense, copal, palo santo, and other shamanic tools, drums and instruments. The space smelt amazing, and there were around three to four others there too. First, we started with Kambo, phyllomedusa bicolor, also known as giant leaf frog, or giant monkey frog, from the Amazonian Forest. It was explained to me that this medicine would cleanse the body and make us purge. Then there was Sananga, which is a powerful plant medicine used in the form of eye drops, which the Amazonian indigenous tribes use to enhance their night vision whilst hunting. During these ceremonies, it's used for energetic cleansing and detoxifying the body. We all laid down, and the shaman made his way to each of us. When he got to me, he told me to close my eyes, put some of these drops into the corner of each eye, and told me to blink, allowing the Sananga to make its way into them. I had no idea what to expect, but did as he asked. I closed my eyes then, after he administered the drops, I started to blink and my eyes immediately felt like they were on fire. It felt like he had put acid in my eyes, and it was incredibly intense – so much so that I nearly had to release a manly war cry through my gritted teeth, which were ground together so tightly, I'm surprised they didn't chip or break off in my mouth.

I closed my eyes as tightly as possible, but it didn't help, so I just had to ride it out, which I did. I spent the whole time with my eyeballs on fire, praying, even though I'm not at all religious, that I wouldn't be blind when I finally got to open my eyes again. Once the initial effect wore off and I could open my eyes again, I was so grateful to still have my vision, albeit a much shaper vision. I remember thinking to myself that I would never do it again.

Now, with our bodies and eyeballs fully cleansed and purged, we were ready for the Bufo. I use the word ready loosely, because I was actually fairly scared. Each time I go into a ceremony like this, I realise fear is very present. It's not a fear of dying, but fear that my mind will leave my body and never return, and that I'll be left as a drooling, eyes vacant, empty shell of the person I once was; but have come to realise that that's the ego, and maybe it's because the ego knows it's about to suffer a death that it reacts like that … although mine needn't worry, as it always seems to find its way back just fine.

The shaman called me over to where each individual had their Bufo experience. I sat down on a yoga mat, removed my trainers and sat with my legs outstretched in front of me. He came and knelt down beside me, explaining that I should inhale slowly and gently until my lungs were completely full and I could inhale no more, then hold my breath for a few seconds. He gave me the pipe, which I held to my heart and spoke my intentions into it. They were: what is the point of my life? Why am I here? Is there a God? He then took the pipe, heated it up, and held it to my mouth for me to inhale. After taking the first pull and holding it in, I already felt my soul slipping away. The shaman then told me to take another drag, which I did, my upper body immediately falling slowly back; and once again, I was no longer in control of my body.

My vision became tunnelled, my eyes closed, I saw some faint red geometrical patterns … and then there was nothing. I was aware of absolutely nothing, I don't know how long for, but the next thing I was aware of was being everything – there was only me, and I don't mean the body of me … just a pure awareness, and I was being shown that it was the same awareness that's in all of us. Everything was all one and the same thing, and I felt absolute oneness. I had never felt this before; with my entire imagination, I could never have fathomed anything like what I experienced, nor will the way I'm trying to explain it here be able to convey the depths of a Bufo experience.

When my eyes opened, I was overwhelmed by tingling all over my body. There was a feeling that I was about to cum harder than

I had ever cum in my entire life, before the feeling transmogrified into an explosion with such magnitude that the only way I can even try to explain it is that the entire universe erupted and exploded from inside of me, affecting every cell in my body. I couldn't stop laughing, and it felt like I had been shown what this thing we call life really is. All worry, sadness, pain and negativity felt laughable – it was so funny. I experienced the entire love of the universe, an unquantifiable love, and realised it wasn't something I was feeling. For those few moments, or however long it lasted, I was it, I was love; I was all the love that there is, has ever been and ever will be. It was like the universe had made love to me.

I felt loved, that there was something out there bigger than me, bigger than all of us, and that it cared for me; it loved me, I mattered, I truly mattered … that I was a part of it. As the feeling started to fade, I was left with crazy, impeccable vision. I could see the clouds in the sky, all the different birds, and altitudes at which they were existing in that moment. The grass was vibrantly green, while my trainers, as I put them back on, were not the flat black I normally perceived them as every day – I could see every shade of black that existed within it.

I looked around at the other people who were there, and wanted to tell everybody how much I loved them all. I wanted them to know, I wanted everyone in the world to know. This was an experience that had given me an insight into what could be … into what is. The 'what' could be: we give birth to negativity with our thoughts, we choose to give life to the worrying and sadness, and we choose to make it real every moment we choose to be unhappy. It isn't real, it doesn't exist, and we could actually just laugh it off. We can choose not to worry, we can choose not to be negative or sad, and we can choose to be happy every day. To what is: we are all one and the same thing, we all matter, we are all important, and we are all love.

On the way back home, I sat there in the taxi smiling to myself, looking at the people on the street, wondering if they knew the universe's secret … and if they didn't, wishing that I could tell them.

Even though I felt like that in this moment, this very special moment, once I got back to work and what I had come to call the real world, it was very easy to slip back into old habits and thought patterns, even though it felt like the universe had picked me to reveal itself to, and to show me its secrets. In hindsight, I now see that at this point, my journey was only just beginning.

MY FIRST MUSHROOM TRIP, JUNE 10TH 2021

I had been wanting to experience mushrooms for some time, and had decided that tonight was finally the night. I had dinner with a couple of friends early, so that by the time I was ready to start the journey, my stomach would be near enough empty. After dinner, we went to a bar called Hooters to watch an ice hockey game. I hadn't ever watched an hockey game, and had never imagined that I would, but as my friends were American and Canadian, it made absolute sense. It was nice, and while I didn't really pay any attention to the hockey, it was cool getting to hang out with them.

As we sat there at our table, our waitress introduced herself. She had an amazing, magnetic energy about her, and came across as very open to interacting and having a laugh. A tattoo reading 'self-love' ran vertically between her breasts, and whilst talking with her, my friend said: "I'm so sorry, but I can't stop looking at your chest area."

She laughed, and said: "Yeah, I know. It's my fault because I have a tattoo there!"

We ordered our drinks, and she came back and forth every so often, asking if everything was alright and having a laugh with us. I hadn't really spoken much to her myself, but as we were leaving, I felt the urge to ask her what her name was, purely because of the energy she carried herself with. She told me her name, which didn't actually matter, because by the next day I would be calling her Angel.

I went back to my apartment, where I had fifty four grams of wet mushrooms that I had bought from my good friend, who cultivates them. I split the mushrooms in half, squeezed lemon over them, speaking the intention: "Show me what it is I need to see," ate them, then laid on top of my bed in the dark, with nothing but my boxer shorts on, listening to opera and classical. Since getting into plant medicine, which I was now starting to call it, after meeting more and more people who were in the circle and hearing them refer to it as such, I started watching everything I could about it on YouTube. I saw videos where there were psychiatrists researching the benefits of psilocybin being used as a therapeutic tool and aid, leading patients through guided sessions using blindfolds, and I loved the idea of it.

A lot of people I know had talked about taking mushrooms in nature, having amazing experiences and being one with nature. As much as that does sound amazing, it wasn't what I felt I needed. By walking around nature with my eyes open, I would be influenced by external stimuli, and although I imagine it to be a beautiful experience, I wanted something different. The experience that was most calling out to me was one that involved being in the dark with my eyes shut, just as I had seen it on the YouTube documentaries, because this meant I wouldn't be influenced by outside stimuli. With my eyes shut, the only things that could possibly come up were those from within … the world inside of me.

I laid on my bed in complete anticipation, not knowing what to expect, then after about 40 minutes, a plant that was in the corner started to dance to the music I was playing, and I realised it was beginning.

"You're going to be okay tonight, but you have to put your trust in me," a voice told me.

I spoke back to it, but it was more of an internal voice: "I've never done this before, I'm a little scared, but okay – I'm going to trust you," which was crazy, because at this point I had absolutely no idea who I was talking to.

"Don't worry, tonight isn't the night you die," it said back to me. "You're going to be okay."

This raised a whole new set of questions: who did this voice belong to, which apparently knew that I wasn't going to die that night? And if it was so sure of that, it implied it knew, with the same level of conviction, the day on which I would die – right?

It then started to tell me: "You always say so many bad things about yourself, you're always so mean to yourself … you have to show yourself more self-love."

I was shown visions of the girl from Hooters, her chest area and her self-love tattoo, then started to feel weird sensations in the parts of my body that I'm insecure and embarrassed about.

The voice then said: "And there's this."

I was shown a question that seemed to be presented by two guiding hands; the one that had lived in the very core of me forever: 'Is there a God?'

"There is a God," said the voice. "But not how most would explain it. It isn't some man in the sky, it isn't a he, and it definitely isn't judgemental."

A lot of the information I was given about this question faded pretty quickly, but one of the things I did remember, which really resonated with me, is that we are all one and the same thing, we are all part of God, and that God is just a word. This made me so happy, because after years of being in the church, hearing people define God and what 'he' is, I grew to dislike the word, and would shut down and lose all interest the minute anyone mentioned it; but now I was being told that you can actually swap the word God for love, for universe, and that each one of us is part of that massive love, or universe.

The lesson continued, and the voice said: "And then there's this …"

It presented me with another one of my core questions: 'Do aliens exist?', then answered simply: "Yes, you are an alien."

I had no idea how to process this, so I didn't, as I didn't want to try and give it some weird meaning that would really just have seen me clutching at straws. It then showed me another question: 'Will I ever find someone to truly love, who will truly love me back?' I was shown images of some of the women I had been with, who scrolled from right to left across my mind space. I believe the women I was being shown were those with whom there had been a real chance of me developing a relationship with.

At this moment, I felt the music that was playing climaxing … like it was building to a peak, as classical music does; but I also had the sense that something big was about to be revealed to me. "You've been sent so many opportunities of real love, but you haven't been able to love them in that way properly, because you're broken," the voice then said to me. "But we can fix this, and we fix this by peeling back the layers and going deeper. And we can do this by eating more mushrooms."

With that, I found myself in the kitchen, squeezing more lemon juice on the mushrooms I had left. I then ate a bunch of them, laughing to myself, by myself, thinking: 'wow I'm crazy, is this really happening?'

I went back to bed and laid down, and a little while later, the voice returned, showing me another question I had, which was:

'Is there life after death?' I immediately felt the music building up again, climaxing, followed by the voice of my Auntie Janice, who died in 2017. I felt her presence, and she called my name. I spoke out loud this time, and said: "Is this real? Is this really happening?"

"Yes, this is real, this is really happening," she responded.

I couldn't believe it, and told her: "I love and miss you sooo much, Janice!"

She asked me about her sons, my cousins, and how they were doing. I told her I hadn't really spoken to Tonye, Janice's other son, in a while, as we had sort of lost contact with each other, but that the family were taking care of her son, Ibim, and ensuring he was okay.

I then felt the music building up again, and the next thing I knew, my dad was there, speaking to me internally.

"Have you ever truly loved me?" he wanted to know.

I guess this was because he had treated my mum really badly, had hurt her and had kids everywhere, so I had judged him and spoken poorly of him on many occasions throughout the years. But that didn't change the fact that I loved him.

"You're my father, of course I love you," I replied without hesitation; and with that, he exploded softly with bright warm light radiating from him, as if a burden had been lifted.

The music then climaxed again, and I knew something big was coming … something even bigger than what had just happened. It felt like my heart was bursting, then Ethan, my brother from another mother, was there. One of the closest friends I'd ever had in this lifetime, I felt like I was going to cry, and wanted to.

"Why did you go?" I asked him. "Why did you leave us?"

I was overwhelmed with sadness in this moment, and had never felt so sad in my life! I miss Ethan so much.

"I didn't want to go, but I had to," he said, asking: "How's my son?"

"I'm still in touch with Anne, and I saw them both in Hull. He's growing so quickly," I told him, and Ethan looked so happy.

All three of them – my auntie, dad and Ethan – then asked if I wanted to go with them. At that moment, the girl I had met in Hooters that very night appeared, but this time she had wings, appearing to me as an angel that was going to escort me to the other side if I decided to go – hence the birth of her new name, Angel.

A vision of my mum arrived right in this moment, saying: "Son, I know you haven't been happy here for a while now, and it'll break my heart if you decide to go with them, but I'll understand."

I began to see visions of my family – my beautiful nieces, little brother, Ryan, and sister, Reannon. I realised that, even though I had felt ready to die for a while now, I'd be okay if I didn't. I wasn't really ready to leave my family and, without even realising it, I had made my choice.

My auntie, dad and Ethan then said: "Okay, you've made your decision, but we can't stay any longer – we have to go."

As the music faded out, they too began to fade … more and more into the distance they faded with the music, until they were gone; and even though I was so sad, my heart felt renewed, and the pain and sadness weren't so overwhelming anymore. I had been given the opportunity to truly say goodbye to all of them.

The voice then came back, and said: "What you truly want in this world is a family, a daughter, and you can have all of this, but you have to stop taking steroids."

In this moment, I felt like I chose steroids, but didn't know why, because this wasn't the choice I truly wanted. The voice then left, and I was left with powerful urges to call my mum and tell her I loved her. It was like I was being told I had to do this, and the feeling had been there all night. I tried to sleep, but when I did, I had recurring visions of an ambulance turning up at the bottom of the building, paramedics running up the steps of the building and entering my apartment to find me dead on the bed. I saw it as clear as day and became scared, as I had decided I had to stay in this life. I didn't want to die anymore, and I think because of this, I was now actually scared of death.

I got up and drank as much orange juice as I could, because a friend had told me it would lessen the effects of a mushroom trip. But it did nothing, and I found myself living infinities within each minute.

I looked at my watch, which said 00:53hrs. I got up, used the toilet, went into the kitchen and tried to down a whole carton of orange juice. I returned to the bedroom, turned the lights and television on, and tried to continue watching a programme I had started earlier. Filled with violence and people getting killed all over the place, it was something I usually revelled in, but in that moment I couldn't take it. It felt repulsive, and hurt my heart to see such violence, so I skipped through the various channels, trying to find something more pleasant.

I couldn't find anything to fit my mood, so decided to watch Moana. I watched it with my nieces so many times when I had been in London during the pandemic, and it was a truly feelgood kind of film … well, in the state I was in, it turns out that it wasn't so feelgood. There's a bit at the start of the film when the grandmother explains how the island's heart has been stolen, and it was so scary I had to turn it off. I had watched quite a few minutes of Moana, and did a few other things in between getting out of bed and switching the film off, but when I looked at my watch it said 00:54hrs. One minute – only a minute! – had passed, but how could that be?

I thought I had imagined it, or that I had incorrectly remembered the time when last checking my watch, but it happened again between 00:54hrs and 00:55hrs. The feeling was that I was living entire lifetimes, that time was elapsing, and that I had done much more in that minute than I could actually remember.

When I started experimenting with plant medicine a couple of years back via DMT, and had worried about having bad trips, as I had heard them called, I assumed people were referring to demons and monsters, when actually demons and monsters didn't have shit on what I was experiencing in that moment. The feeling of being stuck in time is way worse than any demon or monster. I was questioning if I was dead, or whether I had died and was reliving the same moment again and again, and would continue to do so forever.

I called my sister, Gina, so I wouldn't feel so alone in whatever was going on in this timeless void I seemed to have slipped into. I didn't want to admit that I was scared, so just told her that I had taken mushrooms and that I had spoken to dad. She cried a little at the memory of our father. I felt so much love for her during this conversation, but also very uneasy, like I had to go. I said bye to her and, after living through infinity a few more times, and being more scared than I can explain here in words, I thought that the best way to keep an eye on time, and reassure myself that it was actually passing, was to leave the apartment and go walking along Avenido Poblado at 01:15hrs in the morning.

The streets were empty and silent as I made my way down to the main street, carton of orange juice gripped tightly in hand, swinging back and forth. I began calling my closest friends, driven by a compulsion to tell them just how much I loved them. I called my mum, little brother and sister to tell them how much I loved them too. I felt completely overwhelmed by the amount of love I was feeling. It was so intense, it felt like it was going to burst out of me and envelop the entire universe.

I walked for a few hours, contemplating life and everything I had been shown, while sipping on my orange juice. I eventually got back to my apart at 05:00hrs, when I had a shower. This shower was like no other that I had ever had before. As the water hit my skin, bounced off and flowed down my body, it seemed to be washing away what I can only describe as a thick, invisible layer of mud or negative energy. It felt like the first time I had ever actually showered, never having felt such cleansing, then went to bed and slept for most of the day.

The next day, I went back to Hooters and told Angel what had happened. To my surprise, she didn't think I was crazy, having sat in Ayahuasca ceremonies, and was very much on her own path of discovery through medicine. She's now somebody in my circle of closest, most valued friends.

PASIÓN

Having upset Golden so badly, I decided I never, ever wanted to risk hurting another woman in any of the ways I had hurt some of the women who had been in my life to date.

In March 2021, I was back in Colombia on leave and had gone out with some friends. We went for dinner, then onto a club I had always heard of, but had never been to. The entrance is an elevator, supervised by doormen who take the entrance fee and then allow you to ride the lift up to the club. As you arrive at the top floor, before the doors even open, you can hear the music – mostly reggaeton – thumping, and as soon as the doors opened, I saw beautiful, delicious women everywhere.

Dressed elegantly and seductively, with every curve of their bodies provocatively on display, I understood immediately why this club's reputation preceded it. I hadn't had any intention of meeting a lovemaker that night, and hadn't been with one for a while. In fact, I had retired from meeting lovemakers, but it was so nice to be amongst so many beautiful women. Now, I knew that in a place like this, women making eye contact with you was a given, but I still found it intense and a little intimidating. I never know how to react in such situations, so I just smiled nervously.

We ordered drinks and had a laugh. All of the friends I was out with that night were men, though none of them were looking to meet anyone. It was just a nice place to have a drink and hang with some friends, whilst obviously taking in an eyeful of beautifully dressed, hypnotising, trance-invoking goddess type beings. There were all shapes, sizes and colours of women there. I most certainly don't mean to objectify them when describing them like this; more to try and convey all of the different expressions of femininity I saw at this place.

As it got late, my friends had to leave. They all had homes and lives to go back to, so I left with them and returned to where I was living at the time. Once at home, I sat there alone, wishing that I had slyly gotten the phone number of one of the lovemakers from the club. I laid there in bed, thinking: what if I had a regular lovemaker? I could invite her over some weekdays, or at weekends, and just chill. That way, I could have someone in my life to spend romantic time with, without worrying about hurting them, or them hurting me, because it would be an agreement and we would both know where we stood.

So the next night, I got ready and went to the club, but didn't plan on staying long. It wasn't really my thing to be at a club like that alone. It just made me feel intimidated, and question why I was alone, or even at a club trying to meet a lovemaker in the first place. These thoughts all went through my mind, and there was no getting away from them.

I got there early, so that hopefully I would meet a girl and miss the big crowd. I arrived at the lift, paid the bouncer, and went up to the club. Two lovemakers were with me in the lift, and I couldn't help but think that they must have thought I was a loser with no friends, who had to go to a club alone to pick up professional lovemakers. When the doors opened, the club was practically empty. I had gone there too early, but even though everything inside me was willing me to leave, I managed to find the courage to stay.

As I now very rarely drink alcohol (a positive side effect of the medicine), I stood at the bar drinking orange juice, keeping my eyes to myself, as I was one of very few men in the club at that moment. I had felt so much more confident being there the day before with my friends, and the difference in my mindset was marked. I was on my third glass of orange juice by the time the club started filling up, and some of the nervousness I felt started to dissolve. Just like the night before, the club was full of beautiful, attractive women.

I saw a girl that I recognised from the night before, who I had seen dancing and found myself very attracted to. She must have seen me staring, because every now and then I caught her gazing at me, and our eyes met. After going back and forth like this a couple times, I plucked up the courage to approach a woman I'm going to call Pasión. I went to the bar, and stood beside her to order a drink. When she saw me, she smiled, and I asked if she wanted a drink. She said yes, I ordered the drinks, and began a bog standard conversation with her, asking questions like: "How are you? What's your name? How much is it?"

I didn't want to waste any time, and didn't want to be in the club by myself any longer than I had to, but she was a really nice girl. The more we spoke, and the more my nervousness faded, I felt that she would be the lovemaker I would come out of retirement for. Pasión asked if I wanted to dance, but I thought: hell no, I'm not about to embarrass myself in front of all of these beautiful women. I asked her if she wanted to come back to my place, and while she was a bit surprised at the speed at which I was working, she was okay with it. She said she would use the toilet, and that when she came back, we could go.

When she returned, she said goodbye to the friend she had come with, and we left together. Once back at my place, I switched the TV on and we sat together for a bit. I offered her a drink and played the good host, and as she was so fun and easy-going, I asked if she had ever tried weed oil, which by now I was a massive fan of. It allowed me to relax and go to a place of complete calmness and introspection, though I was a little worried that she might think I was trying to drug her. She had never done it before, but said she would give it a go, so I put two complete plungers in my drink, and one in hers.

We sat watching TV and talking, but an hour or so after taking the weed oil, neither of us felt a thing. It had normally kicked in by then, but after heading into my bedroom, I freshened up in the bathroom, after which she did the same. As I laid on the bed, wondering why the weed oil hadn't worked, I heard a random giggle from the bathroom. I asked Pasión if she was okay, and she said that she felt a little strange, and thought the oil was kicking in.

Once she was done in the bathroom, she came to bed and we cuddled. Her body was amazing – slim, but with a very curvaceous posterior – and I hadn't been with a woman in some time, so to feel the bare skin and warmth of a beautiful, naked woman's frame pressed against mine like that would have been enough had it been the culmination of the night. We talked and laughed, and by now I was massively feeling the effects of the oil too. We began to kiss and, for those of you who have experienced what being with someone intimately can feel like whilst under the effects of weed oil … well, you know. It's intense beyond belief, your senses are heightened, and you feel every touch all over your body – every kiss, every touch, every thrust and every moment of intense eye contact feels like it could lead to an orgasm.

I kissed her from her lips to her chin, all over her neck and down to her breasts as she moaned in pleasure. I slowly made my way down from her breasts, and beautiful brown nipples, to her stomach and inner thighs, kissing every inch, then finally made my way directly in between her legs. She was so wet, and I kissed, licked and sucked every last bit of her, whilst she gyrated wildly. I held her hand and we interlocked our fingers. Every now and then, she emitted a little groan or scream, whist squeezing my hands tightly in hers. Eventually, she climaxed, squeezing our interlocked fingers even tighter, whilst forcing herself even deeper into my mouth and screaming uncontrollably. By no means at all am I trying to claim to be a lovemaking legend, but I do know how much more exceptionally intense sex can be on weed oil.

She pulled my face up to hers, but didn't want to kiss. I don't think she wanted to taste herself, but that was okay – it was her loss. Then, breathing deeply and sounding all out of breath, she said: "Condón!" Amid my planning and hast in getting to the club to find Pasión, I hadn't once thought of getting any protection. I had to order some through a home delivery app, which you might think would totally kill the moment, but it didn't – it was intense enough just to be holding each other whilst we waited. The delivery arrived about thirty minutes later, at which point I threw some clothes on and went downstairs.

As I travelled in the elevator down to the ground floor, smiling and feeling quite pleased with myself, something told me to look in the mirror. As I did, I saw that my beard was wet and glistening, telling the complete story of what I had been up to. It was a good thing I looked at my reflection, as I can't imagine what the concierges and delivery guy would have thought seeing me like that. Once I reached the front desk, I grabbed the bag I had ordered from the delivery guy, which aside from the condoms included a drink, some chewing gum and a few other little items, in an attempt to draw attention away from the rubber johnnies, as I'm still very shy when it comes to this. I said good night, smiling like a Cheshire Cat, and the delivery guy must have known that I was as high as a kite.

I got back to the apartment, where Pasión was still very much feeling the effects of the weed oil. We made love, and I felt so connected it was amazing. In the morning, once we were awake, we had a good talk and a laugh, and I was glad to hear that it had been a really good experience for her too. I could already sense that I liked Pasión. Her personality was warm, caring and joyful, and I knew I had made the right decision in choosing her. Before she left that morning, I asked for her number, thinking that I would have her as my regular lovemaker.

Before I returned to work, we met another three times, and then again during my following leaves. Sometimes I called her early in the evening, she came over and we watched a film together, but for me it was never just about the sex – it was about connection; being able to spend time romantically with a woman. As the year progressed, we had met quite a few times, and there seemed to a trust growing between us. She was always very clear and strict about the use of protection, which gave me confidence that that's how she was with all of her clients.

Pasión was the only woman I was having sexual relations with, and she knew that, but if I'm going to be honest, there was a part of me that wanted to have unprotected sex with her … to be truly inside of her and connected, and really feel each other.

One night, that's exactly what happened, and it was sensational. I always felt connected to her when we had sex, as Pasión was an extremely passionate woman in the bedroom; but this time, skin to skin, it was different … it was so much more. I didn't know it then, but this would also be the last time we had sex, and the last time we saw each other.

Pasión was a beautiful woman, and a very cherished memory of mine. She was exactly what I needed at that moment in time.

LOVE

Love was an amazingly beautiful, highly intelligent woman with piercing green eyes. One Sunday evening, after a class on my first Rythmia retreat, I walked into the restaurant there, called Roots, and saw this beautiful lady sat at a table to my right. We caught each other's gaze, her eyes were intense, and for some reason I couldn't look away. I felt compelled to keep staring, and as I did, I saw the most beautiful smile emerging on her face … and by now a massive, heartfelt smile had appeared on mine. We sort of waved at each other and said hi, then I carried onto the coconut water dispenser, got my drink and made my way back to my room.

The next day, during one of the meals at Roots, I saw her at the dispensers, so thought I would go over to get a drink and try to introduce myself. Once I got there, before I even had a chance to say anything, we were staring into each other's eyes and smiling. She said hi, then added: "I keep looking at you and smiling, so I wanted to introduce myself." I was so happy, I introduced myself and told her that I would love to talk to her when we got some free time.

Throughout the day, whilst we were in classes, I found myself trying to locate where she was in the room, then felt overcome by a wave of happiness, and a little sense of nervousness, when finding her. We sometimes caught each other's eyes, she'd show me her beautiful smile and my heart would get excited. The first time we actually got to talk was the Tuesday night after the ceremony. My journey that Tuesday night had been revolutionary, revealing life's biggest kept secret, but we'll get to that later.

After I had this revelation on my mattress, I went out and sat by the fire on a concrete bench.

My elbows resting on my legs and my head resting in the palms of my hands, I was laughing about what I had been shown. Whilst I lightly sniggered to myself, staring at the ground, I felt somebody put their hand on me, and softly stroke my shoulder and back. I looked to the left, and saw these feet stood there; and as I followed them to the legs, then the legs up to the knees, I saw a yellow dress … and as I followed the yellow dress upwards, I saw her stood there with her beautiful green eyes, softly stroking my back.

The only description that could possibly define the feeling I had in that very moment is love – overwhelming love – and I looked at her absolutely speechless. Without even knowing, her touch had been exactly what I needed in that moment, and in that moment, sat on the bench in front of the fire in the middle of the ceremony, I fell in love with her. She walked on after a few seconds, as there's a noble silence that you are supposed to maintain, along with no human contact with others, during the ceremony.

Once the ceremony was closing, and the few who wanted to share their stories had all done so, I found Love's location in the room and made my way over to her. She was sat up on her mattress, talking to the girl sat beside her, but had clearly been aware of me walking over to her, because once I got there, she held her hands up for me to hold and support her whilst she stood up, then gave me the biggest hug, which I hadn't expected. I squeezed her tightly, and didn't want to let go.

As we stood there, her arms around me, and my arms around her, I felt like I was home … and I hadn't felt at home anywhere in a very long time.

"Hey, Mr alien (the name she called me because of the story I shared with the group at the end of the ceremony)!" she smiled. "This may sound crazy, but I feel a connection to you," I told her. "I feel more connected to you than I do to anyone else here." We continued to hug for a moment more, then made our way out of the Moloka. We talked about both of our experiences as I walked her back to her room, before returning to mine. Over the next couple of days, I sat with her whenever possible at meal times and in lessons. On the Friday, I asked Love if we could spend some time together, she said yes, so we sat by the pool on some lilos in the shade and spoke for ages. She told me she had been a CEO and a director of different companies over the course of her life, had been married and then separated. She was an outdoors person who loved white water rafting, travelling and dancing, which was a big thing for her. Having been a shy girl in her younger years, she hadn't had the confidence to dance, but her life experiences had encouraged her to come out of her shell a little.

As I listened to this beautiful, very intelligent human being speak, all I could think was: I want to be with this woman, who I felt completed me. We spoke about our dreams, aspirations and desires for life, of which there were differences – she didn't want to have kids, whereas I did, but it didn't matter, as we were just enjoying the moment, getting to know each other. As the night drew in, the Rythmia closing party began. It was held every Friday for those who had been at the retreat that week, and would be leaving on the Saturday or Sunday. Love seemed to really enjoy it, and danced a lot of the night; then towards the end, she came over to me, we walked to the hammocks and shared one together. I had an app on my phone called 36 questions to fall in love, I asked her if she would like to do it, and she said yes. As we made our way through these 36 questions, which grew intimately deeper with each question, we realised that we had covered a lot of them during our conversation by the poolside. One of the things that came up again was kids, and Love being the honest, sincere person that she is, pointed out to me the one thing I was trying to ignore – that she couldn't possibly give me what I wanted, as children had never been, nor would they now become, part of her plan. I understood and respected this, because while I would have loved to have kids, each individual has the right to desire not to.

When we got to the last part of the app, it asked us to stare into each other's eyes for four minutes. It started off with us giggling and smiling at each other, but as we settled into it, I found it to be one of the most intimate things you could do with someone. I had never stared into somebody's eyes this long, and once the smiling and nervousness is out of the way, it's as if you really get to see the other person. Once a person's face relaxes, and becomes completely expressionless, you notice all the colours in their eyes, and there's a depth to the gaze … almost as if you can feel or see the very life inside them. I realised I had never felt so intimate with someone without having physical contact, which blew my mind. I had heard it said that our eyes are the windows to our souls, and during these four minutes I truly understood why.

The app alarmed at four minutes to let us know that the exercise was over, we smiled at each other, and both leaned in to kiss. The kiss was amazing, and her lips so soft that I didn't want to stop kissing her; but unfortunately, all good things come to an end and it was getting late, so we walked back to her room holding hands. We hugged and kissed each other good night, and I skipped back to my room feeling invincible. The next day, it was time for me to leave. We met as I prepared to board the bus leaving the retreat, we hugged, and I told her that I loved her. I could see that it wasn't something she was expecting, but she kissed me and said that she loved me too. We said goodbye, and I boarded the bus.

We stayed in touch frequently over the next few days through voice messages and video calls, and it made me so happy to see her face. As time went on, we were both back out in the real world – me in Iraq and her still travelling the world – and we began to speak less frequently, but in the moments that we did, I felt loved by her and hope that she felt loved by me.

About six months later, she asked me if I would like to go and see her in Spain, where she would be staying for a few days. Well, of course I wanted to see her, and couldn't have been happier, even though by this point I realised that there wouldn't be a conventional relationship between us. I had come to understand that she too was on her own journey, a journey of self-discovery and inner work, which came as no surprise, given we had met at an Ayahuasca retreat. I was okay with it by now, and was just happy to be getting the chance to spend some time with her. I had also planned and paid for another retreat at Rythmia, which worked out perfectly, as the date she would arrive in Spain came after that.

My next leave came up, I went to Costa Rica, had my second Rythmia experience, then spent a few days in Tamarindo, the closest town centre to the Rythmia resort. After flying back to Colombia for a day to grab some stuff, I travelled to Spain, and needless to say I was absolutely knackered. I arrived in Barcelona, and caught a taxi to the address Love had sent me. When I arrived at the property, Love was waiting at the door to greet me with a massive smile and her piercing green eyes. As I looked at her, I felt the exact same connection that I had experienced at Rythmia, I dropped my bags, and we embraced and kissed.

During our time together in Barcelona, I got to know a lot more about Love. She liked to plan her days out in advance whilst she was travelling, so that she could see as much of a place as possible and make the most of the time she had. We went on guided tours where we were shown parts of the city and its history, which we probably wouldn't have come across by ourselves. We went to a cooking class, which I had never done anywhere, and were taught how to cook traditional Spanish dishes. We spoke with the other couples who were there, some of whom were starting their own software business in Brazil, and I got to hear Love talk about business too.

This was something she was clearly passionate about; it was apparent to me and everyone else in the room that she had the most experience on this subject. I found her intelligence so attractive. I had heard people say that intelligence is an attractive quality, but had never experienced it myself before now. She had sought out different restaurants for us to go to, finding one located in a building on the second floor, overlooking the sea. We ate there on a few occasions, some of which we got to watch the sunset over the horizon. It was definitely the best restaurant we visited, due in no small part to its beautiful, intimate setting.

On the first day I arrived, Love said to me: "I think we should spend this time as though we're madly in love with each other." In truth, I really was. We were very intimate with each other during our time together. In bed, these moments were filled with passion, pleasure and love, while out on the street with the rest of the world, there were times when she held my hand, or in a taxi or the cooking class, when we had a moment to sit, she lightly rested her head on my shoulder, and her hand on my leg. For me, these are the moments, filled with tender displays of love and affection, that really matter, when I would really feel loved by her.

Once, she played a track she really liked, where a man talks over the music. She explained to me that his name was Ram Dass, and that the track exemplified one of his teachings, Love Constant In The Universe, that love isn't something you can give to someone. You cannot take hold of the love you may have for someone and give it to them in their hand, for that love is a state of being, and that state of being exists within you, has always been there, and always will be.

When you meet someone, that person may act as a vehicle, a key stimulus, that allows you to find and unlock the state of being that is love. Because you experience this state of being with another person, you then want to possess that person, because you think they are the source of love you're experiencing, and that if they were to leave and the relationship to end, that love would forever leave with them … when in fact, it exists within and is always accessible if we wish to find it.

This blew my mind, and in that moment, what had just been explained to me absolutely transformed my understanding of love. Because of Love, Ram Dass is one of my favourite spiritual teachers.

I now understood I wouldn't be able to possess Love or make her mine. This isn't to say that people shouldn't have relationships or strive to be with someone; more that before you go looking for love, you should be able to locate that state of being within yourself. This was a lesson I would come to understand through a great amount of hurt which, looking back on it now, doesn't surprise me, as everything I have ever learnt in life, I have always learnt the hard way.

In total, I spent seven days with Love. When it was time to go, I quietly wished that I could have had more time to be with her, but my leave was coming to an end and I was soon due to be back at work, so we said our goodbyes and I flew back to Colombia, and then onto Iraq.

RYTHMIA 1, 2021

I finally managed to get to Rythmia after my original dates were cancelled due to the pandemic and work commitments. I arrived in a taxi, and before even getting out, I was in love with the place. There was greenery and nature everywhere I looked, which I know isn't such a hard thing to imagine in a country like Costa Rica, but I had just finished a rotation in Iraq, so the contrast was striking. It also felt special, like anything could happen … that something special could happen.

As the taxi pulled up at the reception, I saw the massive Rythmia logo on the ground that I had seen so many times on their site, and emails, during the booking process. It was hard to believe that I was actually there. I was greeted at the taxi door by great big smiles from the staff, who assisted me with my luggage, and then everybody took a Covid test as part of the induction. We were met with a glass of fresh coconut water, and some things we would need during the week, like a water bottle and retreat journal, which detailed the week's programme, showing which classes were being held, as well as their times and locations.

We were given our Ayahuasca shot glass and Rythmia wristband, which was programmed individually, so that the classes we attended could be tracked. The aim was that we attended them all, which gave us the strongest chance of receiving what they call 'your miracle' whilst there at the retreat. Once I was given my room key, I made my way to the accommodation, which I was to share with one other, which definitely turned out to be the better option than being in a room by myself.

Whilst I walked to my room, I saw trees and hammocks everywhere. There were statues of the Easter Island heads, Buddha and Christ, beside which were concrete benches. There were also some hammocks, which were amazing to relax on during sunny days when you had some free time in between classes and ceremony, and just wanted to relax, take in the scenery and reflect on how the retreat was going for you … and the effect it had on your life and your beliefs, which the medicine definitely compelled you to. The restaurant, Roots, was a beautiful dining area, with a pool and sun lounger chairs all around it. The food was organically sourced and designed to help with your experience by providing you with a clean, healthy diet – plant-based if desired, but there was also the option of meat and fish.

The staff in all departments were absolutely phenomenal, always approachable, and willing to help in any way they could. Most mornings, I awoke to the sound of howling monkeys. I loved it; it was such a contrast from being in Iraq.

I experienced something new every day, whether it be the yoga class, the spar facility, Roots, one of the lessons, or just lying on a hammock chilling, and the conversations were always amazing. Somehow, you got past any small talk, and straight to the point of why we were there, what had happened in our lives to bring us to this place, and which questions had we been asking ourselves to lead us to this point. I found it so refreshing to be in conversations like these, and to hear and see that no matter what anyone looked like, or where they were from, the one thing a lot of us had in common is that we'd all suffered in some way or another.

I had the opportunity to meet and converse with people I would never have had the opportunity to socialise with normally. There were doctors, actors, CEOs and directors of companies, entrepreneurs, phycologists, the retired, and many more from all walks of life. If I had to use one word to describe Rythmia, it would be paradise. I imagine people have all sorts of experiences there, and some very tough ones too … but for me, and I can only ever speak for myself, this place was a gamechanger.

Monday night on the Ayahuasca

We entered the Moloka, an open, spacious building resembling the shape of a crucifix, except it was longer horizontally than vertically, at 17:30hrs. Filled with however many mattresses are needed per night, each one had a blanket, in case you got cold, a white bucket and a roll of toilet tissue at the foot of it, for whenever you needed to purge.

The Moloka had white walls and a mahogany wood ceiling, with geometrical shapes, patterns and the seed of life carved into big, circular frameworks of wood that had then been mounted on the ceiling. There were massive windows, and sliding glass doors, that were all left open during the ceremony that followed. In the very heart of the Moloka was a small circular alter, on top of which were a number of crystals and other items from each shaman, which had been blessed to bring good energy into the room and ceremony. In front of the alter, at the very top of the room, was where the shamans served the medicine.

Once everyone was in the Moloka and had selected their mattress for the night, they called us into the heart of it, where we sat whilst each shaman and light worker (somebody who has undergone a spiritual awakening, and wants to help others) introduced themselves to us. The shaman who was leading the night spoke a little about what to expect from the medicine, how to surrender unto it, and how to ask for help if we needed it. They then sent us back to our mattresses, letting us know that the time for noble silence had begun, which meant no more talking amongst each other and no physical contact. The shamans and light workers then gathered together and blessed the medicine, which was quite the thing to see, watching them dance with the use of indigenous musical instruments, ceremonial aids and harmonica.

Around an hour after first entering the Moloka, they invited us to imbibe our first drink of Ayahuasca. We formed two lines, each of us with our Ayahuasca cup in hand. When I arrived in front of the shaman, he greeted me, took my cup, filled it up with Ayahuasca, blessed it and gave it back to me. I spoke my intention into it, which that night was: "Show me who I've become." I went back to my mattress, and laid there in silence which, we had been told, would be in place for the first thirty minutes to an hour before any sort of music would be played or another shot of Ayahuasca offered.

As I laid on my mattress in this silence, it was amazing. I could hear the wind blowing through the trees outside, and the leaves rustling, and I could hear all of the different forms of wildlife singing their different songs. As I lay there after a while, I realised that I had been softly drifting in and out of different states of consciousness. It was so subtle, I didn't even realise I had drifted off until I saw faint geometrical patterns.

The first thing that broke the silence was a sudden scream from the other side of the room, then I became aware of someone crying quietly from another area in the Moloka. It sounded and felt so sad, and even though they told us to focus on our own journey, as no matter what we may hear, we never truly knew what someone else was going through in their journey, and could be the complete opposite of what we thought was going on, I couldn't help but wonder what that lady was experiencing, and hoping that she was alright.

After what I imagine to have been an hour or so in silence, the shaman told us all that we could come forward for a second drink. I jumped up immediately to join the queue, and when I got to the shaman, I set the same intention again, drank my shot and returned to my mattress. A little while later, I started seeing patterns again, but it was still hard to perceive them clearly, and I sometimes felt that its effects had already worn off. I went back later for a third and fourth drink. As I laid on my mattress, I started thinking that I wasn't going to experience anything, and even went to sleep for a while, though I'm not sure for how long. At some point during the night, I woke up to the sound of vomiting, screaming, laughter and the girl next to me having a conversation with herself. I felt like I was about to be sick, it was like my stomach had been brewing something inside of it, and now it had to purge it all. I scrambled down my mattress to the bucket, and vomited more aggressively than ever before. I opened my mouth, and it seemed to all fall out at once in one fell swoop, but as I looked at it, it had only fallen around the inner rim of the bottom of the bucket. It was almost a perfect circle, apart from the top, where the circle was broken.

None of it had fallen in the middle, and I remember thinking how strange that was. The shamans told us that after purging into a bucket, we could ask it what it was. It was explained to everyone during classes that a lot of what we purged during these ceremonies were energies that were no longer serving us, and that sometimes, if we asked what something was, after purging, it would tell you. So I leaned into the bucket, asked: "What are you?" and as I knelt there, waiting to see some sign or other, I vomited again; but this time, it only landed and took shape directly in the middle of the bucket, and as I hovered over the bucket, I saw the shape that had formed – the silhouette of a woman holding a baby.

So now there was this unfinished circle, with the logo of a woman holding a baby right in the centre of it. I had a pretty good idea what I was seeing, but asked again, as I didn't want to leave any room for doubt. This time, before I had even finished thinking about what I was going to ask it, my head felt as if it was abruptly pushed a few inches lower, towards the bucket, and in my mind's eye, I saw the word 'baby'. Then came a feeling of overwhelming revelation … a feeling that I would be a father one day; though since then, I have come to question my interpretation of this message. What if I had misunderstood it, and what I had actually purged was the belief that I had to be a father?

It has taken me a few years, but in hindsight I've finally come to understand what this night had really been about. It hadn't been some sort of premonition or foresight into the future that I was finally going to get the family I had dreamed of. Instead, what I had purged was a feeling I had carried for years: the feeling that if I could just create this dream family, I would be worthy, I would matter to someone … maybe even matter to myself.

Tuesday night on the Ayahuasca

I spoke my intention – "Merge me back with my soul at all costs" – into my shot glass, took my first drink, then laid on my mattress – again, in silence – and after what I imagine to be forty minutes to an hour later, I started to feel the medicine; then shortly after, felt completely sober, the states interchanging. When they called us up for the second shot, I drank it and returned to my mattress. Again, I felt the medicine coming on in waves, and after a little while, started to see what appeared to be a small, bright, focal pinpoint of light in the distance of the sparse and boundless darkness behind my eyelids. I laid there for a little while like this, before opening my eyes.

When opening them, I saw the ceiling fan take the shape of something like a trumpet, with a strange eye at the end of it, staring at me. I found that if I moved around on my mattress, the eye would follow me and each of my movements; then, the same as before, I became sober and felt nothing. A while later, they called for those who wanted a third shot. This time, when I returned to my mattress and closed my eyes, for some reason, in this Moloka, full of people, most of them being very vocal with whatever they were experiencing, be it crying, screaming, laughter and so on.

Amid it all, I became acutely aware of my heartbeat. Through absolutely no intention of my own, all of my attention had become focused on it. I could hear it clearly, and feel the thudding of each beat against my chest, and then suddenly, and very abruptly, it stopped. I could no longer hear it; I could not feel it. I had no heartbeat. Before I even had time to try and process what was happening, or even allow myself to feel fear, my mouth expelled a breath like never before. It was deep and far reaching, I felt it throughout my entire body, and with it I felt any sort of connection I had to my body, or to this world, completely severed.

By now, whatever it was that was left of me was scared – so scared. I had just felt my entire body shut down, I was completely untethered from it, and now there was nothingness, except a knowing, deep within, that I had just died. After a while of feeling scared at what was happening, I began to feel euphoric. It was a feeling that just washed over me and, in that moment, I understood that it came from a sense of being completely unburdened by the human body. It felt like I was being showered in ecstasy. To die is a truly exhilarating thing.

Once all sense of fear had been obliterated, I began to travel through what I can only describe as different realms, seeing all kinds of geometrical patterns, shapes and colours, until I eventually arrived at the end of the journey, where I was met by an alien – a biped being, green of colour with a head shaped like an inverted triangle, no mouth, but with small, slight eyes. It had a body, but I couldn't make it out. The only thing that was obvious and clear to see was its arms and hands.

As soon as I arrived there, the being simply pointed towards two places within the space or realm where we were. I looked to where its left hand was pointing, and saw my body, the avatar of Ricardo Chin, just stood there, absolutely motionless and devoid of all life, on a small, elevated square platform. When I looked to where its right hand was pointing, I saw another platform, but this one was empty. I didn't understand, so I spoke to it in English: "I don't understand."

The alien pointed again at Ricardo Chin's body, then to the other platform, and at that moment I felt a mass of information enter my being, as if downloaded, and understood or, rather, remembered that I was not my human body – none of us are.

I went to speak to the being again, but this time my communication was conducted in our native tongue, which was like a long, drawn out "Ommmm," which carried in it more information than any words ever could. I spoke in the tongue a few times, confirming with the being what I was understanding, whilst it communicated back to me in hand gestures, its native form of communication.

It explained to me that I was an alien being, and that I had just died in the avatar of Ricardo Chin. I was told that we, as the beings we are, come to the place I was in at that moment to enter the game that we humans call life … a place where I would be shown characters in the game of life that I could choose from. For example, I could be shown Maria – Maria's character will be born into the game of life and, amongst many other things, give birth to a daughter, and her daughter will grow up to have children; so Maria will experience what it is to be a mother and grandmother.

There could be a character called John – John will have a daughter who will die at five years old from cancer. John will experience the loss of a child, one of the greatest losses we know as humans.

Ricardo Chin – the Ricardo character would be unlucky in love, and experience a great deal of loneliness throughout his life.

As the beings we truly are, there are experiences or concepts we don't fully understand or haven't experienced, so we would go to this realm, see a character that will experience the thing we don't fully understand, pick that character and be birthed into the world, the game of life, with absolutely no recollection of the entirety of being we truly are – therefore, truly believing and experiencing life as the character we believe ourselves to be.

Once I had understood all that the being had told me, it asked me one simple question, offering me a choice. Pointing again at the avatar of Ricardo Chin, it told me that I could go back to that body and character, living out the rest of Ricardo's life and all of the experiences yet to come; or, pointing at the empty platform, it offered me the choice to return to the game of life in another avatar, as a completely different character, starting the game of life again.

Deep in my being, I immediately decided to come back as Ricardo. As soon as I made that choice within me, I didn't even need to communicate it to the being. The next thing, I was aware of was my eyes opening and waking up on my mattress. It was amazing and invigorating to have a body again, I laid there looking at my arms, following them along to my hands, then used my hands to feel the rest of my body, which felt so soft and beautiful. Simultaneously, I became aware of the other people in the room all wrapped up in their own experiences, again hearing the screaming, crying, purging and laughter.

I felt a sense of great revelation, and couldn't stop laughing. The feeling was overwhelming, like I now knew it all, I had all the answers – knowledge that had definitely merged me back with my soul, and answered some of the questions that had been with me forever, like what are we doing here and what's the point of life?

I realised that we are all alien beings who have come here to play the game of life; to experience love, pain, suffering, sex, murder; what it is to die, sorrow, loss – all of the emotions and hardships life is filled with. I went and sat outside by the fire, my mind racing. I thought about my gran, dad, Ethan and Janice. I was having visions of seeing them come to the end of their lives in the characters they had been playing, and running back like excited kids to have another go on the game of life.

The way I imagined it was like a little child whizzing down a slide at the park. The thrill it gives them is so intense, filling them with so much joy, that when they get to the bottom, they run straight towards the steps, screaming out for another go on the slide again.

I sat there in front of grandfather fire (so-called because indigenous cultures have always known fire to be a wise, loving presence, calling the spirit of the fire grandfather), head in hands, giggling to myself, thinking that this revelation had been tremendous; which coincided with Love appearing and stroking my shoulder. It had truly been one of the best nights of my life.

Wednesday night on the Ayahuasca

Tonight, my intention was: "Show me everything." By this, I meant: show me where we are when we aren't here – i.e. not alive in human form – and to show me how the universe works in every way. I drank my first cup of Ayahuasca after asking for this intention, then returned to my mattress, lying there in silence for a while, whilst everyone was served their drinks. Some time later, after the period of silence had elapsed, they started to play live music, and as it played, one of the light workers walked through the Moloka holding a pot in his hand, wafting copal through the room.

I love the smell of copal, and all the sacred smokes. The shamans claim that with the smoke come the spirits; that it's used as a conduit to bridge our world with that of the spiritual. I found this to be true; shortly after, very clear, strong visuals started kicking in, despite having only taken one cup of Ayahuasca, and I was well on my way. At one point, I opened my eyes and, as I went to close them again, I couldn't, as they were stuck at the point prior to complete closure; so I could see the blackness at the backs of my eyelids, but also a blurred, unfocused picture of my surroundings.

I seemed to have no control over my eyelids, and then an alien appeared in the space at the back of my eyelids. It was difficult to clearly define its form, as I could only see the top half of its body, but I was able to make out its outline from the waistline upwards. Its arms were outstretched and in the air, and it said: "We live in the in-between, we live in the folds of life," then my eyelids were allowed to close, and I began to be shown things.

I found myself in another realm where everything was black, with a tint of grey. I became aware of myself, and saw that I had no body – my entire being was one massive eye. I hid behind one of many structures, shaped like a building, but with no doors or windows. As I manoeuvred myself around this realm, I managed to peep around the corner of the structure I was hiding behind, and saw an alien. I don't know what gender it was, but the energy felt masculine in nature. The being was tall – so very tall – had deep black coloured skin, its arms and hands hung from its shoulders, with no real movement from them as it walked, it was very slim in build, and I observed it as it walked on by in the mid-distance.

Then it was almost like there was a voice saying: "And then there's this …," and I was shown a barrage of impossible shapes and information that I couldn't even begin to explain, even if I wanted to. The voice communicated to me again: " … and then there's also this, this, this and that …" The speed and depth of profundity to the things I was being shown grew to a point where I couldn't bare it anymore. I was being shown so much, and could now open my eyes too, so I saw my surroundings in the Moloka alongside all of this unfathomable information in my mind's eye, as clear as anything has ever been to me.

It was so intense, my brain couldn't comprehend what I was being shown. And then, as the information further intensified, I was shown a vision of me grabbing hold of my right eyelid, pulling it upwards over my forehead and back towards the rear of my head, ripping it clean off to uncover a massive, disproportionate eyeball. I didn't understand what was going on, but knew that I didn't want to be in the Moloka anymore with this going on. I felt like I had to get out of there, so got up and went to sit by the fire.

Now outside, sat by the fire, I was shown visions of myself on the floor, rolling around screaming, digging my nails into my neck and face, ripping my skin away from my body. Then, as I looked to the other side of the concrete bench I was sat on, I was shown myself knelt down, holding onto the bench with both hands, headbutting it as hard as I possibly could, over and over again. I began to laugh uncontrollably, and couldn't hold back. What I was being shown was so wild and intense, it was consuming my mind. The feeling was that if I did some of the things I was being shown, it would alleviate the pain and severity of confusion from the many different faces of uninterpretable information I was being shown.

As I sat there watching all of this, laughing out loud like a complete madman, I realised in that moment that I had got my intention. I had asked the medicine to "show me everything," which it had done and was doing, but my puny human brain couldn't comprehend it. I thought to myself that this is what it must be to be psychotic. I understood that I was being shown that the human brain can't handle 'everything', which is impossible. It made me think about people I've seen in the street, and labelled as crazy, when maybe they weren't crazy at all; just receiving more information than they could process, and were struggling to understand it.

I found it so funny, realising that I had received my intention, and that I was now in a battle to not absolutely lose my mind. I was still laughing uncontrollably, despite trying to stop myself, as it was horrendously loud and probably a disturbance to the others in the ceremony. Just as I was starting to gain a little control over myself, a guy came out who was in his third week at Rythmia. Every time I had seen him in ceremony during the week, he had been laughing uncontrollably, and now he came out laughing, which triggered me into another fit of uncontrollable laughter … which in turn fed his laughter. Even though the ceremony was in noble silence, we were unable to stop.

We managed to get a grip of the laughter, and tone it down for a moment or two, during which time a British guy who I had met earlier in the week came out. He had taken his blue t-shirt off, and was holding it in his hand. It looked like he was on a mission, marching over to the last vacant concrete bench by the fire. As I watched him, skilfully managing to hold back my laughter while still being shown visions of myself headbutting the bench and ripping my skin off, he sat down, held his T-shirt up in front of his face and screamed into it. I burst out into laughter again, there was no controlling it, and it hadn't just triggered me – the guy who had been laughing all week exploded into a fit of laughter, followed by the British guy. It was horrendous; now there was a three man laughing choir sat by the fire, unable to control themselves and most definitely disturbing others in the ceremony.

The British guy got up after a while, repeating the phrase "Deary me, deary me!" to himself whilst walking away, in an effort, I suspect, to try and get a grip of his laughter. I shortly followed, leaving the fire and heading back to my mattress in the hope that I would stop laughing. Back on my mattress, the visions started to subside, although the laughter was still very present. I was trying my best to control it, but ended up triggering a lady two mattresses down, who began laughing; and as laughter is infectious, a whole bunch of other people started laughing too. Soon, pretty much the entire side of the Moloka where I was lying was in hysterics. I felt so guilty, although my laughter told a different story.

One of the light workers stood close to my bed. I thought she was going to tell me that I had to go outside, but she didn't (Sarah, the shaman leading the ceremony, later told us that she had told the light workers not to stop us, as she thought it was beautiful, and indicated that the medicine was working at its best, with us purging through laughter). A little while later, however, I got up, went outside and laid on the decking. At this point, most of the crazy visions I was having had calmed down, and I found my body involuntarily talking alien again, with more of the "Ommmming" from the night before. I found that my tongue curled up to the roof of my mouth, and the "Ommmmm" reverberated from the back of my throat.

When it was time for the second glass, I went and got it, saying: "Mother Ayahuasca, thank you so much, but please no more of the crazy! Please just heal my heart." I said this jokingly, and with the utmost respect. With that, I went back to my bed and experienced absolute euphoria, with my body again humming in alien talk, with an understanding of what I was being shown, despite being unable to remember anything about it.

I woke up some time after and thought: 'Oh my God, I'm not sure if I can take another cup', at which point I realised that the shaman was talking to everyone, that the ceremony was over, and that we were now at the sharing phase of the night. For me, this is proof that the medicine (Mother Aya) always gives us exactly what we require, and never more than we can handle, so there was no need for me to have another cup. I had experienced pure bliss and euphoria after drinking that second cup, and it lasted until the end of the night.

RYTHMIA 2, 2022

Monday night

We took our first drink, and I set my intention to: "Show me who I've become." I went back to my bed, then we had an hour and a half of silence before any music was put on and we were offered a second cup. I had been a little scared leading up to this retreat, as I was convinced I was due a really tough experience. I didn't really feel anything during the hour and a half of silence, or after the second cup, though after the third, I started to see patterns and feel it working through my body.

I started to get random thoughts, pictures and scenes coming through. I was shown an elderly person on what I assumed was their deathbed. Either dead or about to die, I really thought it was my gran, as she had died a year earlier; but as the scene drew closer and became clearer, I could see that it was actually me (I looked sooo much like my grandmother!). I felt so much love for him, old man me, which is something I had never really felt for present day me.

It's quite a surreal experience to see yourself on your deathbed, but it was beautiful, and the feeling I had was: 'Oh my God, I made it – I really made it! I love you, old man me'. Since my last retreat at Rythmia, I had been constantly wondering whether you could ask the medicine when and how you would die. And if you could, was it even something you would want to know? And without even asking it as an intention, the medicine knew exactly what had been going on in my mind and the questions I had begun asking myself.

As I laid there, I received prompts to get up and take more medicine, seeing the shot cup in my mind's eye – my right hand would lift up and my finger would point out. Whilst lying there, asking myself if this was really a sign to go and get a fourth drink, my left hand started rapidly tapping the mattress, as if to say: go and get another drink. I continued to lie there, asking whether this was really happening, just to make me get up for another drink of Ayahuasca.

I then felt a bug on my neck, scurrying down the back of my collar and towards my back. I jumped up immediately, flapping around, not finding anything, and got insights coming through that it was a more drastic signal to encourage me out of the bed to get another serving, which I did. When I returned to my bed, my head began to involuntarily and uncontrollably shake up and down, and a weird frequency noise came out of my mouth – it was wild! I then reached the point where I was absolutely stone cold sober, and felt compelled to go to the fire. I was shown a picture of a log fire in my mind's eye, so took it as a signal, got up and went over to the fire.

I sat by the fire for five to ten minutes before a girl came over, sat down and cried hysterically to herself, saying things like: "I'm not going back – I'm not fucking going!" and "Fuck him!" She was having a tough experience, and after a few minutes of this, she got up and broke the noble silence.

"Sorry, I'm gonna go," she said. "I don't want to be disturbing you." "Stay! It's okay," I responded.

"No, I'm sorry."

As she went to leave, I reached out and held her wrist, asking her to please stay. Sitting back down, she continued to speak to me, which I guess was a bit awkward for the other people around, as we weren't supposed to break the silence or touch each other.

At one point, she asked: "Are you my soulmate?"

"I could be."

"What does it mean? Everyone is going to leave, and we're going to stay for another retreat – this is crazy."

I wasn't totally sure what she meant by this, and was a little confused, but I let her talk. I didn't want to say too much, and offend others in the vicinity, but I did want to be there for her and provide a little support if I could. She then wrapped her right arm under my left arm, and held my shoulder.

"Is this really happening?" she asked. "Are we really going to do this?" "What do you mean?" I replied, unsure of what she meant. She looked at me, took her arm away from mine and looked away, as if being shown something, saying to herself: "Ohhh I get it … I get it, I understand." Then, looking at me again, she added: "Everyone kept telling me about you. I get it – you're the healer." She looked me up and down, and said: "You're the plant."

I put my hand on her knee, and tried to calm her. "Are you okay?" She pushed me away, looking annoyed. "This always happens to me. This is always the way." Another guy, who was stood by the fire, tried to offer her support and give her a hug, but one of the light workers immediately came over to separate them, as we weren't supposed to talk to each other or physically touch during the ceremonies.

I thought about this quite a bit, because we had spoken for some time, and I had lightly rubbed her shoulder and back (which you're not allowed to do), to try and offer some support. Nobody had come over or said anything – most likely not having seen us – but this means that, for whatever reason, our interaction had been allowed by luck (does luck exist? Or are things always just exactly as they're meant to be?), the universe, the medicine or mother Ayahuasca, whatever you choose to call it. I realised that the universe is constantly trying to talk to us, and a lot of the time it's through an intermediary, be it another life form, our emotions, or a situation we're experiencing.

As I sat there thinking about what had just happened, it dawned on me that I had just got the answer to my intention: "Show me who I've become." I had become a healer. As I looked back and tried to understand how I could possibly be a healer, I saw moments where friends had sought me out for advice, or even just to have a conversation. They told me that I had a certain energy about me that made them feel good, something I had heard before on a number of occasions.

I understood in that moment that being a healer doesn't mean you have to be a doctor, a shaman, a therapist etc. Sometimes, it just means being present in somebody's moment of need, whatever that looks like: being a shoulder to cry on, just listening – providing a space where someone can think out loud; a warm cuddle; a friendly, unknown face decorated with a warm, caring smile as a stranger passes by on the street. Why? Well, why not? We all have the power to become healers, even if that means just being somewhere with somebody else, sharing the silence as they work their way through their thoughts.

Tuesday night

Tonight, I went in with the intention: "Merge me back with my soul at all costs." I had my first drink, and laid there in silence for what seemed like a lifetime. As always, after a while, we were called up for a second drink, and after returning to my mattress at some point, my entire reality changed. It was as subtle as drifting off to sleep, waking up in a dream, and never knowing how or when you arrived there. I found myself in a room in a completely different realm. It was a small, square shaped room, deep black in colour, and there was a voice that said: "There's something that you've forgotten here in this room. It's very important that you find it."

I began to search this room, which wasn't hard, because it was small and had nothing in it, which left nowhere to hide anything. I searched for what appeared to be quite some time, but found nothing. Every now and then, the voice would repeat: "You need to find it, it's very important." I searched and I searched, but still found nothing. At some point, I became distracted, and thoughts of my Auntie Pauline started streaming into my mind, accompanied by the sense that everything wasn't going to be okay.

I had recently booked my mum and auntie a holiday in Costa Rica for August 2022, as a sort of a small thank you and token of appreciation for all that they had done for us – my brothers, sisters, cousins and I – whilst we were growing up, and all that they still do now. As the date drew closer, Pauline and I spoke one day. She said that she had been suffering a persistent cough and tingling in her throat, and that she had an appointment booked with a doctor to get it checked. The next time we spoke was after the check-up, and she informed me that they had found cancerous cells in her throat, with another bout of tests scheduled to see if they could get some more in-depth results and discover exactly what the cancer was doing, and over how much of the body it had spread. Before she had gone for the second bout of tests, I had come to Rythmia on this retreat.

So as I lay there on my mattress, back in my body and no longer in the black room, I was filled with this sense of impending doom that seemed connected to my auntie. And then I was shown that she was going to die. I can't even begin to explain how this was shown to me; it was almost like a knowing … a downloaded foresight that I had been given from an external force that at the same time seemed to exist inside of me. I knew that what I was being shown was true.

I was devastated by learning this; I didn't want my Auntie Pauline to die.

I began to ask the force that was communicating with me, and showing me all of this, whether my auntie's life could be saved, but then the medicine started wearing off, so I immediately got up and took another drink from the shaman. Once I got back to my mattress, it was as if the journey picked up straight away from where I had left it. I asked: "Please don't take my Auntie Pauline."

"If you want to ask for the life of your auntie, you have to go to the bridge between life and death," said the voice that had spoken to me in the black room.

As soon as I heard it and digested the words, I seemed to appear right there: at the bridge between life and death. As soon as I saw it, a memory inside of me seemed to unlock. I knew this place; I had been there before, many times before, and as I looked over the bridge, I saw a room that I also recognised. It was a white room with random 3D shapes in it, a square, a circle and a rectangle, all white in colour and placed randomly within the room. Three clowns were also present there, and as soon as I saw them I realised that this is where I had been coming to party every time I smoked NN-DMT – I had been partying in the afterlife.

I became aware of an entity who was there guarding the bridge, and in particular her facial features. She had a mouse-like face, a long snout of a nose with a red bubble at the end of it; her skin was yellow, tanned in colour, and looked to be of the same material that teddy bears are made of, with random patches of red sewn into her skin and body … but she most definitely was

254

not a teddy bear, emitting a yellow aura that demonstrated the force and strength of her power.

For the entire duration of our communicative interaction, I was presented with only her right profile. She moved slowly and diagonally from the bottom left corner of my archs of view to the top right corner, keeping her right eye trained on me the whole time. We communicated telepathically, but she would not allow me to cross the bridge, which was strange because she had permitted me to many times before.

"Why won't you allow me to cross?" I asked.

"Because you've come with an intention, to ask for the life of your auntie to be spared." I began to beg and plead with her. "Please don't take her life!"

She said no, I continued to plead with her, and I could feel her getting annoyed with me – to the point that she said: "No, this is how it's meant to be. THIS IS HAPPENING!"

I felt fear inside of me, so asked instead: "Will my auntie at least get to enjoy the holiday I've booked for her?"

There were no words, but the feeling that the being emanated to me was: yes, she would. I was then shown what it would be like when she passed away, and how I would feel. It was as if I was being allowed to experience her future death, and to mourn her. I laid there, aware of the tunes that were being played in the ceremony, and some of them were the saddest expressions of music I had ever heard … or at least that's how I was interpretating them at the time. I felt I was no longer hearing the sad music, but that my soul, my very being, was drifting ever so tenderly and softly over the waves of it. I felt enveloped in sadness, such deep sadness, then something changed.

Suddenly, I felt this glimmer of hope infuse me, and I knew deep within myself that Pauline was so much more than just Pauline. It felt like ancient wisdom that had always been there, but which

I had forgotten. It had been awoken and, with that, I remembered that I too am so much more than Ricardo Chin. In that moment, with that thought, I once again found myself in the black room I had been in at the very start of the journey, and this long since known, but buried, knowledge resonated through my entire being like a shockwave of remembrance. I heard the voice one last time: "You had forgotten your true identity."

I had forgotten who I truly am, which is not Ricardo Chin the human being, but the eternal being I am, when not here in the game of life. I am me, the eternal being me, who happened to be in the human body of Ricardo Chin, having a human experience as Ricardo, and that the eternal being, the true essence embodying Pauline, would be just fine and go on long after leaving her body. With this realisation, the music changed, and all of a sudden it wasn't sad anymore – it was beautiful … a beautiful sadness. I was shown what was in store for Pauline, what came next, and although I can't put it into words, it was so beautiful, it felt like pure bliss – an absolute paradise.

Some day, Pauline the human would pass away, but her essence, the eternal being, would live on, and this made it so much easier to understand, accept and even feel happy for her.

Thursday night

The Colombians came in and led the ceremony for Yage night. Separated into two queues – one for men, and one for women – the yage was a thicker mix, which I found really hard to keep down. After lying down, it wasn't long before a lady in the room was full on feeling the effects of it, screaming so loudly and having such a tough journey that the shamans and light workers accompanied her outside, where they helped and supported her. This mix was so strong that I started feeling tingling all over my body. I then felt the medicine working through all the different parts of my body. My head moved from side to side, then my hands, followed by my entire body, which softly shook – or, more accurately, vibrated. I started making alien noises again – my tongue curled up in the roof of my mouth, and the humming started. My head moved too, in lots of different angles, almost as if to show me all of the different frequencies that could be reached vocally. None of this was done voluntarily, as if my body was being controlled by something else.

My hands lifted up, and my whole body vibrated at a speed I couldn't recreate even if I wanted to. My hands made a flapping noise that resembled the sound generated when a bird flaps its wings, and the noise emerging from my mouth was like a rapid breathing, with my mouth wide open. I saw what seemed to be waves of energy materialise from my mouth and, just as rapidly as it had started, it stopped, my hands dropping to my side. This happened again and again, accompanied by the alien noise coming from my mouth, which was more like a frequency resonating throughout the entire room (It's a noise/frequency that I've tried to recreate, but cannot, as I believe this was alien me/higher being me showing me some of what I can do).

I went out by the fire, and sat there for a while, laughing; understanding that I truly am an alien.

I laid on the concrete bench by the fire, and once everyone else had left the area, I said: "Show me what you can make me do," and all of my body began vibrating, my limbs involuntarily shooting out.

I was sat upright when the call rang out for anybody to come up who wanted a second cup of Ayahuasca. I found my body moving involuntarily, almost like someone who has Parkinson's disease. Ignoring it, when a second call went out, I asked: "Does this mean I'm supposed to have a second cup?" My hands shook and vibrated, and my head nodded rapidly, as if to say yes, so I asked: "Am I speaking with someone?" My hands shook again, and my head nodded, so I then asked: "Am I speaking to my higher being?" Once again, my hands shook and head nodded, and the feeling I had was: oh my God, life is so strange, I have a body, look at what I can do. It was as if my soul was marvelling at the fact that it had a body, and how alien it felt.

KARMA

Karma is probably singlehandedly the most pivotal individual in my human experience responsible for teaching me one of the most important lessons I would ever learn. Meeting her on my second Rythmia retreat, the first time I saw her I had only just arrived, walking towards reception with my friend Gerardo, as she walked past. She was this beautiful, mixed raced woman, her skin was golden and glowing, her hair was dark black, and it just seemed to flow – curly and full of volume, this was one of the most beautiful natural looks I had ever seen. She was wearing a green summer onesie type dress that just seemed to beckon my attention and, in that moment, as I watched her disappear into the spar and wellness building, I wondered if we would end up talking, or maybe even develop a friendship during the coming week.

During one of the mealtimes at Roots restaurant, our paths crossed and we both said hello. This is something you would see every day at Rythmia, with new people meeting each other and the community growing. We introduced ourselves with basic greetings, and asked each other what we did. She told me she was an actress, and I don't know why, but I didn't ask her what she had been in or what she was currently working on. It just didn't seem important at that moment, and in hindsight I'm glad I didn't, as it may have changed the natural growth of the relationship if I had known those things. As it was a mealtime, and we had both been on our way to select food and drinks when we bumped into each other, we said that we would undoubtedly see each other around throughout the course of the week, and that it had been nice to meet each other.

The next time I saw her was Monday evening at about 17:15hrs. I was walking towards the Moloka from my room, and saw her sat with a few others on the concrete bench in front of the ceremonial fire place. I went over and sat on the bench adjacent to her, addressed everyone there and asked if they were excited about what was about to happen … but mostly my attention was on her. Everyone responded yes, though some were nervous, which is absolutely understandable prior to launching a full frontal assault on your ego.

As I had been there before, I started telling them about one of my experiences from the previous year. I explained my death and rebirth journey, and how much it had changed my life. Karma seemed quite interested by my story, which obviously made me happy, as I could talk about medicine all day long – I loved it. When it was time for the ceremony to commence, the doors to the Moloka were opened, I wished her an amazing experience, and we made our entrance.

The next day, we saw each other a few times, discussing each other's journeys and what had bought us both to Rythmia. We were getting to know each other, and it felt nice. The evening came and, after entering the Moloka and selecting my spot for the night, I realised I had forgotten my shot cup, so left my water bottle and retreat journal on the mattress, and returned to my room to fetch it. When I got back to the Moloka, I saw Karma stretched out on the mattress beside mine, which made my heart smile. As I sat down on the mattress, she said: "Oohh, that was your water bottle and journal," and nodded her head in some sort of unspoken understanding – more at herself than at me, as if to say, in a weird way, that it made sense that unbeknownst to us, we had ended up choosing side by side mattresses.

During this night, I made a lot of weird noises that I have come to call alien talk, while Karma erupted into long, loud burps. As I came in and out of consciousness, I sometimes heard a chorus of burping coming from her mattress. I remember thinking, whilst listening to this, that she was so beautiful and her burping so cute.

It's crazy, when you attend something like this and completely surrender to the medicine, you can find yourself in completely vulnerable states in front of people you barely know – a room full of vulnerable people, all purging in many different ways. I think this is partly why it's so easy to really connect, and make true friendships there, because we pretty much lay everything bare, and get to see each other at our best and worst.

We reached a point where we were comfortable enough to make light-hearted jokes about her chorus of burping, and the very strange noises I made during ceremonies. Later in the week, I asked Karma if she would like to hang out in the spar facility, where they had a hot tub, cold plunge and steam room, to which she said yes. So, on the Thursday, the last day of medicine, prior to the ceremony, we hung out together a little in the hot tub. It was really nice, there were others there too, and we all spoke and shared our experiences and feelings –

conversations I still can't have today with some of the closest people in my life, purely because of a lack of open-mindedness. The time came, and we all went to our final ceremony. During the ceremony, there was a moment when I was in conversation with my higher self, asking: "Does Karma know that I like her?"

The answer was yes, so I asked: "If I kissed her, would she kiss me back?" and the answer was yes again. It was funny; I was sat outside by the fire, having a full-blown conversation with myself, which by now seemed absolutely normal.

The next day, we met, and Karma had a massage booked, so I walked with her to the spar.

When we got there, they said she had to get some paperwork from the clinic, which was good as it meant I got to walk with her a little longer. All the way to the clinic, she held my hand and I felt my heart smiling again. We talked the whole way, I told her that I had asked my higher self in ceremony if she knew that I liked her, and she smiled, as if to confirm that she did indeed know.

Saturday came, and that was her week at the retreat over. I really didn't want her to go, and think there was a little part of her that didn't want to leave either, but when the time came, I walked her to the transport. Before she got on the minibus, she gave me a massive hug and a lingering kiss on the lips, which was the cherry on top of this absolutely amazing week. Once she had left, I felt a little sad, and found myself asking whether I would see her again?

The next day, we texted back and forth. She was in the Marriott Hotel, and would shortly be leaving to head to Liberia Airport, and then onto America. Me and Gerardo were preparing to head into Tamarindo for a few days, before leaving Costa Rica. Once we arrived in Tamarindo, which is only about a 20 minute drive away from Rythmia, a group dinner had been organised for later that night, arranged via an Instagram group that had been started by some of the people who had been at the retreat that week, who were also going to be in the town.

We checked into our hotel and, as I was settling into my room, I got a phone call from Karma, saying she hadn't boarded her flight in Liberia. I immediately suggested that she come to Tamarindo, and that she could stay with me, as my room was big and had two double beds in it. Saying that she would get a taxi and join me, she arrived around an hour and a half later. I was so happy to see her, we put her luggage in my room, then made our way to dinner. More people turned up than we had originally expected, everyone shared their retreat stories, explaining how the experience had already impacted their lives, and a good time was had by all. When the dinner was over, we made our way back to the hotel. Once in my room, I wanted to ensure Karma didn't feel uncomfortable or threatened in any way, being alone with a guy she had only recently met. I made it clear that I would be using the bed closest to the window, and that she could have the other one. I wanted her to feel safe, and know that she had absolutely nothing to worry about from me. I took out my iPad, which had a medicine music playlist on it, and left it to play on the table.

We talked about everything, including the ceremonies, our lives and failed relationships. It was really nice to be in her presence. After showering separately, she sat on the side of her bed, combing her hair, whilst I laid on mine watching her – she was so beautiful. When I told her I had braided my sister's hair when I was younger, Karma looked quite surprised and told me that I should braid hers, jokingly calling me out to see if I was telling the truth.

I hadn't braided my sister's hair in many, many years, and Karma's hair was big, plentiful and a lot longer and curlier than Gina's hair had been. I wasn't sure how this was going to turn out, but being the ex-Royal Marine Commando that I am, I got up, put my money where my mouth was, and stood by the courage of my convictions. I sat on the side of my bed, with her sat on the floor in between my legs, trying to manage this mass of beautiful, natural hair. It wasn't easy, I had clearly bitten off more than I could chew, and halfway through, I could see that it wasn't going to be a very pretty looking braid – rather, it looked more like a dreadlock or a braid that had been left for many days and was now beginning to mat together.

I told Karma that she should prepare herself for the most horrendous looking thing she had ever seen in her life. She laughed as she videoed it, saying: "No, it's not!" in her strong American accent. When it was done, she got up and told me how much she liked it. I told her that she would have to take it out, or people would be looking at her like "who shot John and forgot to kill him?" Karma laughed, saying she didn't care, and that she was leaving it in.

As we both stood up, we cuddled to say goodnight. Standing there in our embrace, feeling each other's bodies pressed against each other, with me only wearing a set of pink boxer shorts, and her nothing but a yellow T-shirt and underwear, it seemed to come very naturally in that moment for us to kiss each other. Locked in this intense embrace and kiss, we directed each other back to my bed. I laid her down, and continued kissing her, but was a touch conflicted, as we had just had a week of intense ceremonies and I was a little concerned that we were moving too fast. I think she felt the same way, because just as naturally as the kiss began, it subsided in the same fashion.

We laid there under the sheets, cuddling each other until we fell asleep. I hadn't cuddled a woman like this in a very long time, and had never had a woman cuddle me the entire night. I woke up from time to time, feeling the warmth of her body wrapped around mine, and cherished the loving embrace. I woke up in the morning with Karma lying in my right arm, and to the sensation of her hands wandering over my body. She moved over my chest, then down my stomach, and once her hands were as low as they needed to be, she took a hold of me. By this time, I was very aroused – I mean, what an amazing thing to wake up to. As she began to softly stroke my morning glory with a firm grip, I became increasingly aroused. Keeping my eyes closed, and Karma tightly embraced in my arm, I began to ever so slightly thrust myself back and forth into her hand. Eventually, I rolled over on top of her, threw the sheets off of us and began to take her yellow T-shirt off. I saw her beautiful, natural small cup breast, her nipples were dark brown and thick, our faces drew together and we kissed, which is something I don't normally like to do before at least brushing my teeth … though with her it all felt so natural, as if we were hiding nothing from each other – not even our morning breath.

I began kissing her neck as I moved my way down towards her beautifully pert breasts, which I took in my mouth one by one. I loved feeling her nipples erect in my mouth, and after giving her breasts my complete, undivided attention, I continued to make my way down her body, past her stomach, kissing every inch along the way until I arrived in between her legs. I kissed, licked and sucked her inner thighs before pulling her knickers down. Once they were gone, I was face to face with one of the most beautiful things I have ever seen: a wealth of bushy black hair just above her vagina. At that moment, she felt the need to tell me she hadn't groomed herself in a while, because she had actively not been looking to meet anybody; but she really didn't need to explain this to me, because whilst staring at her as naked as could be, everything I saw was absolutely perfect – she was a beautiful, divine specimen of a human being.

As I began to kiss her there, she was already wet, which made me happy. This was clearly something she wanted, so I kissed, I licked and I sucked, and eventually she came. I don't think there's anything more intimate than tasting the woman you're making love to. As I made my way up the bed and began to kiss her, she slid her hand down and put me inside of her. It was intense, I hadn't been with a woman in many months, and was surprised I had even managed to last this long. She had this way of making eye contact and not letting go, which at times felt a little intimidating, but during this moment it intensified everything so much more, especially having recently been in Ayahuasca ceremonies. It was as if there was a connection that had me locked into her eyes, whilst also watching her facial expressions as her head jerked up and down the bed.

When we finished, we laid there smiling and cuddling each other, before getting up and ready for breakfast. Over the next couple of days, we made love many times and got to know more about each other. Karma could sing, play the violin, and was truly a gifted individual. God knows what she saw in me. I had nothing, and worked in Iraq for eight months of the year. During our time at the hotel, she told me that she was going home to New York to meet with a guy on a date that had been arranged prior to the retreat. I liked this, as we were being honest with each other, and I shared with her that I would be heading to Spain to see a lady I had been speaking to.

When the day came to leave, just before we checked out, I was sat on the bed as she came over and straddled me, saying: "If by some crazy happening I'm pregnant, I think I'd have it."

This didn't seem the slightest bit strange, or out of context, to me. I think we were both so caught up in the moment, and swept away by what we were feeling, that it felt like: why wouldn't we make a baby? My response was that I would want her to have it, I started picturing it in my head, and it became something I actually hoped for.

A while later, she left in a taxi to Liberia, and I left a few hours later on a plane from Tamarindo. We messaged and voice noted each other the whole way back during our separate journeys.

Karma said she was thinking about coming to Colombia instead of going back home, but I knew I would have to fly to Spain in a couple of days' time, and felt bad at the prospect of her flying all the way to Medellin, knowing it would only be for a couple days. To this day, not having her come to Medellin is one of the biggest regrets of my entire life!

When my leave was over, and I got back to work around ten days after we had said our goodbyes in Costa Rica, we were still very much attracted to each other. We spoke every day she was still on hiatus and I was back in Iraq, we video called each other for hours at a time every day, and when we weren't video calling, we were texting.

I came across a card game whilst watching a Ted Talk by Kalina Silverman, whose ethos was: "What if we skip the small talk, and instead talk about what really matters?" I suggested that Karma and I play this game, she downloaded it, and the idea was that one of us would pick a question, screenshot it and send it to the other person, who would answer it; then the other person would pick a question, and so on. This went on for the entire eight weeks I was in Iraq. Many of the questions were very profound and intimately personal, affording insight into someone's deepest thoughts, beliefs and secrets, and making it a very good way to get to know someone.

During this particular rotation, it was to be my 40th birthday, and on the day itself Karma sent a song she had sang for me over a voice note. Her voice was absolutely amazing, I was falling in love with this woman, and every time we spoke or I saw her name flashing up on my phone, my heart got excited. One day, as we were about to end a video call, she said: "Listen, there might be sometimes when I'm going to feel the need to tell you I love you, but please don't feel that you have to say anything back to me." Unbeknown to her, by this time I was already full blown in love with her, so my response was: "I love you too." I told her that I had been feeling it for some time now, which she seemed to accept quite well. I couldn't believe it, it felt like everything was coming together; that 'me', this 'nobody', had managed to meet this beautiful woman who had fallen in love with me. I told a few people at work about her, and laughter featured among their responses. I was told it wouldn't work, wouldn't last very long, and some asked what she saw in me. This was all expected banta from the sort of environment I worked in, and the individuals I worked with, but even though they meant it jokingly, I began to think about what had been said.

What was I actually bringing to the table? I worked in Iraq for eight months of the year, I probably earned a fraction of what she did, she was creative and extremely talented, so in truth, what could I possibly offer this woman? Apart from maybe a few quick-witted responses, and the making of a good cup of English tea, I came up with nothing. But I ignored my doubts, and thought love would rule the day, because I'm cheesy like that. We began to make plans for me to go to New York and visit Karma. She said she would be working through the days, but that we would have time in the evenings and weekends to do stuff, so I booked my ticket for a ten day stay in New York. She messaged me through the days, saying she had planned and booked things for us to do, including going to a Kendrick Lamar concert and a classical concert, knowing I had a fondness for classical and opera music. I felt so loved by her, and excited by the fact that she had been thinking about our time together and planning what we could do.

Her birthday was coming up just before I was due to go on leave, so I asked for her address, which wasn't the way I wanted to get it, preferring more of a surprise, but it was the only way. I ordered a bouquet of red roses and a big teddy bear with some helium balloons that said 'I Love You' on them. Looking back now, maybe this was a bit intense, though when her birthday came round, I got a video call from Karma saying that she had just had a delivery of roses from me and that she loved them. She was hosting some friends at her house for the evening, so I wished her a happy birthday and left her to enjoy her night.

As the end of my rotation drew close, I felt that there was something changing between us. I couldn't tell what it was, but I was aware of it. Karma had told me a couple weeks earlier that Nathan, a new cast member for her show, had just arrived, and that she would be showing him around. I believe she wanted to make him feel welcome, so I guess she introduced him to people, showed him around the city a little, and that they rehearsed their lines together. One morning, whilst on a video call, she told me that Nathan was heading over to cook an omelette for her, in appreciation for all of her hospitality and kindness.

When speaking a few days later, she told me that there was a man in her vicinity who she had flirted lightly with whilst out one evening. I admired her honesty, and up to now we had been completely frank and open with each other about all aspects of our lives. When Karma asked how it made me feel, my response was that flirting was something people in relationships could do with outside parties. I mean, it's nice to be with someone, but also to still feel attractive and desired, and that as long as the flirting is harmless, as in there's no heartfelt desire for it to actually go somewhere, my stance was that it was fine.

Sometime later, she mentioned the guy's name who she had been out with, and with whom she had flirted, and the penny dropped.

It was Nathan, and I started to realise that they must have been spending a fair bit of time together. Given they worked together, I could understand that they would see a lot of each other, but something felt different now that I knew who she had flirted with, and alarm bells were going off. I asked Karma whether she wanted to explore her feelings for this guy, because if she did, there was no point me going to visit her in New York; but that I would understand, as we weren't in a relationship.

I never saw myself as a jealous person, but if I feel that someone has given me a reason to feel jealous, then I do experience that feeling, and it's definitely not one that I enjoy. Karma told me no, it wasn't something she wanted to explore, and that she definitely still wanted me to visit her in New York. I obviously still really wanted to go and see her too, so we stuck to the plan.

The end of my rotation came, and I made the journey from Iraq to Medellin. I had a day to gather my clothes, pack my bags and have a full body wax, which I always got on arrival back in Colombia. I don't like myself when I look all hairy, and by now, from the constant steroid use, I could really grow some hair.

The next day, I set off for New York, and when I arrived, Karma met me at the baggage belt. It was so nice to finally see her again. Her skin was glowing, her hair was in a bun, and she was wearing a beautiful beige summer dress. We cuddled, and all I remember thinking was that she was so beautiful, and that her skin smelt amazing and felt so soft.

We made our way to her car, but as Karma began to reverse, there was a loud noise and the vehicle came to an abrupt stop. She had hit something, and when we got out to see what had happened, we saw that she had reversed into one of the barriers. I looked at her as we stood there observing the small area of superficial damage to the vehicle, and felt that she was a little nervous, so I gave her a hug and asked if she was okay. My intention was to try and show her that she didn't have to be nervous, and that we could just be in that moment of hugging for a little while, then reset ourselves before setting off again.

We made it back to her house without any further incidents, and once I had put my bags down in her bedroom, I joined her in her walk-in closet, from where she was talking to me. I cuddled her from behind, slid my hands slowly up her summer dress, and took hold of her breasts.

Karma exhaled deeply with an accompanying moan, as if to signal her approval of what was happening, then turned around and kissed me before we walked over to her bed. I laid her down, and we continued to kiss. I kissed her neck, I licked and sucked her breasts, lifted up her summer dress and went down on her, just as I had done many times during our time in Costa Rica; but something was different … it felt like no matter what I did, it did nothing for her.

Eventually, she held my head and pulled me up, we began to kiss again whilst I de-robed her, then once we were both naked, I got on top of her, she put me inside of her and we began to have sex.

It felt as if something was missing, and our lovemaking wasn't how it had been before. When we had finished, I asked Karma why she hadn't been able to climax. This was a question in part derived from insecurity … from a feeling that maybe I wasn't the person she wanted to be there, doing that with her. But I also asked the question because sex is supposed to be pleasurable, and enjoyed by both parties involved, and if I'm doing something wrong or there's something I could be doing that I'm not, I want to know so that I can learn, hopefully fix it, and for both of us to enjoy the act of being together.

"Maybe there's a bit too much going on inside my head," Karma told me.

271

"Is that because there might be a part of you that would rather explore whatever there may be between you and this other guy?" I asked in response.

"No, I've consciously chosen to be with you, and I think there's something in that – the act of choosing you over anyone else."

I understood what she was saying, but a part of me also thinks you can't choose who you have feelings for. It's something that happens naturally, without any coercion or dedicated act of choice, though I silenced my ever growing insecurities and fears about what future, if any, we had ahead of us.

I asked Karma to close her eyes, unpacked some gifts that I had bought for her birthday, and rested them in front of her. When I told her to open her eyes, she looked surprised and happy. Opening the final gift, she saw that it was a leather journal and said: "No way! Just give me one minute." She walked over to her bookshelf, and pulled from it a gift that she had got for me which, very much to my surprise, was a leather journal. At that point I had never journaled before, but I would soon start. This journal would quickly become my best friend, in joint first place with my Bose speaker, which I take everywhere.

Before going to bed that night, Karma invited me to go to the set she was working on, where she introduced me to her colleagues and friends. I was so happy, as it felt like this amazing person had invited me into her life, and wasn't scared to make it public knowledge.

Over the next few days, the whole experience soured very quickly. The next night, when we were lying in bed, I rolled on top of Karma, trying to create a moment, and told her to touch herself, which was in alignment with everything we'd ever spoke about when it came to sex. Her reply was: "I don't want to," but it wasn't just that she didn't want to carry out this action … it felt a lot more personal, like she no longer wanted to be intimate with me. I rolled off of her, and laid on the bed beside her, my confidence completely shattered.

"Is this what you really want?" I asked. "Me being here? Us trying to pursue what we felt in Costa Rica? It just doesn't feel as if this is something you really want anymore, and not just sexually, in this moment. It seems as if, whatever you felt for me during our time in Costa Rica, and during my eight weeks' rotation, when we spoke every day and at all hours of the night, is no longer present."

"I don't want you to leave," Karma told me. "Like I said before, maybe I'm a little bit too much in my own head."

Later in the night, she tried to initiate sex with me, but the damage was already done. I couldn't get an erection for love nor money, and not being able to get hard made everything ten times worse. She looked at me with my limp, lifeless penis in her hand, and said: "Maybe you're right – I don't want this."

For me, that was it – talk about kicking a man when he's down.

"I think I'm going to leave," I said.

"I'm really sorry," said Karma. "I'm so sorry."

"It's okay," I told her. "You're allowed not to want this. Is it okay to stay the night and leave in the morning?"

"Yes, of course. But you don't have to leave."

As far as I was concerned, I had to leave. I was in a foreign country, in a city where I knew absolutely nobody aside from Karma, and felt more alone than I had in a very long time. The following morning, she asked me to please not leave until she got back from work, to which I agreed. This particular day, she had booked a chakra realignment massage for us both, and the plan was that I would go with a very close friend of hers, since work commitments had prevented Karma from being able to make it. The massage was truly magnificent, although I couldn't fully enjoy it because I was busy beating myself up about the situation I now found myself in.

Once the massage was complete and I had left the premises, I wandered the streets for a while, thinking. I was completely alone in this massive city, and had absolutely no idea where I was.

After a while, I came across a shopping mall that had a cinema in it, and as I had plenty of time to kill before Karma got home and I would leave, I decided to watch Thor: Love and Thunder. Once the film was finished and I left the cinema, she called me, saying that she really didn't want me to leave, and that she would like it if I came to set, where she was working that day.

I was quite reluctant to agree to this, as I didn't see the point in meeting her friends and work colleagues if she wasn't really interested in me anymore. When she asked again, I decided to go, and a taxi took me to the set. When I arrived, it was a sight to see. I hadn't seen anything like it before – the area where they were working was cordoned off, and police provided an outer perimeter, where spectators and fans stood watching.

A member of staff soon came, ushering me through the cordon to the director's tent. Karma came over during a cut, and cuddled and kissed me, ensuring I was okay and taken care of before returning to the shoot. Once they had wrapped for the night, she briefly introduced me to some of her colleagues and cast members – even Nathan, the guy she had flirted with, who I expected to truly dislike, but who was actually a cool guy. One of the cast members she introduced me to said that he had heard so many good things about me that I had better start being amazing now, so no pressure! He was quite funny, and I instantly liked him – I liked them all.

A couple of days later, we were in bed and I was on top of Karma, kissing her, when she asked if I could feel her energy. I didn't fully get what she meant, yet knew something was off. I had no intention of putting myself inside of her, which she actually ended up doing, so once it was all done – and again, it was like it had done absolutely nothing for her, which by now was a serious issue inside my head – I asked her what she had meant by asking me if I could feel her energy? "I hadn't wanted to have sex," said Karma.

This was like a knife in my heart. I felt completely disgusted with myself. I had just had sex with someone who didn't want to have sex with me. I had never in my life wanted to put somebody through such an ordeal.

"Why did you put me inside you?" I wanted to know. "I wasn't pushing for that."

"You were on top of me, kissing me, so I thought that was where you were trying to take it. It just felt easier to go through with it than to reject you."

At that point I knew had to leave, as I felt horrible about myself. I told her that I had never, ever wanted anyone to be with me out of a sense of obligation, or it being the easier option to go through with it. I packed my bag whilst tears fell from Karma's eyes. She wasn't deliberately trying to hurt me, but you can't help what you feel and, for whatever reason, her emotions towards me had drastically changed. Despite this, we cuddled and said goodbye. I was still very much in love with her, and wanted to end things on a good note.

I booked a hotel for two days to try and figure out what my next plan of action was. I contemplated leaving New York early, and heading back to Colombia, but thought better of it, and instead booked a flight to Costa Rica for that weekend to surprise my mum and auntie, who were there on the holiday I had booked for them. The next day, Karma messaged me, saying that she still had the tickets for the classical concert she had planned, and that I should accompany her. I told her that I would meet her there, and when I arrived, I saw that she had organised a really nice spot with foldaway chairs, a blanket, and had gotten some small bites to eat.

We sat and talked about the music and other random chit chat – pretty much everything, apart from the elephant in the room (what was happening between us). I was very careful not to be touchy-feely with Karma, because she had already demonstrated in the harshest way possible that it wasn't what she wanted from me. When the concert was over, we put our chairs away and left. I sat in her car with her, and ordered an Uber back to the hotel. Karma offered to take me herself, but I didn't see the point in it, so we sat in her car talking.

She apologised for the way things had turned out between us, and I told her it was okay; that you can't force yourself to feel a certain way for somebody. We sat staring into each other's eyes, Karma saying she wanted to tell me she loved me. I told her that I loved her too, and that I only wished her the very best in life. My taxi came, I left, then on the way to the hotel, she called, asking if we could watch a film together. I said yes, despite being frustrated by the constant back and forth nature of our relationship. I couldn't truly understand what was happening, it was all very confusing, and all I knew for sure was that I was in love with her, and that I would keep taking any chances she gave me to be with her, even if it was against my better judgment.

She came over, we watched a movie, then cuddled the entire night with our clothes on under the sheets, as I didn't want her to feel that I was trying to initiate anything. Spending the night and morning together like that was really nice, and a glimpse of how it was back in Costa Rica after Rythmia.

After speaking for a while, we decided that I would go back to her place, and stay there until I left for Costa Rica. During this time, Karma told me that she wished I wasn't going. I explained that I would return once the weekend was over if she felt it was something she wanted; but not to answer the question now, to think about it and tell me when she was sure. We spoke again once I was in Costa Rica, Karma confirming that she was open to me coming back, so I booked the tickets, despite quickly running out of money. Even though I was nearly broke, I just wanted to spend time with her, and see whether we could get back on track to having something special.

When I arrived, it was late, so I got into bed with Karma, we cuddled and went to sleep. The next morning was probably the best that we had together whilst I was in New York. We got up, did breath work that led into a meditation, and I was on a high. I asked if she would come to the gym I had been going to, so that we could train together. I thought it would be fun, something that could bring us closer together, but as it turned out, I couldn't have been more wrong.

We got to the gym, and started doing squats at the squat rack. When it was Karma's turn, I tried to correct her form slightly, but looking back on this now, I realise it wasn't my place to do that – I mean, who am I? I'm not a qualified personal trainer, or anyone of significance in the gym world to be giving anyone advice. When she had finished her squats, she went and sat on a CrossFit box, and looked off.

"What's wrong?" I asked.

"I'm feeling anger," said Karma, her expression mirroring her words.

"Why?"

"Can we not make this about you?"

I tried, but this felt very personal, ruining what had been a decent vibe since I returned to New York.

"Do you want to leave?" I asked.

"We're here now, so we might as well finish."

It didn't feel like a good situation to be in, and I figured it would be better to let her train by herself, but that didn't go down well either.

"Are you just going to leave me to train by myself now?" Karma asked me.

The truth is, I have never been good in situations like this. I hate confrontations and arguments, both of which I take personally, and it felt as if nothing I said or did was right. I felt awkward as we continued the session in near silence, and couldn't believe this was how things were unravelling, so soon after arriving in New York for the second time.

A couple more exercises later, we left, and whilst walking back to her place, Karma began to tell me quite angrily: "I don't understand why you have to make everything about you! Believe it or not, people sometimes go through things that are unrelated to you, so stop making it about you!"

"How would you have felt if I had gotten angry and the roles had been reversed?" I asked.

I wanted to say more, but she cut me short, yelling: "Why do you always have to turn things around like that?"

I looked at Karma, whose expression was saturated with anger and irritation. It broke my heart to see that someone I loved so much could be talking to me and treating me like this.

As I opened my mouth to try and reply to her, my voice cracked. I couldn't complete my sentence, my words were broken, I felt overwhelmed by emotion, and tears started to fall from my eyes. I felt so weak and embarrassed, I quickly wiped my eyes and tried speaking again, but the words still wouldn't come and the tears kept falling. I couldn't believe it, and felt so silly. I was this 102kg ex-Marine, big gym goer, and was stood there crying, for the first time since I was sixteen years old, the last time my mum slapped me.

I decided it would be best to just keep quiet, to stop me from further embarrassing myself. I think Karma saw that I was having a difficult moment, so said nothing as we continued the walk back in mutual silence, broken every now and then by my pathetic sniffing and sharp, shallow breaths. When we got back to her place, we entered via the back, and she led us to sit in the gazebo type structure in her garden.

She sat there, staring at me whilst I tried to compose myself – unfortunately to no avail. I had my forehead propped in my right hand, covering my eyes, which were still streaming tears. I didn't want her to see me like this – I never wanted anyone to see me like this – and I certainly didn't want to see myself like this, but I had absolutely no control over the situation. Once I had managed to dial the tears and sniffles back a little, I began to talk, although every now and then, I was interrupted by my cracking voice.

I told her that I had suggested we go to the gym together, thinking it would be fun and that we would have a laugh training together, but instead she had gotten angry. I said it felt that her anger was very much directed at me, and then on the walk back, that I had been verbally attacked, and that I felt as if I couldn't say or do anything right for her.

Karma came and sat next to me, put her arm around me, resting her hands on my shoulders, and asked if it was alright for her to hold me like that. She then repeated back to me her interpretation of what she had heard me say. She was a very active listener, and had understood it all. She also had tears falling from her eyes at this point, and it seemed to me that these were now the moments when we were able to connect most, which was quite sad, because it wasn't how I had envisioned things going. We spent some time in the gazebo, talking things out and dialling back the intensity of everything.

We spent the rest of the day in a park amongst nature, and though things were still a little awkward, they were much better than they had been. We were expecting a call from a friend of hers, Heather, who facilitated MDMA guided sessions, and who she had already introduced me to. The call was for us to get acquainted with each other, so that she could see what sort of energy I had, get a little feel for my history and what it was I hoped to get out of the experience. Eventually, we had the call, which I thought went well. Heather asked if she could sit with it for an hour, then let me know if the energy felt right for her to proceed. The hour passed and she called back, saying she was happy to go ahead with it, and that there would be another facilitator present at the session called Zoe. I was really happy, and while it was something I hadn't expected, it was definitely what I needed in that moment.

The session was set for eleven o'clock the following day. Karma took me to Heather's house, stayed for the introduction and intention setting part of the session, then left and came back when it was over. It was one of the most powerful truth revealing experiences I've ever had, and I'll never be able to thank Heather and Zoe enough for what they brought to the session. The rest of my time in New York had a few ups and downs, but in the main, things were good.

We had been invited to two gatherings with her cast members, held in their homes on consecutive days.

Saturday's gathering was really nice. The home of her cast mate was phenomenal, about an hour's drive outside of the city, surrounded by beautiful countryside, with greenery and trees everywhere. Everyone was so welcoming to me, they were an amazing group of people, and Karma came and cuddled me from time to time, which felt nice. I loved feeling affection from her, which made it feel like we might still have a future together.

We stayed there all day, leaving at night to make the drive back to hers. We had sex together, and while it was good, I couldn't make her climax; but it felt like she was present, and that she actually wanted to be intimate with me.

On the Sunday, we went to another cast member's gathering. Again, it was an amazing home about an hour's drive away from the city, but this day was very different from the previous one. Karma barely spent any time with me, and with a few of us adding some legal cannabis squeezes to our drinks, it didn't take long for me to get high. Sat on my chair alone, I began to feel really awkward and self-conscious, because everyone else was talking to each other in various groups, in different parts of the room. I thought that Karma might see me alone, and come over to spend some time with me, but she saw me and left me to it.

I felt silly, like a third wheel that nobody needed, especially Karma. I sat in the kitchen, watching a cartoon that was on the TV in the distance, in the living room, trying to pretend that I was so interested in it that no one would see how awkward I was. I felt like a loser, but thankfully the cast member whose house it was came and sat next to me to have a chat. I was so grateful to him for coming over and giving me some of his time, and will never forget it. It was such a small gesture, but it meant so much to me in that moment. An hour or so later, people started leaving, so we too said our goodbyes and headed back. My flight was the next day, and I was high and tired.

When we got back to Karma's place, we spoke for a little while, and I ended up mentioning how I felt, being left alone. She said that she was sorry she hadn't thought about it or realised, and that she was truly sorry. I struggle with this a lot, because as far as I'm concerned, if you really care about someone, it's not something you have to think about – it just comes naturally, which led me to believe she didn't really care for me at all.

A. Nobody

I used to think that if you really wanted someone, you fought for them. You fought for it to work, but after Heartbreak and Karma, I realised that you should never have to fight for someone to love you, or to make someone want to be with you. Relationships that are meant to be will always just be.

MDMA

Karma and I arrived at Heather's home, a beautiful house in suburban New York. When she and Zoe opened the door to us, they made their introductions and welcomed us into the house.

After explaining that she had only recently bought the house, which accounted for the absence of furniture, Heather showed us the property's three different floors and her two beautiful dogs.

She showed us to the room where the guided session would be conducted. Small, with a big window in it that let in loads of sunshine from what was a beautiful sunny day, there was a mattress on the floor with a pillow. There was a vision board propped up against the wall underneath the window, candles and incense. Zoe explained that she had cleansed the room with sage, which I absolutely loved the smell of by now. I felt like it was the perfect setting to have an amazing experience, even though I had only ever seen MDMA as a recreational party drug. I remained open to it, as I had read articles about it, where it was explained that trials had been, and were being conducted on, people suffering from PTSD and depression, with some very positive results.

The four of us sat and spoke for a while about the medicine, and what I wanted to get from the experience. Heather explained that she had a speaker for music, but that I could instead use the headphones she had told me to bring along. I asked if I could use my own playlist, and she was fine with that. At that point, she said she would like to set her intentions for me, before Zoe and Karma doing likewise. Their intentions for me were so loving, caring and warm, I felt truly cared for. When it was my turn, my intention was very simple: I asked for a little help, saying that I felt a bit lost at the moment, and please could the medicine give me some guidance as to what I was supposed to be doing with my life.

At that point, Karma gave me a hug and left. Heather explained that I was to sit with my intentions for a little while, and that when I was ready, I was to light the candle, take the tablet, and that she and Zoe would join me in the room shortly. So, when I was ready, that's exactly what I did. I then put my headphones on, and played my favourite playlist, which has opera, classical and an assortment of very sad, heartfelt songs that I've accumulated over the years and always love listening to.

I laid back on the mattress, rested my head on the pillow and put the blindfolds on (a necessity if wishing not to be influenced by outside stimuli, and for whatever arises; to come from within). I laid there for a while, then felt them enter the room. I couldn't really hear them, but could feel the vibration of them walking. A strange thought came over me: I didn't actually know these two ladies, yet there I was blindfolded whilst they were creeping around the room. I pictured them standing above me with massive kitchen knives clasped in their hands, waiting to rain down a savage attack on me.

Luckily by now, I knew a little about the ego and how it tries to manifest when it thinks it's about to get dissolved; so knew that they weren't actually creeping around the room or about to attack me, and that it was just a feeling that had manifested in me. Having now done some medicine, I knew some of the questions to ask when moments like this arose … so I asked myself: 'what is it that I'm feeling?' What came back was vulnerability and distrust – I had only just met them, and was laid there blindfolded and completely vulnerable.

In ceremony, the shaman always said to ask yourself when you had first felt a certain feeling, or feelings, so I asked myself this question and, at that moment, it felt that it had been during my time with Heartbreak. I felt Heather take my hands, which I had placed on my chest, and move them both to the sides, gently lifting my headphones from one ear to say: "Let's keep your heart and chakras open, and just surrender to the medicine." As my sense of distrust subsided, I found myself becoming overwhelmed by sadness – a deep, heartfelt sadness that it seemed there was no escape from.

As I laid there in the sadness and the melancholy songs rolled on through, I felt my left arm begin to tremor, with my finger rapidly tapping the mattress, before my right arm began to shake, followed by my stomach, then my entire body. As I lay there shuddering, my hands involuntarily lifted up from my side, softly placing themselves palm side down over my heart. Still trembling, my hands began to repeatedly shoot out a few inches away from me, as if something was being released from my chest. My feelings explained to me that this was my heart crying, and that it was the only way that it could purge the sadness from my body, as I had never allowed myself to cry.

At this point, I felt Heather stroke my arm softly, and pull the left headphone away from my ear to ask if there was anything I wanted her to write. I said no, it was okay, she softly placed the headphone back on my ear, and I returned again to the enveloping sadness. At some point, I felt my higher-self arrive, and he sat there in the sadness with me for a little while, before nodding his head, as if to egg me on, saying: "Go on, ask me the question you want to ask." "Why does the world have to be so sad?" I asked.

"It has to be sad, so that we can experience the beauty in it."

"Why do we have to hurt each other so badly in the ways we do?" I asked next.

"We need to hurt each other so that we can create and experience the sadness." He then asked: "Do you want to finish the experience early?"

He meant this life, this human experience, that I was currently in, and this was the third opportunity I had been offered to not exist here anymore.

"No," I replied. "I'll see it out." In that moment, I realised it was also the third time that I had wilfully chosen to stay, and that there was something in that.

Lying there in the realm of emotions, conversing with my higher self, I realised that the sadness I was feeling actually had a beauty to it. I could feel this beautiful sadness, which had visited me during my first mushroom experience, and then again whilst on Ayahuasca, mourning the future death of my auntie.

I felt Heather stroke my arm, and lift the headphones again. This time, she said: "Please will you drink some water," so I sat up and drank some of the water I had brought with me. She asked again if there was anything I would like her to write, and I asked whether it would be alright if I wrote something down. She gave me the pad, and I jotted down the questions I had asked my higher self, along with the answers he had given me. Zoe touched my arm, and as I turned around and looked at her, she seemed like she wanted to cry for me, saying: "You know you can ask for help, from us, your guides … from anyone, from anywhere, that feels safe to you. It's okay to ask for help."

I saw that Zoe and Heather could both feel the weight of everything that I was experiencing in that moment. They were clearly two very empathic, caring human beings who made me feel safe and cared for, even though I wasn't sharing exactly what was going on with them. I said thank you, then handed the notepad back to Heather and got straight back to it. With the blindfolds and playlist back on, I was fully submerged in the beautiful sadness. As time passed, I floated on the music and trembled.

I felt Zoe stroke my arm, and lift a headphone to say that she was receiving a message from my body, which was screaming out: "I'm not a machine!" I said: "Okay, thank you," and understood that she was offering me a moment to vent, share … maybe even just cry a little, or to express whatever I was feeling, but I didn't know how to do any of those things in that moment. She placed the headphone back on my ear, and I went back to the journey.

I hadn't had many visuals up until now, on what had hitherto been an emotions-based experience, but then I was shown a vision of me walking towards a table in what appeared to be a café with another person. In the vision, as we both sat down, my higher self said: "This is what you want to do – you want to talk to people about the sadness," so I sat up, raised the blindfold up to my forehead, and asked Heather for the notepad and pen.

I sat there for a little while, notepad in my lap, pen shaking in my hand, when I suddenly had waves of strong emotions wash over me that seemed to be carrying a sense of unspoken feelings that had existed in me for many years. I began to write down what was coming to me in these waves: 'I've been so unhappy and sad for so long, it's become the norm to me. I'm tired'. The waves continued to come, so I carried on writing: 'I'm so annoyed with myself for not being able to show myself love … I want to be in a job where I get to talk to people about the sadness … how dare I love myself when I have caused other people pain and sadness … I've been so sad for so long! … why would someone else love me when I can't even love myself? … other men have so much more to offer than me … look at me – I have nothing, I'm a nobody, so why would anybody love me?'

With this, came the revelation that I had absolutely no self-love. The penny had finally dropped, and I finally understood what was meant when people say: "Love starts at home. If you don't love yourself, nobody else is going to love you." I had never understood this before, and it had taken this MDMA journey for it to become clear to me.

I gave Heather the notepad and pen, put the blindfolds and headphones back on and laid down, appreciating the profound emotional depth of music on my playlist, and thinking about everything that I had just been shown. At that point, I had a vision from my higher self, stood in a field, waiting in line at the bottom of a gangway that led to a space ship. Smiling, he shouted to me with a thumbs up: "Are we good? Is everything gonna be okay?"

"Yes, thank you, man," I shouted back at him, giving him a thumbs-up. "Thank you, everything's gonna be okay. I'm good." With that, he boarded the spaceship, which then left. With his departure, I felt and understood that the journey was over, an understanding that I relayed to Heather and Zoe.

WHAT I LEARNED FROM MY MDMA SESSION

From the MDMA session, I learnt more about self-love than I had ever understood. The adage, love starts with yourself, which I had heard many people say over the years in real life, and in many of the chick flicks and other movies I used to watch, finally made sense. The phrase alone sounds very wise, but in all the years I had heard it said, I had never heard anyone explain why no one would love you if you didn't love yourself. When I think back on it now, I had never had this conversation with myself, I had never asked myself whether I loved myself, and maybe if I had, I would have realised many years ago that self-love was something I was lacking, and could have started working on a lot earlier.

I think the reason I had never had this conversation with myself was that I hadn't been mature enough, or even openminded enough, to understand the need to love one's self. I thought love was something that was given to you from other people, like familial love, romantic love and friendship love. During my session, it had all become clear, and I could see and understand that without self-love, I could have never shown myself any love, nor could I have ever shown myself any respect.

I realised that women are very empathic, and that they could sense it, whether it be at the conscious or subconscious level, so in some cases they may not even have been aware that they'd picked up on it. Sometimes, lack of self-love is demonstrated in the smallest of things.

One example is if I had just started to say something, and then the woman I was with happened to speak at the same time, I would stop and say: "You first."

"No, you go," she would say in response.

"No, please – you go first."

If occurring once or twice in a conversation, this might be considered normal practice; but when it happens time and time again, I might as well say: "No, please, you go first, because what you have to say is way more important than anything I could ever have to say."

Another example is if I was busy, and a love interest said that she needed something, I immediately dropped everything I was doing, which she hadn't even asked me to do, to try to accommodate her needs. I did these things thinking that it would demonstrate how much love I had for them, and how important they were to me, but it was never perceived like that. To the contrary, it's perceived as though you have no value for yourself, and what woman who truly values herself is going to want to be with a man who doesn't value himself? And even if she did, it wouldn't say much about the woman either, would it?

I could see that this is what I had been doing. I had been looking for my self-worth in the women I met. The unspoken feeling I had was: if I can just get this beautiful woman I've chosen to love me back, then maybe I'm not such an ugly, unlovable, wretched individual after all … but they never did, at least not in the way that I needed them to. And as for the few women I had come across who had loved me, and shown a deep sense of care and affection for me, I found that it felt incomplete. I'd be with them, and feel that something was missing, so I wasn't able to love them the way that they deserved to be loved, and ended the relationship.

I would feel so horrible because these were good women, and I really didn't want to cause them pain, but I also knew that the only other thing worse than ending a relationship would be to keep it going out of fear. What happens then is that you grow to resent each other, wasting valuable, precious time that neither of you can ever get back, and then things are so much worse than if you had ended the relationship when you first realised it had no future.

In this journey, I learnt that self-love and self-worth had been missing in me, and that it had absolutely nothing to do with the beautiful, amazing women who had shown me love. I realised that what I thought had been missing in the relationship was actually missing from inside of me, and that rather than the relationship feeling incomplete, I had felt that within myself.

I then understood why I had been going to the gym since I was 15, and taking steroids since I was 23. I realised that every time I had taken tablets, injected myself with steroids, insulin or HGH, I had merely confirmed that I wasn't enough. I was telling myself that I wasn't enough as I was, that I was less than, and needed to be more; and as I was now 40 years of age, it meant I had been telling this to myself for 17 years. The sense of being physically and aesthetically less than had become ingrained in me, and was now part of how I identified with myself.

I had always disliked my belly, which had never been as ripped or as slim as I had wanted; and, I believe, from taking insulin, that it had distended a little, adding more mass to it. There were days when I would feel worse than others, and on those days I looked in the mirror at myself, and my stomach specifically, and felt so angry at how it looked that I would shout, swear and punch myself in the belly. The medicine had allowed me to see all of this, and I knew that I had to stop the course of steroids I was on – at least for now, or until I could learn to love myself for all that I am, my defects included.

Self-love is the acceptance of all that you are, imperfections included. It's the knowing that you are worthy – you are deserving of this life. It's realising that without self-love, you cannot truly love another, as the love you give would be coming from a place of need, as opposed to a place of love.

It's like asking someone who has no money for £50 – they don't have it to give. It's impossible to give something you don't have, so instead of giving love, I would be giving my need for love… my complete lack of self-love, which would be masquerading as love. I realised that this is what I had been trying to give women all these years, every time I told them that I loved them or that I had fallen in love with them.

INTEGRATION
THE START OF THE HARDEST
ROTATION OF MY LIFE

This would, without a doubt, be the hardest rotation of my life – I just didn't know it yet. It started out well, I was making progress and healing and, dare I say it, I even thought I was actually healed. I was out preaching to people like I was an enlightened being, telling everyone to do some medicine, though little did I know that my healing had only just begun. I was watching and downloading everything I could on consciousness, reading books, I ordered some mala beads and got my good friend, Fraser, to bring them in for me.

I started wearing them every day, and while in the vehicle en route to location, I fed them through my fingers, using the mantra: "I love you, Ricardo; I love you, Ricardo; Ricardo, I love you …" until we reached our destination. I downloaded Insight Timer, and listened to night time meditations with affirmations of self-love, happiness and inner peace. I found guided meditations by a lady called Sarah Blondin, and fell in with her work. In the mornings, I listened to Reawaken Yourself To Love & Joy, where she encourages you say out loud the things you are grateful for. These are simple things, the little things in life that we take for granted, then at night time I would listen to Surrender To The Stillness.

I found such joy in these meditations, self-development techniques and reading materials, then discovered Gaia. What an amazing streaming platform, there was no stopping me after that, and I deleted all other streaming platforms on my devices. I couldn't believe it; I would be out at work, looking forward to getting back to camp so that I could meditate. I was doing everything that I would have rolled my eyes at people doing before, and if anybody had tried to persuade me to give them a try, I would have completely dismissed them.

I once heard it said that meditation is really a means by which to find a moment of deep intimacy with yourself, with your heart, with your soul, and intimacy with the world inside of you. I now know this to be absolutely true.

READING *A NEW EARTH*

This book had come into my life two years earlier, when given to me as a present by one of the most important people in my life, Golden, although I hadn't been ready for it then. Reading had never really been my thing, so I had just stored it away with my things in Colombia. One day, during this rotation, I had selected something to watch on YouTube, and during the adverts at the start, there was one for a podcast with Oprah Winfrey and Eckhart Tolle. As the advertisement described the podcast and its contents, my attention was called to it intensely, so I downloaded the podcasts on my phone and began to listen; and the more I listened, the more I knew that I had to read the book. Obviously, I didn't have the book on me, so I downloaded a kindle app on my iPad, followed by the book itself.

After reading the first chapter, I knew that this book was very special, and when I got to Chapter Two, I read something that would change everything for me. I read a line that said: 'One thing we do know: life is going to give you whatever experience is most needed for the evolution of your consciousness. How do you know this? Because it's happening right now'.

Halfway through reading this, something came over me, and before I even completed the sentence, I seemed to know exactly what it was going to say. When I had finished reading it, it was like being in a ceremony – that sense of something coming, and when it arrives, you realise it's a moment of revelation, something that deep down you've always known, even without consciously knowing it.

It was the same lesson I had learnt in my second Ayahuasca ceremony, where I experienced a death and rebirth; but hearing it come from Eckart Tolle, in the way he had so eloquently put it, and with the last bit – 'How do you know this? Because it's happening right now.' – something inside of me had awoken, and I was able to watch the story of my entire life play out in my mind's eye. With this came the understanding with resounding clarity that nobody – absolutely nobody – comes into your life by accident, and with that I understood that Karma had entered my life to help me suffer, and set the scene for me to have another attempt at the lesson I had failed so miserably all those years earlier with Heartbreak. She also introduced me to Heather, who facilitated my MDMA journey, where I came to fully understand self-love in its entirety, and my lack of it.

When Karma and I met in Rythmia, the medicine allowed us to become unidentified with the stories of who we thought we were. It gave us a temporary blank canvas, if you like, and in that space, the love/oneness inside us both recognised itself in the other. Then we went back to the real world, and started to re-identify with the stories of who we thought we were and what the ego told us we wanted. She was Karma the actress, daughter, sister etc. I was Ricardo, who worked in security in Iraq, son, brother; and by the time we actually got to see each other again, she didn't recognise me and, because of that, I didn't recognise her and, because of that, our relationship was destined to fail.

With this came the understanding that Angel had come into my life to set the stage for this second chance at the most important lesson of my life: self-love. As already explained, during my first mushroom journey she had played a massive part with her tattoo of 'self-love', which helped me understand that I hadn't been treating myself very kindly and needed to show myself more love.

I also realised that I was broken, which I hadn't fully understood at the time, and that what I had understood as not showing myself enough love was actually a complete absence of self- love. With that came the realisation that this had been the real message behind my higher self telling me: "You're broken." I hadn't understood this message in its entirety, which is why in the same journey I had chosen steroids over what I was shown I could have had.

I now realised that Heartbreak had been sent by the universe to help me suffer, but that I had been so focused on the suffering, and the events of the experience, that I had totally missed the lesson at the heart of it, which of course was self-love; and that nobody will truly ever be able to love you if you don't love yourself.

WALKING EFFORTLESSLY

One day during my rotation, having read A New Earth and still trying to integrate its lessons, and those of the MDMA guided session, I left my room to go to breakfast. Whereas I normally walk fairly fast to everywhere I'm going, something inside me decided to walk really slow. I had Beethoven's Piano Concerto No.5 in E-flat playing on my phone in my pocket, and the weirdest thing happened: I felt the breeze on my face, a feeling I'd never had before.

I had felt the wind many times when the weather was rough and inclement, but I'd never felt this breeze. I felt the sun beating down, and washing over my face, whilst my body absorbed its energy, which made me think about the sun and how its position can't just be a coincidence – any further away from the earth and we wouldn't feel it the way we do; any closer and it would probably be unbearable for us humans. I asked myself how the sun ended up in the perfect position in relation to our planet.

When I arrived at the dinner hall after walking so slowly, I still had so much time left, It felt like time was on my side. I kept this up in the days that followed, and right up until the end of my rotation. Some colleagues and other people saw me walking like that, and wondered what I was doing and what was wrong with me. Someone even asked me if I was alright, and I guess to him I looked broken. To anyone observing, it probably looked as if I was walking aimlessly, when in fact I felt that I was walking effortlessly. Every step happened naturally, nothing was being rushed, nothing was being forced, and I felt more at peace and more present than ever before. I heard the birds singing, and I loved it.

When I got into medicine, I started to get the feeling that life was such a gift and that it was so precious; but now I was coming to the realisation that I had been missing the bigger picture. Life is indeed all of that, but what is even more of a gift, and truly precious, is to awaken in this life … to awaken from the story of the character you're playing, to be present and to notice all of the things that are constantly happening all around you, but which some of us miss because we're so caught up in our characters.

MEDITATING ON WHEN I FIRST FELT UNLOVABLE

I was sat in the classroom one day, having had an integration call with Heather the night before, going through weapons training with my team and the training manager. Whilst sitting there, two questions that I had been asked came to mind: one from Karma, and one from Heather.

After crying in front of Karma, and trying to fight back the tears, she had asked me if anyone had ever told me that it was wrong to cry, or that I shouldn't cry. At the time I had answered no, but as I sat there in the classroom, I remembered what my mum used to say to me and Richard whilst disciplining us: "Stop your fucking crying, or I'll give you something to cry about!" I felt my eyes welling up, but had to get a grip of myself as I was in the middle of a weapons lesson in the training office, and there was a room full of men and AK47s – this was not the place to be crying.

I then thought: if Karma was right about that, what could it mean about a question Heather had asked me? During our first integration call, she had done some exercises with me, one of which is called the drama triangle – two minutes of letting myself moan and rant about something that was triggering me, and then just seeing where it went and what came up: villain, victim, hero (the three toxic roles of victim (the primary role), the villain (who the victim blames for their suffering) and the hero (who steps in to relieve the victim's suffering).

It transpired that I felt unlovable, which I already knew at this point, but had never wanted to admit to myself, let alone anyone else, because it made me feel weak. Heather then asked me if I would close my eyes, and see if I could find the part of me that felt unlovable, which wasn't hard because I'd felt unlovable for years by now.

I told her I had found it, and she asked me if I could sit with it for a while, and find out who that part of me was and if it had a name, which to me felt a little silly. I nonetheless sat there feeling it and thinking on it, but nothing came up, so I said: "Chin (the name I'm known by at work, was known by in the Marines, and was called by all of my friends in school)." As soon as I said it, it felt wrong, and I knew who it was that felt unlovable. The name came straight out of my mouth – "'Ricardo! Ricardo is the one who feels unlovable." – at which point, Heather said: "Interesting. We'll find out who Chin is later."

She then asked if I could go back to my childhood, and think about the first time Ricardo had felt unlovable. I knew where she was going with this, and didn't want to entertain it at all. "How was your relationship with your mum growing up?" she asked.

"My mum has always been there for us, and I always felt loved by her." "How about your dad?"

"He was never there. Loads of black kids never had their fathers around, and I never felt I needed him, because I was the man of the house."

"All children need both parents while they're growing up," said Heather. "And all children need the love of both parents."

"Well, that doesn't resonate with me at all," I responded, dismissing her suggestion … but, oh my God, how wrong was I! Whilst sat in the weapons lesson, now thinking about that question from Heather, I started to remember the days when we would ask: "Mum, when's dad coming back? When will we see him again?" Other memories started to surface, including the times when we sat at home after school, waiting for him to arrive, dad having told mum that he'd be round to see us. Late afternoon turned to evening, evening turned to night, and when darkness set in, it became clear he wasn't coming. I guess my mum could see that we were feeling disappointed and upset, and said things to try and cheers us up, like: "He'll come tomorrow." Other times, she would say: "You dad is a wotless (West Indian slang for being worthless) man!" and as I sat there, recalling this, I welled up again.

I thought it better not to dwell on this whilst sat in a room full of men having a weapons lesson, and that I would return to my room and meditate on it, which by now I had come to love doing. So, when the lesson was over, I took the weapons back to the armoury, then headed to my room to meditate. I have this beautiful ashtray, bought for me by Karma, that I absolutely cherish, and which I used for my incense, Sage and Palo Santo, much to the delight of the lads who lived next to me, who asked: "What the hell are you burning in there? I'm surprised the fire alarm hasn't gone off with all of that smoke!"

I lit the sage and copal incense stick – oh, how I love the smell of copal! – and just before lying down to meditate, I lit the Palo Santo. I laid down on my bed, and played my favourite sad playlist, which I had used during my first mushroom trip and MDMA session with Heather.

After meditating a while on these two questions, I became emotionally overwhelmed and, as had been the case whilst reading A New Earth, I was shown everything in my mind's eye, just like being in ceremony.

I started to cry and was shown: dad showed mum his pain body, she showed him hers, and together they both showed me, Richard and Gina their pain bodies. Dad abandoned us, and mum was left to pick up the pieces all by herself, raising three kids and suffering heartbreak. Dad wasn't there to show her or us any love, and at times I thought: why won't he come home?

Why doesn't he want to spend time with us? Without knowing it, I think this unspoken question turned into: he doesn't love us, he doesn't love me – he can't if he chooses not to be here. Growing up, Richard and I pushed mum to her limits. As already explained, she sometimes beat us and told us we were just like our father. Looking back on this now, I realise this was a broken women showing us her pain body, and it wasn't just her pain body from dad, but from the relationship she had with her mother and father, who had both shown her their pain bodies.

If we cried when she beat us, she said: "Stop your fucking crying or I'll give you something to really cry about!" and I believe this might account for part of the reason I feel ashamed to cry, so I don't, feeling weak if I allowed myself to shed tears. So, because of this, I hadn't cried since I was sixteen years old, the last time my mum beat me, until I reached 40 years of age.

I realised that the relationship, or lack of, I should say, that I had with my father was the sole reason why if I ever had a child, I'd never want a boy. I now saw that the relationship I had with my father had affected all of the relationships I've had with men. I've never told my brother that I love him – not even once. I tried to tell him once, after my first mushroom experience, by writing him a text message saying how much I see him struggling to be able to provide for his daughter. Life hasn't been very kind to him, things never seem to go right for him, and it makes me so sad, and yet I still can't tell him that I love him. He's such a good father to his daughter, and I hope I can be like him one day, if I ever have a child.

I also realised that my dad is the reason why I've never been able to understand why some of my work friends told me their fathers were their best friends, and that when returning home on leave, the first thing they planned on doing was going to a bar, pub or restaurant to have a drink or meal with them. I just can't imagine it, and have never been able to comprehend why anyone would want to be best friends with their dad. I think I even saw it as weak, but now realise it was because I was never shown that a father and son could have that kind of relationship.

When dad was there, there was a sense of love, but then he left to go on whatever adventure he had planned, or visit another one of his families, even though the only woman he was ever married to was my mum. I have absolutely no idea what he did when he wasn't with us, which was most of our lives, so I can only guess. Once he was gone, we were again left wondering when we would next see him. God knows what my mum was thinking or feeling about her husband, who was never home with his wife and kids. Still in the meditation, I saw that I then went out into the world and started showing people my pain body. I joined the Royal Marine Commandos because I really wanted to kill people – where had this desire even come from? Gina was still at home, getting shown mum's pain body, and Richard was a grown man who started to show his pain body back to mum. I would come home on leave from the corps, and whenever those two argued, I found it unbearable. I then realised that family tensions, coupled with rejection from women, which had now become frequent in my life, were the reasons why I didn't feel that the UK was where I wanted to be anymore.

A. *Nobody*

Whenever I returned to 26 Guildford Road, my childhood/broken family home, there was a sense of not wanting to be there any longer than absolute necessary, and I then realised it was because of the negative energy that had built up in this house from years of people showing each other their pain bodies; and that it had lived there since I was a child, and all it had done was grow. I love my family, but couldn't stand that house.

Ryan and Reannon, my adopted little brother and sister, then came into our lives. I love them so much, though they have already been shown so much pain and suffering at such a young age – more than I can ever imagine being bearable – but that will be their story to tell. Mum shows Reannon her pain body, and Reannon shows hers right back.

History is repeating itself: Gina is having a tough time with her ex-fiancé, and father of her child. They both show each other their pain bodies regularly, even though they don't live together, and God knows what their daughter, Ava, is thinking or feeling.

I saw that I had been looking for love and self-worth in women because my dad had made me feel unlovable at such a young age. So if I could form a relationship with a woman of my choosing, and persuade her to love me, then maybe it would mean I was worthy of love after all.

With all that my mum went through, I never once saw her cry, and still haven't to this day.

FINISHING THE HARDEST ROTATION OF MY LIFE

Once I started experiencing my awakening, as I came to call it, I went to bed many nights thinking that I would die. There was almost a feeling that I was understanding too much too soon. I went to bed feeling fearful – I felt as if I'd realised my life lesson, and was now awakening, so what if my purpose in this lifetime was over? With that came the thought that I might not wake up, or would die soon … or maybe there would be another lesson to learn – what if I was to become blind, deaf, paraplegic or be burnt badly in a fire, and my future lesson would be to see how my soul evolved through that? This sounds crazy, I know, but it's how I felt.

I meditated, and in the stillness, thoughts and feelings surfaced. I saw that my mum, brothers and sisters had all come here to suffer too, and that although we were all family and loved each other, everyone had come here on their own journey – to suffer, to help others suffer, to feel the sadness and then, when it all becomes too much, to hopefully awaken. Sometimes, parts of my body involuntarily shook during meditation. My left hand and arm trembled, my head sometimes nodded uncontrollably, and violently to the left and right, or up and down; and my entire body occasionally became stuck in a trembling fit.

I was constantly overwhelmed by the feeling that it was okay to die, that my family and loved ones would be alright if that was what was supposed to happen, and hopefully evolve through it. I was engulfed by the understanding that all of the women I'd ever encountered in my life, in whatever capacity, were also on their own journey. They hadn't come to hurt me, and I hadn't intentionally wanted to hurt them, but we helped each other with whatever life lesson we were experiencing at that moment.

I woke up in the mornings, assuming that I hadn't dreamt, then as I settled into my morning meditations, before getting up and ready for work, downloads of a dream I'd had in the night hit me; and as I worked my way through it, the dream I had before that would all of a sudden reveal itself. Most mornings, I remembered four to six wildly vivid dreams.

Whilst all of this was going on, things between me and Karma had taken a turn for the worse. I felt that we were drifting further and further apart, and it wasn't what I wanted. She would say she was going to call, then I wouldn't hear from her and it was devastating, as I still had this dream in my head of things maybe working out between us. At one point, it simply became too much for me, to be in Iraq in my room by myself, constantly waiting for someone to call. I wanted to see her face, hear her voice, have a laugh, feel cared for and engage as best as possible, given there were thousands of miles between us.

One day, I got in my vehicle and drove down to the armoury with a colleague to put weapons away. Once I'd parked up and he got out, I was shutting down the vehicle; and as I glanced at the passenger seat and saw the rifle in the footwell (where we keep them whilst on mission), it was like my mind's eye opened up and I was shown an entire scene unfolding, as if a movie. I saw myself pick the rifle up, and put it in my mouth. It was so real, I could feel the sensation of coldness from the mettle muzzle on my lips. I saw myself squeeze the trigger, and pretty much felt what it would be like to have a burst of automatic weapon fire penetrate my head.

It was strange, feeling as if I was observing the scene from outside my body, yet experiencing it firsthand too. There was no pain, as if the rounds ripped through my head so quickly that there was no time to feel anything. Then, as I was shown myself sitting there, head all opened up, brains everywhere, I was able to experience what it would be like to momentarily feel the cool breeze on whatever was left of my intact brain. I was also shown the reaction of my work colleagues, all shouting "NO! What have you done?!" with their hands resting on their heads in complete dismay and disbelief.

It was like I would still be able to understand what was happening at that moment, despite my body having shut down, and feel nothingness, with no pain whatsoever. What most struck me was the feeling of being sat there, having taken this decision and still being able to comprehend what was going on around me for a few moments, not being able to move, and knowing that I was now completely on the side of no return.

It felt like infinity, but this was all shown to me within seconds. Obviously, this wasn't something I was able to share with people, especially in my line of work, as I would lose my job – and for good reason. You can't have people with access to weapons and ammunition walking around with suicidal thoughts, although I didn't see my situation like that. I didn't want to kill myself, but I was definitely very unhappy.

Every day for the rest of my rotation was the same: whenever we drew weapons out from the armoury, the memory of the vision I was shown played out, as if seeing the weapons triggered it. It was like I was being shown that if I was going to feel so ungrateful for this gift of life, if it was such a burden and inconvenience, and I was going to allow myself to be so deeply unhappy every single day, there was another way out.

I can only imagine how dark and lonely a place it is when somebody decides to take their own life, and actually goes through with it. I've known a few guys over the years who have taken their own lives, and they were never, ever the ones I would have expected to commit suicide.

I felt like I was being taught the lesson of letting go of someone and something that wasn't meant for me, so I sent a message to Karma saying that I loved her and always would, but that I could feel her pulling away more and more, and that I was struggling to accept the new dynamic of our relationship. She messaged me back in the morning, asking if I would be open to having a couples' counselling session. I was so surprised, and hadn't imagined her asking that, so agreed, as it felt like she was truly open to working through whatever was going on with us. She organised it all, with Heather playing the role of mediator, and I trusted her unequivocally from the guided session. Karma put us all in a group chat together, and titled it 'A Loving Conversation', held over Zoom, and it was amazing. There were ups and down, but Heather held the space so caring and lovingly that it wouldn't have been possible for it not to have gone well.

Coming out of the Loving Conversation, I realised that I had been trying to control the way Karma showed me love. I realised it was just as unfair as if she had told me how I should show my love for her.

I think that behind a lot of the sadness I was experiencing, along with the undeniable, inevitable ending of whatever there was between us; was this feeling of fear, that as I was now forty years old, any dreams and aspirations I had of meeting someone, and having the daughter I had always craved, were probably coming to an end.

No matter how the dynamic between us changes throughout the years, I will always love you, Karma. I would love you deeply as my wife, I would love you deeply as my girlfriend, I would love you deeply as my friend; and if a day ever comes when we no longer talk at all, I will still love you deeply, just for being who you are. I will love you deeply from afar.

The lesson the universe taught me through Karma was a reconfirmation of Ram Das' teaching of love: how I could love her without being possessive, and the lesson of acceptance … accepting that everything is exactly as it's meant to be, it always has been, and always will be.

I realised that there was a part of me that had constantly identified with the role of victim; that I was always the one being treated unfairly. I realised that everyone has their go to emotion, and for whatever reason, sadness was the one that I most identified with.

For other people, it may be anger, fear, shame or guilt, but whichever emotion features most prominently for you will be one of the biggest teachers in your life, and it's actually trying to show you or guide you to the bigger state of unrest that lies within you – all you have to do is listen.

One day, during this rotation, whilst all of this was going on, I met a lady in the coffee shop on camp. She stood out to me because I always saw her waving and saying hello to everybody on camp whenever she was out and about, which might sound normal, but it isn't – especially not in the environment in which I work, where acknowledging strangers and saying hello seems to be a basic courtesy not many people are capable of. Some people feel that they're above the need to be polite, and share simple decency with others who they deem to be beneath them, others may be too shy to respond, or may be going through some personal issues, so I guess we never know the story behind the face of the person who chooses not to say hello back.

This day in the coffee shop, a simple hello led to a mutual introduction, followed by a random conversation, which started when I mentioned how I saw her saying hello to everyone, asking whether she noticed that a lot of people don't say hello back.

"Yes," she replied immediately. "But it doesn't matter. We can change that, and I'm not going to stop saying hello to everyone." She radiated kindness and positivity, so it felt very easy to talk to her. I saw her from time to time in the coffee shop, we always had a little chat, and as she had also read A New Earth, we often spoke about that.

"I haven't been very lucky in love, and don't think I've ever shown myself much self-love," I told her one day – quite the thing to be telling someone you barely know over a coffee. Whilst I'm sure she had many things to do and a busy working day, she nevertheless asked if she could pose a question.

"Is there a perfect love? And if there is, who is it? And what does it look like?" She then looked at her watch, and said that she had to leave, as a team was waiting to take her out to site, but that I could think about it and tell her the next time I saw her.

As I left the coffee shop, and walked back to my room, I couldn't stop thinking about her question. I've grown to love questions like this, as they make me introspect myself. By the time I got back to my room, I had my answer:

"Is there a perfect love?" Yes, I think there is a perfect love, but sometimes it's hard to find and it's not something that comes easily.

"Who is it?" It's yourself.

"What does is look like?" It looks like complete acceptance of all that you are, and all of your imperfections. The perfect love is to discover how to love yourself. The perfect love is perfectly imperfect.

I came to cherish my conversations with Espacio, which is what I came to call her, because whether she knew it or not, during our little conversations she provided a space for me to think out loud, which I've now realised is one of the states in which I most thrive. I have been quite lucky because, even though my work environment, where I spend the majority of my time, isn't necessarily a very friendly one for the school of thought and concepts I want to discuss, there are still people I can talk to. And while I can count these people on one hand, I'm so grateful for them.

RYTHMIA 3, NOVEMBER 2022

I was really looking forward to this Rythmia because I had three of my friends going with me, two of them being Gerardo and Justin, who were now two of my very closest. A friend called Ryan, who I had known a while, came along too, our friendship growing exponentially at the retreat.

Just before heading to Rythmia for the third time, Karma called me, saying she wanted to release me so that I wasn't waiting around believing that there might be something between us. At this point, this was already pretty clear to me, although it was still tough to hear. It took a few days to process, but then I realised it was exactly what I needed to hear, providing the closure I needed before going back to Rythmia.

I realised that the visions of suicide had nothing to do with Karma – instead, it was a deep sense of loneliness that was making me feel like that, and have those thoughts. I realised that women had become my kryptonite, and that it was nothing that they had done wrong. I had made them my kryptonite. I had made them my weakness.

Monday night

I went into the first ceremony of the week, and set my intention by asking: "Who am I?" What came back couldn't have been further from all of the different possible outcomes I had envisaged, and dreamt up in my head, in the months leading up to the retreat.

I was shown that my mum had birthed me into this world to experience aloneness. I had left home at 19 years of age to join the Marines, taking myself far away from all of my loved ones, friends and family because I hadn't felt at home in London. After ten years in the Marines, I worked on the ships for two years, which meant being even further away from home for even longer periods of time. Then after that, I got into close protection and went to Iraq, where I have been for the last nine years; and when I'm not in Iraq, I'm in Colombia, at times not seeing my family for well over two and a half years.

I got shown that I had unconsciously orchestrated my life to be this way. My upbringing had to be the way it was, I had to fight those boys, and get sacked from my apprenticeship, so that I could join the corps and really get set on my path to loneliness. It's why my relationships with women always ended up the way they did – it was all by design, so that I would find myself on this journey to awakening.

I was shown that in every moment of happiness that Ricardo had enjoyed, there had always been the presence of a deep, underlying sadness. This sense of aloneness is something that runs so deep, but also something that could reunite the world, because it's something so many of us suffer from. I see now, that to experience solitude is something so special, and only through its acceptance can we begin to heal and realise that aloneness is not loneliness.

A sentence began to appear in my mind's eye, posing a question, my intention … and a reply. 'Who am I? I am aloneness.'

'By myself I am alone, and when we come together as a people, we are alone. We are aloneness'.

I was shown the ethos I had been living by, which was: 'I was born alone, I will die alone'.

In fact, I couldn't have been more wrong because 'by myself I am oneness, when we come together as a people, we are oneness – we are God'.

'Alone is just another word for one, and aloneness just another synonym for oneness'.

I had to love and nurture that part of me too, and felt that this might have been the purpose for my existence – to understand this lesson, which would in turn provide the space for whatever it is that needs to be born from that.

Justin came and knelt down next to my mattress, saying: "I love you." By the time I turned around and started to say: "I love you too, brother," he was already up and walking away. He later told me that he had been thinking for a while about breaking the noble silence to tell me that, and I'm so glad he did, because it was exactly what I needed to hear in that moment.

Again, another example of the universe speaking to us through others at precisely the right moment, in which we need to hear what it is that they have to say – I am not alone, I am loved, always have been and always will be … I am love.

At this point, I started getting random downloads and understandings pop up in my mind space.

*The purpose for my existence was to 'be', and to be alone.

*The greatest love of my life is my aloneness – 'it' has always been there for me.

*We hurt each other because of a deeply misunderstood sense of aloneness, which we misinterpret as loneliness.

*I have such a deep appreciation for all of the women I have had the pleasure of knowing in my life. That so many women sacrifice so much for the progression of humanity is truly commendable.

Women are all that men are, and more. I used to think that it was a miracle that man and woman could create life together, but now I see clearly that man and woman could never create life. Man and woman create a vessel which, don't get me wrong, is still a thing to be marvelled at, but consciousness is the life energy that then embodies what would otherwise be an empty vessel. Then consciousness is birthed into the world through woman and the divine feminine.

Women can do whatever I can do, maybe sometimes to a lesser degree, and maybe sometimes to a better degree, than I could ever hope to achieve in my life, but the one thing they can do that I cannot is give birth to the human form of consciousness, bringing us into this world and enabling our unique journey of evolution.

There are over eight billion people breathing oxygen here on planet earth, and that's only possible because some mother somewhere decided to give birth to each and every one of us.

*There are so many different angles to it that, as humans, we will never be able to comprehend how existence came to be.

*What a gift it is to be able to marvel at the universe.

*I realise this is why I had moved so far away from my family, and had pushed the few good women who have loved me away.

*I realise now that this was another confirmation that I'm not Ricardo Chin, because I'm not alone. None of us are – we are all one and the same thing.

Tuesday night

After my first cup, and using the intention "Show me who I've become," I felt a deep sense of loss, then a while later, after a second cup, I slept to the very end of the ceremony.

Wednesday night

My intention was: merge me back with my soul at all costs, and heal my heart. I drank two cups of Ayahuasca and had the feeling that actually I was okay, I didn't need another. I became aware of a love that I felt for myself, and that maybe the sleep I had in ceremony the night before had helped heal me at a much deeper level. I went to grandfather fire, where, I was told, you can dispose of habits or things that no longer serve you.

You do this by looking at the fire and saying your full name, followed by your mother's full name, then your father's full name, and then you say what it is that you want to give away – the habit that's no longer serving you. I asked grandfather fire if he would please remove these weird thoughts I had of hurting people whilst talking to them, in moments that I would describe as perfect. The next day, I nearly went the entire day before having one of these types of thoughts.

The next day, I did it again, introducing myself, then my mother and father, and asked grandfather fire if he could take away the remnants of what was left of this habit. I made a motion with my right hand, as if grabbing something out of my forehead, just like I had done the night before, then made a gesture to indicate I was throwing it into the fire. It still happens, but with a lot less then frequency than it used to.

Thursday night

Tonight, I asked to see mother Ayahuasca, who started to come through after drinking my second cup. I saw Garden of Eden type pintas, images and visions of kaleidoscopes of fruits, vegetables, nature and beauty, but then she told me that there was something in my body that wouldn't let her through.

I started thinking about how I had never loved myself, all of the bad things I had said about myself, all of the pain I had caused others, all of the pain and sadness I had felt during my upbringing and life, and how I had pretty much isolated myself from everyone close to me. An overwhelming feeling came over me, my higher being arrived and told me that it had to be this way: "I'm sorry, I never meant to hurt you, but it had to be this way or you wouldn't have got it."

I had to suffer all of this pain, hurt and loneliness – otherwise I wouldn't have understood … I would never have been able to awaken from the dream of Ricardo Chin, and realise that none of this matters … absolutely nothing matters, but that's exactly why everything matters so much. Life only matters as much as the meaning we choose to give it.

We come here, to the game of life, for the purpose of experiencing and awakening, and in doing so, to evolve as a consciousness. I realised that on my mushroom trip, when I heard a voice saying: "I'm sorry, I never meant to hurt you," that it had been my higher being referring to our taking the role of Ricardo Chin, and experiencing all of the sadness he felt.

I then knew with my very being that I wasn't Ricardo Chin. I could see it, feel it and understand it with more clarity than I ever had before. How could I have ever been Ricardo Chin? I already existed before that name was ever given to me; that name was given to me after the fact that I existed. I realised that if I'm not even Ricardo Chin, if I'm not even my name, then how could I possibly be any of the things that came after that?

I saw that I had spent forty years trying to become Ricardo Chin, and everything I thought he should be, everything my family told me he should be, everything society told me he should be, when actually I just am … I AM.

My entire life, I had been my biggest enemy, and obstacle. The hardest thing I've ever had to do is to become myself.

Why does nothing matter?

Ultimately, nothing matters. The price of living is dying. Each life costs exactly one death. The only award for successfully completing life is the expiration of it. There's no goal other than life experiencing itself, and evolving through the experience, which would happen whether humanity existed or not. It's like, if I died, who would care? Some family members and friends would, but then what if they too, and every human life on Earth, were to die? Who would care then? No one – absolutely no one – and the Earth would continue spinning. Then what if all forms of life that have ever existed on Earth, and have come to know it as home, were to die? Mankind, land dwelling life, sky dwelling and ocean dwelling life, are just some examples of the infinite expressions of life that are out there. If planet Earth ceased to exist one day, it would just be something that the universe/life experienced, and it would continue just fine without us.

Why does everything matter so much?

It matters because I want to wake up every day in the one unique expression of one idea of infinite ideas of what life could be. More simply, I choose to wake up every day as Ricardo Chin, even though life has at times felt unfavourable. I choose not to take my life, which would mean missing the point of why I came here in the first place: to experience life from the perspective of Ricardo Chin. The fact that I choose that is powerful … that those of us who choose to continue along our life path is powerful. We can always just give up, and identify with suffering… give in to despair, depression, and ultimately take our lives, but we choose not to, and there's power in that.

I wake up every day, and I want to see, I want to be seen, I want to hear, I want to be heard, I want to touch, I want to be touched, I want to feel, I want to care, I choose to care. I want to love, I want to be loved, and it's through that that the seed of meaning and mattering is born. We all know that we're going to die. None of us get out of this alive, so existence can appear futile; yet every day we can consciously choose to get up and continue to live, and hopefully be nice to one another … love one another, be there for one another and help those less fortunate than ourselves. It's from that very feeling, the desire to apply ourselves lovingly to life every single day, even though ultimately we're doomed, which gives meaning and mattering to our existence.

LONELINESS

I began to become aware of my loneliness during my time working on the ships. Since then, it had grown exponentially, and by the time I met Karma, I was aware that a deep sense of loneliness existed within me. Over the course of many years, I realised that there were moments when I could manage to make it subside a little, by having one night stands or spending time with lovemakers. It wasn't until later that I realised this came at a price, and I don't mean money – I mean the damage that I was doing to my inner self.

These women would be beautiful, friendly, caring and even loving sometimes. With the one nights stands, most times at least one, or both of us, were drunk and, I guess, looking for a moment of connection, or to experience pleasure, which would ultimately be superficial and devoid of the kind of connection I was really looking for.

With the lovemakers, I knew exactly where I stood. Most of them were definitely about the money, which I absolutely understand, while some went a little beyond their job and I was able to connect with them, and even feel a tender sense of warmth. I had dinners with some of them, I've watched movies and cuddled on the sofa with some of them, but undoubtedly with the same dynamic as one night stands – the illusion would be over in a matter of hours.

Once they left, the unescapable sense of loneliness always returned to keep me company. What was loneliness for me? Loneliness was a sense of not feeling at home, despite being surrounded by family … a feeling that something was missing, and not wanting to be there. It was travelling the world, and not feeling that I belonged anywhere. It was going out for dinner alone or with friends, and seeing couples everywhere, who in the main seemed happy in their togetherness.

Loneliness was being at work in Iraq and not having someone I loved, who loved me back in the same way, to call at the end of my working day, and feel a sense of belonging … that there was someone out there who wanted to talk to me and hear about my day. Loneliness was finishing an eight-week rotation, and having no one to greet me at the airport, where I saw many couples embracing tightly after spending time apart. It was having no one waiting for me once I got home. It was going out for the night, whether it be with friends or by myself, then going home alone.

Obviously, there were moments when I had some of these things in my life, but they were fleeting, few and far between, and I still felt lonely and incomplete. The only person I had spoken openly to about being lonely was Heather, during an integration video call. I wouldn't ever have spoken to anyone else about it, or allowed myself to be vulnerable like that, because speaking of loneliness made me feel weak. I didn't even want to admit it to myself, let alone anybody else. No doubt this came from some unwarranted (and invalid) sense of male pride or machismo, and because the environments I was in weren't conducive to subjects like this.

After my second Ayahuasca journey, on my first retreat, I had begun to think that my lesson in life was to experience loneliness, but now I understand that for me loneliness was actually a side effect of having no self-love. Because I didn't love myself, I was never going to be able to have someone in my life romantically. Because I didn't love myself, I was never going to feel complete.

SADNESS

There are many, many ways to discover sadness, and I discovered it through loneliness. Sadness is a deep, deep void. I realised that there's something in me that likes to revel in the sadness, and I found that sadness; although sadness also has a beauty to it. I feel it when I'm most truthful and intimate with myself, and it's during these moments that some of my biggest revelations have occurred.

Being the man I am, I would rather suffer in silence and solitude than to ever reach out to someone and tell them that I was struggling, especially if it's to do with loneliness or sadness. There's this feeling of: what am I moaning about? What gives me the right to feel sad when there are people out there who have truly suffered? Nothing that bad has happened to me, but the truth is, sadness wants to be felt, and it wants to be expressed.

I'm aware that I've dealt with my sadness, but I'm still able to listen to powerful, sad music and watch sad movies that move me in such a way that I can tap into the sadness that still exists within me. We all have the ability to access deep lying sadness, and while I'm not suggesting that everybody should, I found that by accessing and exploring my own sadness, it's not something I ever want to cause another human being or any type of being to feel. To enter that space of sadness of your own freewill is like conducting a controlled experiment – you know what you're doing to some degree, but to inflict that sadness on another being, and put them in that space through some action of your own doing, especially if you're aware that what you're doing could put them there through no volition of their own, then you need to stop.

Through the understanding in that space of sadness, you come to realise that you don't ever want to be the reason that somebody else is there, because that would bring the sadness directly back to you, whether it be tomorrow, a month, a year from now or in the next life experience. If I hurt you, I hurt me, as it's impossible to hurt another person without hurting yourself.

I realise now that being sad or unhappy is a choice. When I wake up in the morning, it's me who chooses whether to be sad, or when something happens to me throughout the day, I choose how I'm going to allow it to affect me. Up until now, I had always chosen to be sad, and when I asked myself why, I realised that I was purposely choosing to be unhappy or sad, because I wanted to punish myself for having hurt the people I've hurt, and for allowing myself to be hurt. Sadness can be an addiction, but only if you allow it to be.

DEATH

There have been moments where I have been so worried that if I died, it would cause great pain to my family and anyone who may care for me, but I understand now that as much as I don't want to cause them pain, when it happens it will be part of their journey and something they will have to come to understand, deal with, overcome and evolve through.

I have become so fascinated with death and dying, as it's such an amazing subject. One of the things that has always fascinated me about death is that people are called by their name until they die, but beyond that they're known as 'the body' – e.g. they're taking his or her body to the morgue. It's almost as if, at some deeper level, we all know that the body is just the thing that embodies the energy that's truly who we are.

Life is a tightrope, submerged in death, on which we live our lives. We walk on it during the day, and sleep on it at night. Death is what surrounds that rope on either side and at both ends, which we could slip and fall into at any given moment. Some of us will be pushed into it, some of us will choose to leap into it of our own freewill, and that's okay – it's okay to die.

I am most definitely not saying that we should commit suicide, but I am saying that death will come to us all in whatever form it takes, and whenever it chooses to, no matter how much some of us may try to hide or run from it. I'm saying it's okay to die when it's our time, and that in death, we will remember that what we have come to call 'death', and however we have come to understand it as human beings, is actually the space in which we truly exist. By that I mean the higher being us; the eternal us. This is the space in which we come from and return to, before and after every experience we chose to have for the evolution of our consciousness.

When you come to realise what life truly is, you also come to truly love it; and if you love life, then you love everything that comes with it. Yes, you come to love death too, not as the character you're playing here on Earth, but as the eternal being you are!

On my dying day, when I finally become acquainted with my own death, I hope that I can surrender completely and just breathe into it, just as I have in all of the ceremonies I've ever been in. There's a knowing deep inside of me that death is just the essence of who we truly are, slipping away from this corporeal form, and that when that happens, we will no longer be burdened with the fears and worries that have troubled us as humans. You won't be worried about the pain that as a human you thought you would cause your loved ones by dying. You won't be worried about any of the problems that anybody in the game of life is facing, because you'll be able to see it for what it truly is: a journey in which suffering is truly a gift; and your loved ones, and everybody else in the world, are on their own journey of self-discovery and awakening, whether it be in this lifetime or the next.

Many of our relationships with death come from a place of negativity. It's hidden from most of us when we're young, and becomes a taboo that most of us don't want to talk about, so when it actually happens to a loved one, we're caught completely off guard, asking why and how it could have happened. It happened because that's the circle of life. We are born, we are romanced by the world and its opportunities, we love, we hurt, we cry, we enjoy some of life's most wonderful moments, but along the way we suffer. Hopefully, we awaken somewhere along the journey, and at some point, we die.

This should be being taught in schools, for if it was, we would rejoice in the passings of our loved ones, instead of mourning them. Death is an escort that accompanies us from one life to the next, it surrounds us all every single day, and there's absolutely nothing we can do about it, except change our attitude towards it. We have to embrace it, love life, love everything and love death too.

If I had the chance to be in that hospital room with my Auntie Janice again, when she told me she was scared, I would tell her: "Don't be scared. Life is a dream – a beautiful, beautiful dream – but you're about to wake up now."

What is death? Death is the grand finale in the illusion of the character we came here to play.

A letter to my dad

Dad, I judged you my entire life for the way you treated mum, the pain you caused her, and the fact that you were never really there for us. I realise now that not only am I in absolutely no position whatsoever to be judging you, but that I too am responsible for hurting people who had entrusted their hearts with me – people I loved and cared for deeply.

Hurting someone doesn't just come in the form of unfaithfulness, and not being there for your children. It also comes in the form of carelessly allowing good people into your life, and onto your journey, when you're still suffering yourself.

Ultimately, it always ends in pain. I had never once stopped to truly ask myself: "What was your upbringing like?" What were the things in your life that made you suffer, and then hand out your own form of suffering to other people? I've always loved you, dad, but it's taken me many years to understand that I could never be your judge or hold resentment towards you. I love you deeply as my father, I always will, and even though you've been gone for many years now, I hope there was a part of you that knew it then, and knows it now, wherever you are in the universe. I'm sorry, please forgive me. I love you, thank you.

A short letter to Richard

I feel I haven't been the best big brother, especially to you. I've never been able to tell you that I love you, and I don't know why, because I truly do with all my being. Sometimes, I'll have dreams where you die, and I'll wake up momentarily confused, absolutely heartbroken and so sad, because it felt so real and there's this feeling of insurmountable loss. I just want to cry, but as I start recognising my surroundings, I realise it was only a dream.
I may not say it, but I hope you know it. When your daughter, Eden, was born, the love I felt for her was endless – absolutely immeasurable – and why would that be? I didn't even know her yet – it was because of the love I feel for you, which is unfathomable.

A short letter to Ryan and Reannon

I haven't been the best big brother to you guys either, though it's definitely not through lack of love. I love you both more than you'll ever know, and I think of you both every single day. I've been so caught up in my own journey, not understanding who I truly am or why I'm even here, that I haven't been able to be there for either of you as the big brother I should be, and I'm so sorry for that.

I want you both to know that I feel so blessed to have you as my little brother and sister. I always have, and I hope that somewhere inside, you both know and feel that to be true.

Apologies and Gratitudes

Karma – thank you for saving me from myself, for helping me suffer, and for shining light on the entrance to the path of self-love, the most important lesson of my entire life. I will love you forever for that.

Love – you will never know how much meeting you impacted my life in that moment, at that time, and through the now and beyond; and that's not because you can't understand, it's because words in voice or on paper, here in this book, will never allow me to fully express it to you.

Amor – sorry for trying to change you. You were and are perfect, exactly the way you are. The person who had the problem, and the one who needed to change, was me. Thank you for showing me love, and for still being there for me now.

Heartbreak – life hadn't beaten me down enough yet when we met, so I would never have been able to understand the lesson our somethingship was trying to teach me about self-love. Luckily, though, through the many beatdowns life has given me since, I was just about able to understand it when I met your friend, Karma, years later. Sorry for being too unconscious to understand it the first time.

To Golden, and all the women – there is absolutely no valid excuse for any of the pain I have caused you, or any of the women who have been in my life, and it will never be enough to simply apologise. Nevertheless, that is all I have, so, wholeheartedly and with the entirety of my deepest being, the being I now know myself to be, I would like to offer you a sincere apology and tell you I'm so very sorry for all of the pain I ever caused.

If you're reading this, know me, and I have caused you pain, you'll know exactly who you are.

Gratitude to all of my family, friends and support network, who have constantly been there for me throughout this journey, providing space for me to think out loud, and some of you even accompanying me to ceremonies and guided sessions across the world. Some of us may not be of blood, but I see you all as family – my soul family. Thank you, my little sister Gemma, Mo, Gerardo, Justin, Charles, Derrick, Mauricio and Graham. All of you have supported me so much, I only hope that I've been able to reciprocate some of that support over the years, and that you're all aware of how much you mean to me.

Karl – I have so much appreciation and gratitude for you; for giving up your precious time, and being the first person to read this entire book, even in its most raw, unedited form.

Auntie Pauline, Rachel and Lauralee – You beautiful beings, I would like to give thanks to each one of you for dedicating your valuable time to read my book and giving me such welcomed and appreciated feedback.

Fraser – I would like to show my deepest gratitude for you always allowing me to talk at you. God knows if you wanted to hear half the things I spoke about. Most others would have dismissed me as insane, and the things I was saying as the delusions of a crazy man, but you never did, so in recognition of the constant ear bending you received every evening during our walks to dinner,

I want to say thank you for providing space for me to think aloud. In addition, a recognition of gratitude to Chris, Danny, and Harley, who also provided space for me to think aloud at times – it's appreciated more than I imagine you know.

To my teenage enemies – I would like to apologise for the role I played in the conflicts we had, to thank you for helping me suffer, and for being a part of my journey.

To anyone I've ever hurt and caused suffering to, be it family, friend, lover or an absolute stranger, just know that I feel the weight of it every day. Although I know we're here to help each other suffer, I still have to account for the role I play in causing others to suffer, and for that I am truly sorry.

With all of the tales I have told in this book, I recognise that there are always two sides to a story. So all I have tried to do here is tell my story as I see it, understand and remember it. I know that two or more people can experience the same event, but each individual may well see, experience and recall the event completely differently to anyone else who was there.

This book cannot even begin to express my gratitude to everyone who has been, is, or will be in my life. All of you have helped me arrive at where I am today, in this deepest feeling of joy for my life. I love you all so much that words will never ever be able to quantify or explain it.

FINAL THOUGHTS

Sometimes I'll be walking and get the feeling that I'm about to wake up.

The opportunity to peak behind the veil of life is a such a beautiful thing. What a beautiful gift it is to be able to love and be loved – how lucky are we?! I am perfect imperfection.

I feel that madness is feeling every emotion all at once, and not being able to express it. Being sad is a symptom, feeling lonely is a symptom … hopelessness, unworthiness … these are all symptoms that we aren't getting it – it being the point of why we're here, and the crazy thing is that we have to feel all of these things, or we wouldn't get it. It's a paradox.

It's like becoming sick, only so that you can understand why you had to get sick in the first place. When we see people suffering, we want to help them and alleviate their suffering. We want to let them know that they're not alone, but even though our intentions come from a place of love, and not wanting to see them in pain, hurting, to rob them of their suffering would be to deny them the chance of realising why we're truly here – self-realisation. It has to be, or we would never believe it.

That doesn't mean not helping people. It means that we can only help by allowing them to suffer, and hope that if it gets too much, they'll reach out, or that they'll come to find their own truth, which is all of our truths. We are here to suffer, but if we can find the beauty in that suffering, in the suffering of the entire world, then the suffering becomes beautiful, and beauty isn't a thing to be suffered. This is how I've come to understand the phrase and film title,

Collateral Beauty, and what it means to me: to be able to see the beauty in and amongst the suffering, and allowing it to evolve you.

It's the totality of everything; it's in those moments of true presence, when you're able to look at your life and see that all of the love, the joy, the sadness, the pain, the loss, and all of the moments of lack of self-love were needed to get you to that moment of awakening, so that you could become one with it all. We are in the universe and of the universe, so if we can love the beauty of it, we also have to love the ugliness of it, because the universe is always making something happen, or allowing things to happen. No matter how beautiful or ugly it may seem, it's a part of 'us', and a part of who 'we' are … and it's the universe that permits it all to be.

It would be so amazing to have someone to share my life with, but even if that person never manifests for me, I will continue to live my life completely in love with the universe, which I already feel and know to be absolutely amazing.

As you read this book, I hope that you can see that all I am to you is a character portrayed within it; and when you close it, I hope that you can see that you are just a character, a character in an even bigger book, but sometimes you may not even be aware of it because you're reading the book of life interactively.

I am absolutely not suggesting that anybody go out there and do any of the things I've done, although it would be so amazing and transcending if the entire world could just heal. I also understand that it's a process, and that we are all on our own paths – hopefully one of self- discovery, and an ever-evolving state of consciousness.

I know for sure that as long as I'm here in the world, alive and breathing, I will always be challenged with moments of suffering and hardship, so there will be more healing to be done. All I hope is that I can continue to learn, show gratitude and evolve through it all; wake up every day, be the best version of myself, and to continue my journey into the exploration of consciousness, and my true identity.

This is my intention for the rest of my life.

THE ROAD OF LIFE

In my mind, I see this road. It's long and winding, and filled with many other people making their way to the other end. I don't quite know what's at the other end of the road; I just know that I'm on it, and I'm alone. Soon, I see a woman that I feel an attraction to, so once I get close enough, I ask: "Will you keep me company and walk to the end of the road with me?"

She takes one look at me, says no, and points ahead to another woman, who's just ahead of us. I keep walking and, once I catch up with this woman, I ask: "Would you like to accompany me to the end of the road?"

"Yes," she smiles.

I'm happy, we start to talk and get to know each other. After a little while, she doesn't want to talk to me anymore or keep me company, and points on ahead. I'm heartbroken, the road turns dark, and I can't see anyone anymore. I'm alone. After what seems like an eternity of walking by myself in the dark, there's a little glimmer of light. The sun is rising, I can see people again, and I see that many of them are partnered off, holding hands and walking together on the road of life.

Seeing these couples, I feel more alone than ever, but I'm inspired. It makes me feel like there's hope again – maybe I can find someone who wants to walk and hold hands with me. So as I make my way through all of the couples, who seem to be absolutely engrossed with each other, walking as slowly as can be, with no apparent urgency to get anywhere, least of all the end of the road, I see a beautiful woman walking alone. I feel drawn to her, but before I have the chance to catch up with her, I feel a tap on my shoulder. I turn around, and there's a beautiful woman standing there.

"Can I walk with you?" she asks. "Yes," I say.

We start to walk, and she holds my hand.

"I've been walking alone for a very long time," she says. "I'm so happy to be walking with you now."

Whilst we walk, we see someone sat on the side of the road with their knees scrunched up to their chest. They seem oblivious to the fact that we're there, walking past them. I ask the beautiful woman holding my hand: "What's wrong with them?"

"I've seen it many times before during my walk," she starts to explain. "They're people who have been pointed on by someone they'd been walking with, but it's broken them so deeply that they've given up and are surrounded by darkness, unable to see anyone. Some of them will eventually get up and continue their walk, but I've seen others who've never broken free from the darkness and will stay sat there for the rest of time."

We continue walking and talking for some time, but soon enough I become aware of a feeling that something is missing. The feeling intensifies and, before I know it, my hand is pointing this beautiful woman, who has been my companion, onwards. She cries, and I see a look of sadness and despair on her face. She lets go of my hand and makes her way to the side of the street, where she sits down and scrunches her knees up to her chest.

I walk on, not knowing what to say or do; but before long, I'm overwhelmed by a sense of disgust and dislike for myself, for having made someone feel how I had felt when I had been pointed on. The road gets dark again, I can't see anyone, my feet get heavy and my body doesn't want to move anymore. I sit down on the side of the road, scrunch my knees up to my chest, and cuddle my legs with my arms. Again, I'm alone, and completely overcome by a deep sadness and sense of loneliness. I'm sat there for what seems like forever. I try to get up, but it's absolutely hopeless.

I feel like I'm sat there in the dark for a lifetime, and then, out of nowhere, I feel someone take hold of my hand. I look up and see the most beautiful face I've ever seen. I don't understand how or why this is happening, but she says: "Come on, walk with me." All of sudden, I feel a surge of energy, and a new lease of life radiate through my body. I spring up on my feet, and we begin to walk hand in hand.

"I've been in the dark too," she says. "And know exactly what it's like. The road can be tough sometimes, but we owe it to ourselves to make it to the end, if nothing more than to see what awaits us there. I've also been pointed on, and have pointed others on many times, but this is the journey and I've come to realise that there was never any bad intention behind the onward point – it's just the nature of the walk."

As she finishes talking, she lets go of my hand and points me on. I'm devastated, and can't believe this has happened to me again. I ask myself why she would pick me up, only to point me on. Then the road gets dark darker than I've ever seen it before, and I'm completely alone again.

Just as I decide that I'm going to sit down on the side of the road and never, ever get up,

I feel a tap on my shoulder. I turn around and I see me, but this 'me' is glowing, radiating like the sun. I can't hold back, bursting into tears.

"I've been so alone for so long," I tell him. "Even when walking, holding hands with loving companions."

He shakes his head in disagreement. "You've never been alone. I've been there with you every step of the way, but in order for you to notice me, it had to become the darkest it had ever been." Staring at 'me' in all his essence, and his perfectly imperfect imperfections, I fall in love … a deeper love than I ever thought possible. A strange feeling comes over me … a feeling I've never felt before, and I realise that it's the feeling of being enough all by myself. It's the feeling of being complete.

Henry David Thoreau wrote: "Most men lead quiet lives of desperation, and go to the grave with the song still inside them."
Well, this is me singing my song as best as I can, in the only way I know how to at this moment.

This book is my goodbye letter to the world; my farewell letter to the world as I knew it, and my hello to the awakening of a whole new world I had never dreamed possible.

The only reason everything hurts so much is because we choose to care, so bring on the hurt.

In the scale of the world, I sit here a nobody
No worldly possessions, but what my creator has given me
So, I breathe in the air and thank God I'm alive
A nobody, but I'm rich with the value of life.

I hope that on my dying day, when I finally meet death in this body of Ricardo Chin, I will meet it not as an enemy, but as an old friend; to breathe and surrender into it completely

Printed in Great Britain
by Amazon

41384862R00199